CW01465569

HOW THE ARMY MADE BRITAIN A GLOBAL POWER, 1688–1815

JEREMY BLACK

CASEMATE
academic

Oxford & Philadelphia

Published in Great Britain and the United States of America in 2021 by
CASEMATE PUBLISHERS
The Old Music Hall, 106–108 Cowley Road, Oxford OX4 1JE, UK
and
1950 Lawrence Road, Havertown, PA 19083, US

Copyright 2021 © Jeremy Black

Hardcover Edition: ISBN 978-1-95271-508-2
Digital Edition: ISBN 978-1-95271-509-9

A CIP record for this book is available from the British Library

All rights reserved. No part of this book may be reproduced or transmitted in any form or by
any means, electronic or mechanical including photocopying, recording or by any information
storage and retrieval system, without permission from the publisher in writing.

Printed and bound in the United Kingdom by TJ Books

Typeset by Lapiz Digital Services.

For a complete list of Casemate titles, please contact:

CASEMATE PUBLISHERS (UK)
Telephone (01865) 241249
Email: casemate-uk@casematepublishers.co.uk
www.casematepublishers.co.uk

CASEMATE PUBLISHERS (US)
Telephone (610) 853-9131
Fax (610) 853-9146
Email: casemate@casematepublishers.com
www.casematepublishers.com

Front cover: A view of the taking of Quebec, 13 September 1759. Engraving based on a sketch
made by Hervey Smyth, General Wolfe's aide-de-camp. (Library of the Canadian Department
of National Defence)

For Yasmin Thierry

Contents

Preface

I thought formerly I could easily form an idea of a battle from the accounts I heard from others, but I find everything short of the horrid sense and it seems almost incredible that any can escape the incessant fire and terrible hissings of bullets of all size, the field of battle after is melancholy, four or five miles of plain covered with human bodies dead and dying, miserably butchered dead horses, broken wheels and carriages, and arms of all kind … in the morning on the ground in our tents were pools of blood and pieces of brain.

RICHARD BROWNE, BATTLE OF MINDEN, 1759.[1]

Between 1760 and 1815, British troops campaigned from Montreal to Manila, Cape Town to Copenhagen, Washington to Waterloo. The naval dimension of Britain's expansion has been superbly covered by a number of excellent studies, notably by Roger Knight and Nicholas Rodger. There has not been a single volume that does the same for the army and looks in particular at how and why it became a world-operating force, capable of beating the Marathas as well as the French. With the long 18th century currently a vibrant area in the histories of war and imperialism, this book will offer a new perspective, one that concentrates on both the global role of the army and its central part in imperial expansion and preservation. There will be a focus on what the army brought to power equations and how this made it a world-level force.

The multi-purpose character of the army emerges as the key point, one seen in particular in the career of Wellington: while referred to disparagingly by Napoleon as a '*sepoy* general', in other words as a commander of Indian troops, Wellington's ability to operate successfully in India *and* Europe was not only impressive but also reflected synergies in experience and acquired skill that characterised the British Army.

No other army matched this. The closest in capability was Russia: able, in 1806–14, to defeat the Turks, Sweden and Napoleon, but without having any of the trans-oceanic capability and experience enjoyed by the British Army. The experience was a matter in part of debate, including over doctrine, as evidenced in the tension between the 'Americans' and 'Germans' – a reference to fields of British campaigning concentration during the Seven Years' War. This synergy proved best developed in the operations in the Peninsular War in Iberia (Portugal and Spain) in 1809–14, with logistical and command skills used in India employed by Wellington in a European context in which they were of particular value.

How this army was achieved despite the strong anti-army ideology and practice derived from the hostile responses to the standing armies of Oliver Cromwell (r. 1653–8) and to James II (r. 1685–8) is a key instance of the subjects of civil-military relations and military cultures. Perception and politics are both part of the story, as well as the exigencies and practicalities of conflict, including force-structure, command issues, institutional developments, and strategic, operational and tactical culture, tradition and doctrine. Funding was a major key link between politics and conflict, which means going back to the consequences of the Glorious Revolution of 1688–9. That will be the start of the book – a dramatic one, as it was the last successful conquest of the British Isles. At the same time, there is no inevitability about British success over the period of this book, and it is necessary to consider developments in the context of other states. In particular, there is an emphasis on the quality of the army. The reasons behind why British forces did well reveal that Britain was not dependent on naval effectiveness alone.

I have benefited greatly from the comments and criticism of Stan Carpenter, Charles Esdaile, Bill Gibson, Nick Lipscombe, John Peaty, and Mark Stevens on earlier drafts. None is responsible for any of the errors that remain. I know how much effort is involved in commenting on drafts and how far it makes books in effect a collective work. So, again, thanks. It is a great pleasure to dedicate this book to Yasmin with much love from Sarah and myself.

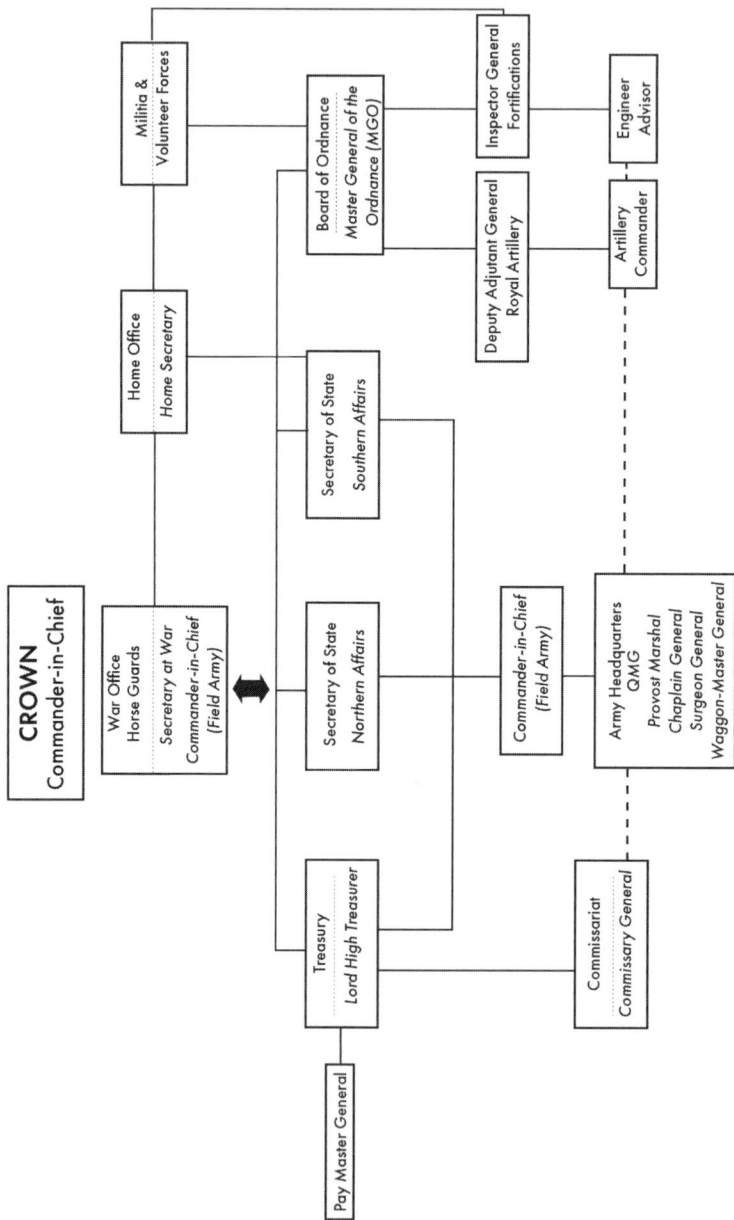

CROWN
Commander-in-Chief

War Office
Horse Guards
Secretary at War
Commander-in-Chief
(Field Army)

Home Office
Home Secretary

Militia &
Volunteer Forces

Board of Ordnance
Master General of the
Ordnance (MGO)

Inspector General
Fortifications

Engineer
Advisor

Deputy Adjutant General
Royal Artillery

Artillery
Commander

Secretary of State
Southern Affairs

Secretary of State
Northern Affairs

Commander-in-Chief
(Field Army)

Army Headquarters
QMG
Provost Marshal
Chaplain General
Surgeon General
Waggon-Master General

Treasury
Lord High Treasurer

Commissariat
Commissary General

Pay Master General

Note: Before 1782, the responsibilities of the two Secretaries of State of the Northern and the Southern Departments were not divided up in terms of area of authority but rather geographically. Both were responsible for England and Wales. The Secretary of State of the Northern Department, the more junior of the two, was responsible for foreign relations with the Protestant states of Nothern Europe. The more senior Secretary of State for the Southern Department was responsible for relations with the Catholic and Muslim states of Europe. In 1782, the two Secretaries of State were reformed as the Secretary of State for the Home Department and the Secretary of State for Foreign Affairs.

Command, Control and Administration of the British Army circa 1730.

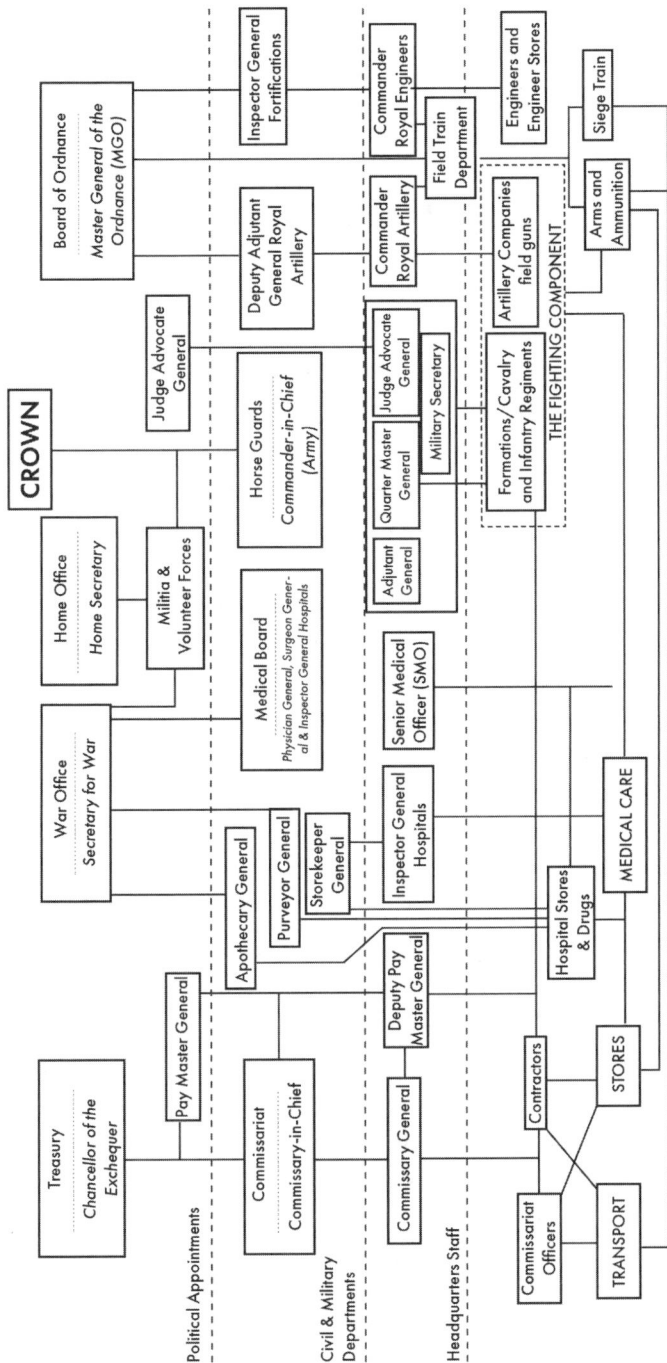

Command, Control and Administration of the British Army circa 1800.

Introduction

Necessary for Britain's survival, the army was an institution, a way of life, a collective and an array of individuals. Their experiences were very different, and dramatically so when men survived while their neighbours were shot down. The army's history in a tumultuous period of British history needs to be understood both on its own, and also in the context of other European, indeed global, forces of the period, and this certainly provides important context in assessing its relative capability.

As this book shows, the tasking of the army became particularly world-wide during this period by the standards of the other armies of the period, whether Western or non-Western. For example, a comparison with the successful Prussian army of Frederick II, 'the Great' (r. 1740–86), supposedly the cutting-edge of the Western military, is unhelpful, as the Prussians needed only to fight in Europe and, indeed, within a few hundred miles of their bases. The British Army, in contrast, had to face rebellions, both in the British Isles and in the colonies, had to mount amphibious operations, both within Europe and further afield, had to campaign overseas in Europe, for example in Portugal, and had to fight on distant continents in very different (and far from uniform) physical and military environments.

These requirements interacted, but not to the same degree for Britain's opponents or comparators. To argue, for example, that Frederick was a better general than his relative William, Duke of Cumberland, or George Washington than his opponent Charles, 2nd Earl Cornwallis, would be to compare commanders with very different challenges: Cumberland had to face rebellion in Britain in 1745–6, and Cornwallis also to command in India and Ireland. So also with more junior commanders and officers, and with their soldiers. The French fought outside Europe, but none of their major commanders did so, bar Napoleon who went no further than the Middle East.

Capability is always difficult to assess in the abstract because of the major issues posed by the circumstances of particular wars. Timing, for example, was a key cause of the problems facing Britain during the American War of Independence (1775–83), with the British failing to end the revolution before France entered the war in 1778. In turn, in that war, the French did not have to face a challenge comparable to that confronting the British, in large part because France's colonies lacked a comparable political complexion.

It was not until the French Revolutionary crisis, when the slave colony of St. Domingue rebelled, that France faced a large-scale colonial rising, and then could not mount a major response as it had more pressing challenges in Europe. Furthermore, it was not until after the Peace of Amiens with Britain in 1802 that the French sought to recover St. Domingue; although initially successful, the attempt was vitiated by the difficulties of the task, specifically yellow fever. Moreover, like France, Portugal and Spain failed to suppress the revolutions in their colonies in the New World in the early 19th century; rather than seeing Britain, and its army, as uniquely unsuccessful, it is helpful to look at the more general political and military problems of tackling colonial rebellion. Similar points can be made about campaigning in Asia. If the British were defeated by the Marathas in 1779, the Chinese had totally failed in successive advances into Burma (Myanmar) in the late 1760s.

The need to maintain forces in the British Isles for home defence, the scale of Britain's global commitments and the proportion of the army tied up holding outposts around the globe exerted such a huge drain on the limited manpower that comparatively few troops could be spared for offensive operations on the European mainland or elsewhere. Moreover, the political context was not particularly helpful for military capability, as the lack of a militarised culture, both generally and in politics, can be seen in the absence of a united military command structure that would be able to devise and sustain coherent peacetime programmes of planning and improvement. This had a serious impact in limiting developments in capability between conflicts. This drawback reflected the anti-military ethos of British politics, the difficulties of enforcing discipline and diligence on aristocratic officers who owned their positions, and the more general absence of a bureaucratic ethos, certainly as compared to the Royal Navy where, due to the responsibilities and roles of captains, supply issues were more commonly linked to those of command. Again, however, comparisons are valuable. British logistics, for example, were more impressive than those of Russia.

Opposition Parliamentary speakers (such as the ever-melodramatic William Pitt the Elder on 3 February 1738, in a House of Commons' debate on the size of the army) pressed for a reduction in the size of the army in order to safeguard the constitution and cut taxation, and thus, in their view, reduce popular discontent.[1] Other MPs, however, had a different view. That year, William Hay, a ministerial Whig MP of independent mind, told the Commons that it was important to keep up the army: 'I never think on this subject but I consider this island as situated in the neighbourhood of France. I consider France as its natural enemy, and at the same time as the most powerful of all nations.'[2] Just as arguments about the role of the navy reflected divisions within Whig politics, and more broadly in British political culture,[3] so even more with the army.

At any rate, parliamentary votes of money were crucial, and no other major state had a comparable constitutional constraint. On 16 March 1786, in the debate on the Mutiny Bill, Philip Francis, a prominent opposition speaker in the Commons, 'laid it down as a maxim, that the great security which this country had for its liberty, was the dependence of the army for its subsistence on that House.'[4] Well aware of foreign awareness of opposition criticism of the size of the army, ministers took care to emphasise the ability of the government to get the necessary legislation through Parliament, as John, Lord Carteret, Secretary of State for the Northern Department, did in 1743.[5]

Views critical of the army did not preclude an understanding of the need to build it up when necessary. Thus, as the War of the Spanish Succession (for Britain, 1702–13) gathered pace, Parliament voted through funds for 31,254 troops recruited from the British Isles in 1702, 50,000 by 1706, and 75,000 by 1711. There were also large numbers of foreign troops that were paid, in whole or part, so that, by 1709, Britain had, at least in theory, a total of about 150,000 troops available for campaigning. In 1714, peace brought a reversion to an establishment set at 18,000 troops.

The American War of Independence (1775–83) also saw a transformation: the British and Irish army establishment at the beginning of 1775 was about 36,000 strong, but war brought rapid expansion, and the envisaged strength for 1776 was 96,314, comprising 24,811 in Britain, 8,003 in Ireland, 5,635 in Gibraltar and Minorca (including 2,373 Hanoverians), 3,501 in West Africa and the West Indies, 13,842 in Canada (including 5,780 Germans and 615 Loyalists), and 40,522 in the army under Sir William Howe that was intended to suppress the American Revolution, including 12,982 Hessians, 2,000 Marines and 1,038 Loyalists. In turn, the Army Estimates provided to the House of Commons in December 1779 noted a rise to 179,500 troops, but of these 42,000 were in the militia. Of the 90,000 men then deployed abroad, 15,000 were in the West Indies and West Africa, and 12,000 in Gibraltar and Minorca.

Numbers brought costs in recruitment, pay, equipment and supplies, as well as much business to manufacturers and farmers; hence the clothmakers making uniforms opposed to the Peace of Utrecht with France in 1713. Those were not the sole costs; there were also those of deployment and support. Thus, it was calculated in 1744 that the siege train required by the Allied army in the Austrian Netherlands would 'amount to 10,000 horses and 2,000 wagons', at a cost of £50,000 for six weeks.[6]

The troops raised and money expended were expressions of both nation and empire, and also helped mould them, providing links within the empire that in part could be a matter of coercion and/or intimidation, but that also developed common interests. There was an inclusive Britishness about the army, and notably so as far as Scotland was involved. In addition, the large number of Irish Catholics in the army in the later decades of our period underlined the extent to which the relationship between Britain and Ireland worked.

Separately, ministers were well aware of the risk of invasion, and the challenge it posed both in peace, for example when relations with France deteriorated in 1731, and in war. For most of the period from the 1570s, England's prime overseas opponents were Spain, and, in 1652–74, the Dutch. France took over this role in 1689, and, thanks to its position, resources and military, was in a better position to invade England, to intervene in Ireland, and to threaten what became the nexus of Britain's alliance system: the Low Countries. Partly as a consequence of this challenge, a great requirement for military manpower pressed on Britain, a society with only modest population growth prior to the mid-18th century, and one for which the navy clearly came first in terms of its strategic requirements and public debate.

The risk of invasion appeared even stronger when France and Spain combined, as they considered doing in 1762[7] and unsuccessfully tried to do in 1779. The risk of a French or, less commonly, Spanish invasion repeatedly posed a strategic challenge that threatened to fix the army so that it could not act abroad, becoming a key inhibitor to its potential global role, and therefore a dimension that needs to be addressed in its history. This was one of the contexts that it is all too easy to forget or at least underplay, for the history of the army is very much about strategy as well as battle. Thus, in February 1740, François de Bussy, a senior French official who spied for the British, noted in his reports to London information from Spain that its preparations in Galicia (northwest Spain) for a possible invasion of Britain '[were] only to create fears in England, and to slacken their [the British] ardour for America [the Caribbean].' That August, however, James, 1st Earl Waldegrave, the envoy in Paris, warned that the French could assemble troops for an invasion relatively easily: 'Certainly if the French intended to draw a body together for any attempt against us, the garrisons of Calais, Dunkirk, Gravelines, Lille, Arras, Cambray, Bethune etc. would supply in four or five days a considerable body of men.'[8]

Allowing for the importance of the changing military contexts faced, and their crucial influence on both funding and tasking for the army, there was also an autonomy of military operations in their context, character and success. Issues such as unit cohesion, morale, weaponry, leadership, and tactics were neither minor nor explained by structural factors including, notably, resource availability. As opposed to an emphasis on theoretical constructions, the specificity and granularity of military history recur frequently, as, for example, in contrasting the successes of Marlborough in the 1700s with those of his British counterparts in Spain or, indeed, William III in the 1690s.

And so repeatedly, for, whatever the strengths and weaknesses of a military system, it was the ability of men under pressure to achieve their goal that was crucial. This can lead to a set of interests and values that are antithetical to those of much of society in modern Britain, a contrast encapsulated in 2020 by the pressure to discredit, discard, or move from attention the statues of three military heroes of our period, Robert Clive, Sir John Moore and Sir Thomas Picton, who were castigated for their roles in imperial expansion and, in the latter two cases, the treatment of slave opposition. Criticism of such conduct was on occasion voiced at the time, and the wealth Clive obtained in India was a matter of controversy. At the same time, this situation did not lessen the bravery, skill and success of the individuals involved, and these factors are still worthy of note today.

CHAPTER I

Winning the Home Base, 1688–1746

To begin with a period book-ended by two episodes of total success (and therefore failure, for a total success for one combatant is a complete failure for their opponent) on home turf is to be reminded of the intensely political character of military capability, let alone victory. Linked to that comes the folly of assuming that the national interest is necessarily clear, a point that is particularly true when civil wars are concerned, but not only then. Assessment of national interest in part arises against this background. Moreover, the ability of an invading force, a largely Dutch one, to overthrow the government in 1688 and of another, a Jacobite one, in 1745 to advance from the western coast of Scotland as far as Derby underlined a vulnerability that suggested that, if the Royal Navy was unable to operate effectively, as in these two cases, the English/ British Army would not necessarily succeed.

Protecting the home base was the key need for rulers, and it tested armies, units, their commanders, and the support system, to an extent greater than any other challenge. Civil war was more serious than international conflict in this regard because it did not offer the opportunity for political compromise seen in the latter; the recent history of the British Isles had shown its deadly consequences in the 1640s, consequences kept alive by the memories of families, communities and nation. Loyalty was a particularly important element in such conflict, and it could test greatly the interaction of military and civilian, as well as the situation of the army within the state, and, in particular, the choices and careers of commanders.

The potential of military power had been seen in mid-century during the civil wars (1639–53)[1] and subsequent Interregnum (1649–60), as a large force had been assembled, the New Model Army serving as an expression of the political thrust of the Parliamentary revolution,[2] only for it to be disbanded as part of the return of royal power in the person of Charles II (r. 1660–85). In turn, Charles sought to establish a new army under his control, but political concern, both about royal power and about the possible consequences of such a force, led Parliament only to provide for a modest force. However, Charles successfully sought alternative funding in the shape of secret grants from his first cousin, Louis XIV of France (r. 1643–1715), although this source, first given under the secret Treaty of Dover of 1670, was unreliable. By the end of Charles's reign, the army was 9,000 strong, with another 8,600 on the Irish establishment: in other words, based in Ireland and paid from its taxation, but under the control of the British government.[3] In comparison the peacetime French army was over 200,000 strong.

The succession of Charles's Catholic brother James II (VII in Scotland) in 1685 led to an unsuccessful rebellion under Charles's illegitimate son, James, Duke of Monmouth. Its total failure revealed the greater effectiveness of professional troops and the limited capability of an untrained force, notably at the battle of Sedgemoor, where Monmouth was crushed. The battle and its consequences prefigured Culloden in 1746.

This encouragement to James to increase his army led him to tell the English Parliament on 9 November 1685, 'there is nothing but a good force of well-disciplined troops in constant pay that can defend us from such as, either at home or abroad, are disposed to disturb us.' In the face of parliamentary hostility to his determination to build up the army and appoint Catholic officers, James prorogued (sent home) Parliament, and built-up the army. Whereas Charles's army had cost £283,000 in 1684, under James it cost £620,322 per annum. James's domestic policies, including the quartering of units on towns judged factious, helped link a strong army with unpopular policies. That James was also associated with Louis XIV, in whose army (and that of Spain) he had served in the 1650s, increased anxiety.

In the event, his nephew and son-in-law, William III of Orange, an experienced commander as a result of war with France in 1672–8 (and the leading opponent of Louis), was able to land at Brixham, Devon without resistance in 1688. Blocking William's advance on London, James's larger army, however, was wracked by poor leadership. With the officers divided and the irresolute James fleeing, the army largely dissolved through desertion.[4]

The subsequent defeat of James's supporters in Scotland and, even more so, Ireland, was a far larger task, and one that required an effective army. The challenge was greater than that which had faced Oliver Cromwell in Scotland and Ireland, as France backed the Jacobite (from Latin for James) claim, as it was to do in successive conflicts until the Seven Years' War (1756–63). After this, the French moved on to support first American (in 1778–83) and, later in the 1790s, Irish opponents of British control; this indicated the extent to which the British government and army could not readily separate home defence from foreign war.

At the same time, the legacy of the 'Glorious Revolution' of 1688–9 was a strengthened hostility to a standing (permanent) army, which was associated with tyranny by critics of James II and Louis XIV. In political terms, however, this issue was less significant than keeping the military within the law and ensuring the constraints of an army effectively under parliamentary control as a result of the government's need for taxes. A standing army became illegal without Parliament's approval granted annually in a Mutiny Act which was essential for discipline in the army. The first Mutiny Act was passed in 1689 and sought to restrain monarchical control over the forces as well as the power to impose martial law. Even so, the legislation was still attacked with reference to the 'terrors of a Standing Army, in such absolute subjection to the will and pleasure of their officers.'[5]

The conundrum was expressed in 1757, in the *Discourse of the Establishment of a National and Constitutional Force in England*, a work reprinted in 1794. The author, Charles Jenkinson, who was to serve as Secretary at War in 1778–82, pressed for a militia of non-professional soldiers called up when there was need on the grounds that a strong army threatened national liberties, a repeated claim in British history:

> We are in this dilemma, either to keep our army so low as to be inadequate to the purposes for which it was intended; or to raise it so high as to make it one time or other dangerous to our constitution; for certain it is that any number of troops which will be sufficient to repel the strength of France, will have the power, if they should have the inclination, to enslave us.[6]

The political context, which included the unacceptable character of conscription for the army, was more significant for Britain's strategic dimension than the question of specific army size, which essentially helped to define operational possibilities. Including the Irish establishment, the peacetime army was only about 30,000 strong in the first half of the century, and 45,000 strong in the 1760s. However, the well-known practices of padding muster-rolls for the profit of officers meant that the number of effectives was lower than that of the formal establishment. This was an aspect of the informal economy of the military.

Numbers increased in wartime, but then rapid demobilisations at the end of wars lessened the combat effectiveness of the army, as well as exposing individual soldiers to often very harsh misery in a congested labour market with no social welfare for able-bodied men. Some men therefore turned to crime. The demobilisation after the War of the Austrian Succession ended in 1748 was linked to a perceived social crisis, not least a crime wave and rioting. In part, this crisis reflected the key role of war in the nexus of labour and power relations, and the consequent interaction of the unstable market economy and the needs of the state.[7] More generally, the military labour market was very different to that in India, not least as the British one was affected by the availability of troops from Europe. Moreover, the possibility of raising imperial forces in the colonies reduced the opportunities there for military manpower from Britain.

There was a particularly politically contentious demobilisation after the Nine Years' War ended in 1697, with the opposition to William III using Parliament to force a reduction in size despite William's well-justified fear both that war with France might break out anew over the Spanish Succession and that his diplomatic efforts to arrange a satisfactory solution of the issue would be handicapped by the foreign (both hostile and potentially Allied) response to British troop reductions.

On 8 March 1701, the House of Commons refused to support an army big enough to fulfil their promise of troops to help the Dutch, only for attitudes to change later that year as political opinion turned away from France and toward William. It was this change that enabled William to prepare to take part in the War of the Spanish Succession.

The issues involved in recruitment had long been a theme of comment and satire, as in Shakespeare's *Henry IV*, and they remained significant, as with George Farquhar's comedy *The Recruiting Officer* (1706). Set in Shrewsbury, this was one of the most successful plays of the century, as well as the first staged both in New York and New South Wales. Whatever the comic aspects, aspects of social life, however, helped ensure familiarity with violence. Duelling was a product of concerns with rank, reputation and masculinity, and, it has been argued, an aspect of the imperial state, with its aspirations fronting a society in which status had to be affirmed while masculinity as linked to display and aggression.[8] Masculinity was also associated with horsemanship, even if the proper nature of the latter was debated.[9] At a different social level, poaching, thanks to clashes with gamekeepers, was another manifestation of a familiarity with violence, although, as with duelling, without any unit cohesion or real discipline.

The problems of raising troops in Britain encouraged the hiring of foreign units, a policy also favoured by a number of European powers including France, Spain and Austria, but with Britain particularly reliant on this expedient, and especially so when invasion of either Britain or (after 1714) Hanover threatened – as it did for Britain in January 1756. Henry Fox, Secretary of State for the Southern Department, wrote:

> If we have secured the metropolis [London] it is all. There is not in all the west or north of England a single soldier … if invasion or threats of invasion from France can effect the keeping our fleets and troops at home, while they send regular troops with their fleets to North America, the object of the war will be lost in the first year of it…. we have required both Dutch and Hessians.[10]

Thirty-seven percent of British strength in America in 1781 was provided by German auxiliaries.[11] In part a prudent response to the demands of the navy and the opportunities of the domestic economy, the small size of the army, however, made rebellion particularly challenging. It was still possible to increase numbers by the use of volunteer forces, notably militia, who offered numbers that might be useful to deter possible dissidence. Nevertheless, the militia did not provide the military value against the Jacobite threat that was produced instead by the alternative of deploying subsidised regular forces from Continental allies. In 1715, John, 2nd Earl of Stair, the envoy in Paris, presented Hanoverian forces to the French as a resource for George I against the possibility of Swedish intervention on behalf of the Jacobites:

> There were 10,000 or 12,000 men on the Elbe, in case the King of Sweden or any other foreign power thought fit to support the rebellion, and that Staden and Hamburg were at least as near Scotland as Karlscrona, or any other port, from whence the rebels could be supported.[12]

The Dutch were willing in 1715—16 to send troops to act against the Jacobites and were asked anew in 1722 when Jacobite action was anticipated.[13] Martin Bladen, who had been a colonel in the War of the Spanish Succession before selling out from the army in 1710, was to tell the House of Commons in 1731 that the Hanoverians were a military resource: 'We have 22,000 Hanoverians for no expense.'[14] In 1753, in contrast, when Hanover was threatened, the hopes were of Russian troops who would be able to intimidate a hostile Prussia.[15] This was a remedy pursued on a number of occasions during the period from 1734 to 1756 when Russia was allied to Britain, and then again after 1763.

Reliance on foreign troops in Britain, however, was not to be pursued during the crises caused first by French entry into the War of American Independence, and later by the French Revolutionary and Napoleonic Wars; the new situation drove the need for a greater reliance on militia and volunteer units.

The Jacobite Wars, 1688–1746

The key military success in home control is apt to be underplayed because it did not occur in England. Instead, the warfare in Ireland ensured that that country was under the control of London in foreign policy and defence. This warfare was more serious and sustained than the unsuccessful attempt to reverse British control by rebellion in 1798. In the event, the Jacobites, the supporters of James II, were totally defeated at the Boyne on 1 July 1690 and Aughrim on 12 July 1691, and William III's forces conquered the island, repeating the success of Oliver Cromwell and thus registering an important continuity in English military history.

The Boyne campaign was crucial to the fate of Ireland. The French advice to their ally James II was to play a waiting game, rather than to risk battle. James was urged to burn Dublin, to destroy all the food and forage in William's path, and to wait for a French fleet to interrupt William's seaborne supply route, the subsequent privation to demoralise and weaken him. James, however, understood the need to consider political as well as military contexts. Grasping Dublin's symbolic and strategic significance, and fearing that the logistical and political strains of delay would lead the French and Irish to waste away before his opponents. James therefore decided to fight – rather as George Washington did in 1777 to block the British advance on Philadelphia, then the capital of the Revolution, only to be defeated at Brandywine. This was position warfare.

Outmanoeuvred at the Boyne, James fled and his army collapsed, providing William with a clear victory very different to the battles in the Nine Years' War on the Continent. The conquest of Ireland was difficult, but in a way less threatening for the British government than later Jacobite rebellions in Scotland, because the latter provided an opportunity to advance on London without needing to gain control of the Irish Sea. Yet, had William failed in Ireland, his position in Britain and especially Scotland would then have been precarious, as the Jacobites would have had their own territory in which to recruit and raise funds. Moreover, France, as the ally of the Jacobites, would have been in a stronger position to intervene in Britain. Such counterfactuals ('what-ifs') might seem idle speculation, but they were present to ministers and commentators aware of the challenge posed by Ireland, not least if it was supported by a foreign power, as it had not been in the mid-17th century.

The key elements in 1689–91 deserve attention, because the victories for William were those for a hybrid or mixed force, which was very much to be a pattern of British military activity on land (although far less so at sea). In August 1689, William's troops, many of them Huguenots or Dutch, had landed and occupied Belfast and successfully besieged

Carrickfergus, as in effect a sequel to the invasion of England the previous year, but failed to force a battle and lost heavily that winter through disease. The following year, William benefited from a larger army than that of the Jacobites and French, by approximately 35,000 to 21,000. The deployment of this force, and William's arrival in June 1690, reflected the significance he attached to Ireland. In contrast, he did not go to Scotland, where, despite victory at Killiecrankie in 1689 – the Jacobite charge defeating static musketeers – the Jacobites collapsed in 1690–1. In Ireland, with an army increased by English recruits and 7,000 hired Danish troops, William succeeded at the Boyne and in capturing Dublin, but failed when he tried to storm Limerick in August 1690. A separate force, benefiting from naval support, played a key role in capturing the fortified ports in southern Ireland. Commanded by John Churchill, then Earl of Marlborough, who proved a vigorous commander, this force took Cork in September and Kinsale in October.

In 1691, William was not in command, and a new French commander, Charles, Marquis of Saint-Ruhe, was sent with arms. Nevertheless, on 30 June Athlone fell to the Williamite forces after hard fighting and a very heavy bombardment. On 12 July, after attacks on the well-deployed Jacobite force (which benefited from its position on a hill) had failed, Hugh Mackay turned the Jacobite flank at Aughrim by leading his cavalry across a bog on which he had laid hurdles; the Jacobite force broke, their infantry suffering heavy casualties in the retreat. For both sides, casualties were heavier than at the Boyne. After Aughrim, Galway and then Limerick surrendered, and the war in Ireland came to an end.

Both the major engagements had been won by the attacking force, and, in each case, tactical considerations relating to the terrain and to the ability to take advantage of developments had been crucial, while the vulnerability of defending armies to flanking attacks had been clearly demonstrated. The context was also crucial in terms of the greater priority attached to Ireland by William than Louis XIV, and the resources available accordingly.

French invasion preparations on behalf of the Jacobites proved fruitless in 1692, 1696 and 1708. However, the Jacobite rebellions of 1715 and 1745 posed a threat to the Hanoverian dynasty that had come to the throne in 1714. The 1715 rebellion ('The '15') involved large-scale hostilities, notably the battles of Preston and Sheriffmuir, but did not gain the tempo and dynamic that was to be seen in Jacobite campaigning in 1745–6. The rising in 1715 saw a hostile response from the regular forces as well as those of the local militia, but it was the Regulars who proved crucial. Indeed, the Cumberland and Westmorland militia offered no resistance when a Jacobite force that had mustered at Kelso invaded north-west England in early November. Regular forces under Lieutenant-General George Carpenter and Major-General Charles Wills saved the situation. Carpenter had stilled the Jacobites in Northumbria, and he and Wills then drove the Jacobites in the north-west on Preston, where a Scottish force had been defeated by Cromwell in 1648. A government assault on the town, which the Jacobites had hastily fortified with barricades, failed on 12 November; instead of attacking them or trying to fight their way out, however, the Jacobites allowed their enemies to surround the town, and their commander, Thomas Foster, unconditionally surrendered on 14 November. Fragile from the start, the '15 in England was at an end.

Carpenter (1657–1732), the son of a Royalist in the Civil War, joined a regiment raised by James II after the suppression of the Monmouth Rebellion of 1685 and served in the Nine Years' War (1689–97), first in Ireland, fighting at the Boyne and Aughrim, and then in the Low Countries. In 1703, Carpenter purchased a colonelcy and fought in Spain in the War of the Spanish Succession (1702–13), being badly wounded at Brihuega. After the '15, he served as Governor of Minorca from 1716 to 1718 and as Commander in Scotland from 1716 to 1725, and gained an Irish peerage in 1719. Wills (1666–1741) also served in Ireland, the Low Countries and Spain, but also in the West Indies, including in the unsuccessful attack on Guadeloupe in 1703. After the '15, for which he was promoted lieutenant-general, Wills became Governor of Portsmouth, an MP, and, eventually, general commanding the Infantry in 1739. These men were typical of the continuity of experience and command in these years.

In Scotland, the '15 proved more difficult for the government and lasted until 1716. The Hanoverian forces in Scotland under John, 2nd Duke of Argyll (1680–1743), a veteran of the War of the Spanish Succession, were outnumbered, but the Jacobites, under the indecisive John, Earl of Mar, who lacked the necessary military experience, failed to gain the initiative. The two armies fought at Sheriffmuir on 13 November 1715. Unaware of the other's dispositions, each general drew up his forces so that his right wing overlapped the other's left, which was instrumental in the defeat of the left wings of both armies, but Mar failed to exploit his numerical superiority (initially about two to one, and probably far more after the defeat of Argyll's left) and did not use his reserves. Indeed, Argyll was left in possession of the battlefield, while the indecisive nature of the battle was to his advantage, as Mar did not continue his advance and needed a victory to keep his army united and to maintain the momentum of success.

The Jacobite claimant, styled 'James III and VIII', arrived in Scotland on 22 December 1715, but failed to bring any French support. Instead, the Dutch had provided the government with 6,000 troops, many of whom were sent north under Lieutenant-General William Cadogan, an effective organiser who proved a more determined general than Argyll. The two men worked together for a while. Despite the bitterness of the winter and a Jacobite scorched-earth policy, Argyll marched on Perth on 21 January. Unable to confront Argyll in the field, and unwilling and unprepared for guerrilla warfare, the Jacobites had lost the initiative and their army suffered badly from low morale and desertion. Rather than facing a siege of Perth, James abandoned the city on 31 January, throwing his cannon into the River Tay, and retreated, first to Dundee, and then to Montrose, before sailing to France on 5 February, leaving his army to disperse. This repeated the pattern seen with his father in 1689 and must have eroded Jacobite confidence: refuge in France was a benefit to the Pretender, but problematic for his followers.

In London, political and military favour moved from Argyll to William, 1st Earl Cadogan (1671–1726), who restored control over northern Scotland. The key military figure after Marlborough, who suffered two serious strokes in 1716, Cadogan was his protégé and, in 1722, successor as Master-General of the Ordnance and senior army commander. An Irish Protestant whose grandfather had served in the New Model Army,

Cadogan joined the Army of the North formed by the Ulster Protestants in 1689 and subsequently served in Ireland until, in 1694, he transferred to the Low Countries. Appointed Quartermaster-General in 1701 by Marlborough, whom he had met at the siege of Cork in 1690, he, in the face of the hostility of the Tory ministry, went into voluntary exile with Marlborough in 1712, being reinstated in the army by George I in 1714.[16]

After the '15, there was another Jacobite attempt in 1719, but the supporting Spanish force was largely dispersed by a violent storm, which discouraged most of the Jacobites from rising. Those that did were defeated at Glenshiel on 10 June, their low morale helping the government forces gain and use the initiative. The Jacobites then went home, while the small Spanish force surrendered.

Attempts were subsequently made to strengthen the government's position in Scotland against another Jacobite rising, George I himself in 1725 feeling it necessary to recommend 'the careful execution of his orders by Major-General George Wade with respect to disarming the Highlands.' Appointed commander in chief in Scotland that year, Wade was instructed to continue the construction of fortifications and barracks in northern Scotland; Charles, 2nd Viscount Townshend, a Secretary of State, wrote: 'The King looks upon securing that weak part as extremely necessary to discourage the Jacobites.'[17]

In practice, Jacobite hopes in the 1720s focused on a rising in London supported by an invasion. In 1722, the Atterbury Plot involved such a rising assisted by the Irish regiments in French service: the 14,000 strong Irish Jacobite army had left under the Treaty of Limerick of 1691 and entered French service, joining about 6,000 men already there. In the event, the French government warned the British government in 1722, recalling Irish units from the Channel. The British requested the Dutch hold 3,000 ready to be sent if required, had an army camp prepared in Hyde Park to overawe London, and summoned regular troops from Ireland. There was no rising.

In 1726, the Jacobites sought Austrian military support, claiming that domestic support would act as a force multiplier and that the British government was not in a state to assemble 6,000 troops in any one place. Prince Eugene, one of the leading Austrian ministers and a former battlefield ally of Marlborough, was dubious, not least because he was not prepared to rely on large-scale desertions from the British Army nor on the Jacobite assurance that George I could not move troops from London to oppose an invasion as the city was rebellious.[18] None was mounted.

The Jacobite army, the alternative British Army used in 1715–16 and 1745–6, was in the event, like Monmouth's army in 1685, a newly created volunteer force. It was therefore a very different type of army to that provided by regular forces, with non-bureaucratic supply and recruitment systems which necessarily affected its methods of operation, not least in matters of logistics and control and command. Having landed in July 1745, the Jacobites outmanoeuvred the government forces and advanced on Edinburgh. At the first battle, at Prestonpans on 21 September, a Highland charge overcame defensive firepower. To a degree, the tactic reflected a degree of Jacobite indiscipline and lack of organisation that hindered more formalised tactics, but it was also effective: the government forces fired only one round before the Jacobites were upon them with their broadswords, and the forces then fled. This rapid victory consolidated the Jacobite position in central Scotland.

When Charles Edward Stuart (Bonnie Prince Charlie) pressed on to invade England, his hardy troops were not too badly affected by the weather; combined with a lack of food,[19] however, the weather did prevent Wade, now commander in chief and a field marshal, from marching his Regulars from Newcastle to Carlisle to block the Jacobite invasion. Subsequently, in late December, Wade, ordered to march from Yorkshire to Newcastle 'as fast as the bad roads and this rigorous season will admit of', feared that 'we shall reduce our army to nothing by long marches and encampments at this time of year.'[20] The weather also prevented the French from mounting any supporting invasion of southern England, although the British fleet was also important in deterring the latter.

The Jacobites were helped by the unfortified nature of most of the British Isles, which ensured that, having taken a poorly fortified Carlisle, they did not have to fight their way through a series of positions, losing time and manpower as they did so. This absence also meant that the regular army lacked a network of bases that could provide shelter and replenish supplies.

Shifts and expedients could be seen with both sides. Invading England, Charles Edward ordered 6,000 pairs of shoes from the city authorities in Edinburgh, obtained several thousand fresh pairs in Preston, and demanded 6,000 from Glasgow on his retreat. His opponent, William, Duke of Cumberland, similarly had to obtain footwear for his men, and, between 30 May and 3 July 1746, Robert Finlay of Glasgow supplied 3,058 pairs of shoes. In such matters, the government forces benefited from the availability of ready money. In a moment of real concern in the campaign on 4 December 1745, when Cumberland was pressing his father, George II, for footwear, the general's secretary, Sir Everard Fawkener, asked the local JPs (Justices of the Peace) in the West Midlands to assemble as many horses as possible the next day, two shillings being offered for each that could carry an infantry soldier. By 9 December, Cumberland could transport 1,000 infantry that way.[21] The campaign also saw both sides seeking to obtain food on the march. As the head of estates, the local élite were pushed into providing: arriving in Penrith on 18 November, the Jacobite advance guard successfully demanded hay and oats from all but one of the local great houses. Correspondingly, on 3 December, Cumberland wrote to William, 3rd Duke of Devonshire, a key landowner in Derbyshire, 'Should we come your way I hope that we shall find meat and bread for the soldiers.'[22]

Charles Edward had only limited control over his officers and men, and had to keep them going with promises. As a consequence, his army could not sustain its advance on London beyond Derby, which it reached on 4 December 1745. Turning back on 6 December, Charles Edward made an effective retreat, thwarting efforts to block it, although the garrison he left in Carlisle fell to siege by Cumberland on 30 December. Once in Scotland, he defeated the government forces at Falkirk on 17 January 1746: a Highland charge was effective, whereas the government troops were hindered by fighting uphill, by growing darkness, and by the heavy rain wetting their powder, all of which also helped make their artillery ineffective. Alongside the vigour of the Jacobites' Highland charge, these factors were presumably responsible for the lack of fighting spirit noted by Brigadier-General James Cholmondeley:

> They [the cavalry] began the attack with spirit which did not last long … our foot gave a faint fire and then faced to the right about, as regularly as if they had had the word of command, and could not be rallied until they got a considerable distance, although I do not think that they were pursued by two hundred men.

Assisted by resting and resupplying his forces in Aberdeen in early spring, and by waiting for better weather, Cumberland's army, in turn, could sustain its advance in 1746 beyond Aberdeen. That helped Cumberland to gain the initiative, which was a key element in the successive closing down of Jacobite options. Moving forward from Aberdeen, his troops crossed the waist-high waters of the River Spey, and, unlike their opponents, found their supply needs met. Cumberland was helped by also being able to deploy Hessian units.[23]

The Jacobites ran out of the advantage – strategically, then operationally, and, finally, tactically. At Culloden on 16 April 1746, the size of Cumberland's larger army provided defence in depth, and this helped make the firepower more effective. The discipline of the infantry blunted what would otherwise have been sensible preliminary Jacobite lunges. In earlier engagements, at Prestonpans, Clifton and Falkirk, the government cavalry had plunged, or been plunged, into the fray regardless, and the control of the fighting had passed to the Jacobites. In contrast, at Culloden the cavalry was fed around the two flanks, ready to intervene when the favourable opportunity offered. For the first time, the action on the side of the government forces was initially left to the artillery. Cumberland's artillery, firing canister shot, and infantry so thinned the numbers of the advancing clansmen that those who reached the British line were driven back by bayonet. Any gaps in the front line could be filled. Cumberland had the advantage of a larger army, superior firepower, an excellent site, and a foolish opponent whose options were running out. Many factors led to confusion amongst the Jacobites: the slant of their line, the nature of the terrain, which was partly waterlogged, the difficulty of seeing what was happening in the smoke produced by the guns, and the independent nature of each unit's advance. John Maclean, a Jacobite officer, recorded:

> When all that pleased or were able to follow their colours march out and was drawn in order of battle about two musket shot from the enemy, they were waiting for us in very good order with their artillery before them and the wind and snow in their back. After a short stay and all the disadvantages an army could meet with as to their numbers, they double or triple ours, and all advantages of ground and wind and weather, our cannon began to play upon them, and they upon us. After we stayed about ten minutes, we were ordered to march hastily to the enemy, which we did boldly. They began a smart fire of their small guns and grapeshot from their cannon, till we were beat back with great losses. Our right wing was flanked and surrounded by the horse which did great execution.[24]

Cumberland wrote:

> ...the Royals and Pulteney's hardly took their fire-locks from their shoulders ... Barrel's regiment and the left of Monroe's fairly beat them with their bayonets... In their [Jacobites'] rage that they could not make any impression upon the battalions, they threw stones at them for at least a minute or two before their total rout began.

His aide-de-camp, Joseph Yorke, noted:

> The broadswords succeeding so ill, the rebels turned their backs, and in flying were so well received by the cavalry under Hawley and Bland, who had broke down two stone walls, and unperceived had gained their rear, that a general rout and slaughter ensued.[25]

Whereas the government side had survived defeats at Prestonpans and Falkirk, the heavy casualties at Culloden marked the military end of Jacobitism. The remains of the Jacobite army would not have been able to mount an effective resistance as they lacked supplies in the barren Highlands. Guerrilla resistance was more of an option, but, lacking the space enjoyed by the American colonists, the Jacobites would have been penned in between Cumberland and those Highland clans that were hostile, while, without the presence of the fugitive Charles Edward who fled to France, the resistance now lacked focus. The way was clear for Cumberland's repression of those clans that had supported the rising, for significant changes in the governance of the Highlands, and for renewed expenditure on the forts in Scotland.

The integration of the Highlands into the British state after Culloden was brutal, but was swiftly followed by a significant increase in the already-important Scottish role in the army. In troops, officers and commanders, the Scottish contribution was disproportionate and significant, and notably so in both India and North America. The *Monitor* asked on 27 October 1759: 'Can Britain ever forget how much she is indebted to a [Brigadier-General James] Murray, whose example and intrepidity taught and led on his Highland laddies to mow down the enemy with their broad swords, like grass under the scythe?' Of the Scots Jacobites, the *Briton* of 19 June 1762 claimed: 'the survivors have since literally washed away their offences with their blood; witness their bones now bleaching in almost every quarter of the globe.'

This recruitment was an aspect of the major improvement to the structure and practice of the British Army stemming from the defeat of Jacobitism. This improvement was due in part to the recruitment of Scottish Highlanders, attracted by conditions of service including land grants, and in part to the experience gained through fighting opponents different to conventional European armies,[26] this experience coming from a variety of sources including notably colonial conflict. The Scottish Highlands offered the support of a robust military system and culture wherein previous service to the clan leadership was now transferred to the state at large, resulting in an outpouring of highly motivated and loyal warriors. Typically in a Scottish Highland regiment, at least two of the ten companies were raised in Ireland. Although efforts were focused on Ulster Protestants, many of these troops were Irish Catholics. Irish recruitment particularly took off after the Catholic Relief Act of 1778. By 1813, close to one-third of the army was of Irish descent.

The Suppression of Disorder

Control of the home base was not simply a matter of suppressing rebellion. Indeed, the army was the essential force used to check public disorder and thus give a cohesion to society. That might seem a long way from the conquest of empire across the oceans, but that conquest was dependent on a secure home base, while an important part of the empire was itself the British Isles – a point underlined by the significance of Ireland, and also by the only recent extension of control over Scotland.

In mainland Britain, there was not always a military response to popular unrest: for example, the Sacheverell Riots in London and many of the mid-century food riots. However, troops were used to suppress some riots and to oppose certain types of large-scale lawlessness; as a result, military support to the civil power underpinned control, as it also did in the colonies. Conversely, the use of this power, for example the St. George's Fields Massacre in London in 1768 and the Boston Massacre of 1770 ('massacres' in which six to eleven and five people were killed respectively), could lead to bitter hostility, although that was not always the case. Thus, the suppression by Wade of a large-scale tax riot in Glasgow in 1725 did not become the basis for such opposition, nor the use of the army against rioters in Newcastle in 1740 or in Cornwall in 1757 and 1773. In Newcastle, workers seeking to pressurise the city authorities over the price of food after a poor harvest were resisted by the town guard before order was restored with the arrival of troops from Morpeth and Berwick. In Cornwall, the tinners were frequently ready to turn to violence in a county where authority was precarious. The situation was far more difficult in 1766, because the food riots of that year were widespread and the government could not meet the requests for troops from local authorities.[27] In 1780, in the face of the Gordon Riots in London, George III summoned the Privy Council which empowered the army to employ force without the prior permission of a magistrate. In turn, the suppression of the riots did not lead to bitter hostility.

More mundanely, the absence of a significant police force led to reliance on troops, although they were insufficient in number for the widespread lawlessness, and other means had to be used. The *Newcastle Courant* of 28 May 1743 reported:

> Yesterday Mr William Aynsley, Water Bailiff, with near 20 men on horseback, well armed, set out for Bellingham, in order to take possession of an estate which the country people by force of arms, have deprived the right owner of, and murdered a bailiff the beginning of this month.

In 1773, an effort to serve writs on two Cardiganshire JPs was forestalled when the server was forced to eat them before being beaten viciously and thrown into a river, feigning death. Another warrant was served on them only with the aid of a pistol. Continental commentators, such as the Comte de Cambis, French ambassador from 1737 to 1740, were amazed at the extent to which popular disturbances were not punished while law and order were flouted; with one of the two Secretaries of State, he attended the Haymarket Theatre in London in 1738 when a riot stopped a performance by a troupe of French actors. The small size of the army limited action, but most riots were very specific in their aims, often seeking to fix the price of bread in times of dearth.

As well as acting against rioters, troops escorted valuable cargoes, especially of bullion and coin. Others guarded prisoners en route to trial, jail and execution, as well as theatres, which were potential foci for riot, with troops deployed for example during the aforementioned riot at the Haymarket theatre. Tax collectors and revenue officers were given support, and smuggling was opposed, a task that was more difficult in Ireland, Scotland, Wales and Western England than in the more law-abiding South-East.[28] Thus, the small detachments of the army stationed in peacetime Wales, at Aberystwyth, Carmarthen and Aberdovey, were there mostly to support the Customs and the Excise. Such small detachments, however, did nothing for training and little for discipline.

The army's success in overcoming opposition in the home base during the Jacobite risings was an important adjunct to British power, both thwarting serious French attempts to overthrow the British government, and guaranteeing Britain as both base and ally. This was important to the rise to imperial power. That, ironically, had been displayed in 1746 when the opposite had occurred. The recall of British forces from the Austrian Netherlands to confront the Jacobites, as well as the dispatch of the British-paid Hessians to the same end, enabled the French to conquer most of the Austrian Netherlands, one British general, John, 2nd Earl of Dunmore, correctly predicting that the under-strength garrison at Antwerp would fall rapidly. To regain these losses, Britain had to accept a peace in 1748, in which it returned its imperial gain of Louisbourg.

John, Lord Glenorchy had written to his daughter the day before Culloden:

> I have often repented taking out the iron bars from the windows and sashing them, and taking away a great iron door, and weakening the house as to resistance by adding modern wings to it. If it had remained in the old castle way as it was before, I might have slept very sound in it, for their whole army could not have taken it without cannon.[29]

However, this view was restricted to that emergency. In contrast, in 1762, Elizabeth Montagu could reflect: 'A virtuoso or a dilettanti may stand as secure in these times behind his Chinese rail as the knight on his battlements in former days.'[30] Indeed, surviving castles were very much an echo of the past. Richard Wilson, who visited Okehampton Castle in 1771, soon after painted a Romantic vision of the hilltop castle with its ruins silhouetted against the evening sky. During the Middle Ages, defensibility was a characteristic of the grand houses of society, but no longer. Blenheim, the palace built in the 1710s for the victorious Marlborough and named as a continued reminder of his prowess at the battle in 1704, was no fortress. Fortification, instead, was reduced to fantasy, as in mock-castellated walls, for example at Castle Howard, the new seat of the Earl of Carlisle.

On the other hand, there were the defended installations of the state, notably the naval dockyards. To overawe the Scottish Highlands and prevent a recurrence of the Jacobite risings, the government built forts – notably Ruthven (1719–21), Forts William (1690–8, 1725), Augustus (1729–42) and George (1727; rebuilt 1748–69), all named after the post-1689 order – as they had done in North Wales after conquering it in the late thirteenth century. Wade built about 240 miles of military roads and 30 bridges to link these positions. However, these forts were different to the form of traditional castles, and none were in private hands. Despite the part of aristocrats in helping raise units during national emergencies, especially the '45, the role of providing defence had been largely replaced by a state monopoly. There was reliance instead on the Royal Navy as well as military power, the latter comprising both the regular army as well as the militia.

The Army and the State

As with the Church, and more than in the Royal Navy, command positions were generally deployed for political purposes in order to reward political allies. Opponents lost their posts; for example, the young William Pitt, an ensign, was dismissed from the army in 1736 for having spoken and voted against George II in the House of Commons. As a result, Pitt was, during the Seven Years' War (1756–63), to be a great war minister who had never fought: like Lloyd George, but not Churchill. The dismissal of officers for voting against the government in Parliament was also an issue on a number of other occasions including in 1733 and 1765.

Dedication and, to a degree, morale were not high among officers and soldiers. Consequently, absenteeism, cronyism, and the pursuit of the financial benefits of command occupied the time of most officers. This was a reflection both of the extent to which the army shared in the values of society and of its institutional character. The bitterly contested field of military appointment was particularly significant, because it reflected, but also redefined, the practice of patronage, which was presented as a matter of recognising and recommending talent. As with the Church of England, this was also a system that had consequences in terms of the 'end-product.' George I (r. 1714–27) and George II (r. 1727–60), who each had experience of military service in Hanoverian forces on the Continent, supported the principle of long service as the main way to advancement, and did their best to counter the purchase of military commissions (appointment as an officer).

Under George I, military patronage was also very much directed to political purposes by a king struggling to cement his position, first in 1714–16 in the face of concern about Tory loyalty and Jacobite opposition, and then in 1716–20 in the face of developing divisions within both the Whig élite and the royal family, divisions that were to lead to the very bitter 'Whig Split' of 1717–20. This crisis saw George, Prince of Wales (later George II) and his ally Argyll in opposition to George I and his major military ally, Cadogan, and military patronage was used to strengthen George I's party in the House of Commons. In turn, there were opposition attacks on the size of the army, notably in December 1717 when an attempt was made to reduce the army on the British establishment from 16,000 to 12,000 men in order to keep the land tax at two shillings (the pre-decimal equivalent of 10 p today) in the pound, instead of three (15 p).[31] The government won the divisions (votes of 185–117 and 172–158), but the issue showed a point of vulnerability.

The rivalry between Cadogan and Argyll carried forward the military factionalism of the War of the Spanish Succession. Also in 1717, the government only narrowly defeated in the Commons (by 204 to 194) an attempt to charge Cadogan with embezzling the funds entrusted him for bringing over Dutch troops to help suppress the '15. Cadogan remained a major political figure, although he lost influence due to his rivalry with Sir Robert Walpole, First Lord of the Treasury from 1721 to 1742, and because he was unwilling to respond positively to the French alliance which lasted from 1716 to 1731. In 1724, Henry Pelham, a figure close to Walpole but not Cadogan, became Secretary-at-War, moving into a key position, responsible for the correspondence between the monarch and other departments. Initially, it seemed that Cadogan's authority was to continue, albeit being confined within narrow limits, but in 1725 he was no longer appointed one of the Lords Justices when George went to Hanover, and was replaced as Master-General of the Ordnance by Argyll. Cadogan died in 1726.

By not, as king, backing a figure comparable to Cadogan (certainly until he promoted his second son Cumberland), George II retained greater power in the army. He personally signed the commissions and, as the instance of the way in which patronage was not incompatible with rewarding merit, was keen on competence, using his formidable memory for names to good effect in keeping oversight of the leading members of the officer class. The monarchs were far less interested in and knowledgeable about naval affairs, a situation that did not change until George III (r. 1760–1820), and then only because he had no personal experience of service in either branch, although he sought to reward merit in both.

George II, who had served bravely as a young man at the battle of Oudenaarde in 1708, frequently reviewed his troops.[32] Like his brother-in-law, Frederick William I of Prussia (r. 1713–40), George believed that the military reviews he conducted were the most obvious and impressive display of his power and importance, and a way to test readiness and efficiency; and Horse Guards in London was in part redesigned by William Kent to this end. In Sir John Thornhill's depiction of the royal family in the Painted Hall at Greenwich, George, as Prince of Wales, was shown, like his father, George I, wearing armour. Once king, George II held a series of regimental reviews which gave him an opportunity to acquire a close knowledge of the army. He had the Guards' regimental reports and returns sent to him personally every week. When he reviewed his troops, he did so with great attention to detail, which in part tended to mean an emphasis on appearance. This is recorded, for a review of the Hanoverian troops held at Bemerode in 1735, in a large painting by J. F. Lüders.[33] Reviewing in London was generally conducted in St. James's Park or Hyde Park, and was a prominent and public activity that was attended by courtiers and diplomats.

Reviewing was a preparation for war, and George derived great pleasure from his participation in the victory of Dettingen in 1743, a victory in which both British and Hanoverian forces served. This was to be his last command, in part because he was getting old and in large part because his role was subsequently taken by Cumberland. While the War of the Austrian Succession continued, however, it was not obvious to contemporaries that George would not serve again; indeed, in 1748, it was briefly suggested that he would go to the Low Countries in order to command the army.[34]

Unlike George III, who displayed no such particular favour, George II enjoyed the company of military men, such as John, 2nd Duke of Argyll, Sir Charles Hotham, William Stanhope and Richard Sutton. Indeed, the last three were each given diplomatic posts, with Stanhope also becoming a Secretary of State and Earl of Harrington, the latter a considerable achievement as George was careful about his promotions to the peerage. In addition, Charles Churchill, a protégé of Walpole, was close to the King, whom he served as a Groom of the Bedchamber from 1718 until his death in 1745. Born in about 1679, he was slightly older than the King, who made him a general in 1727 and subsequently promoted him in 1735 and 1739. Churchill was symptomatic of an aspect of military culture in that he claimed never to have read a book.

Moreover, George's long-time Hanoverian mistress, Amalie Sophie Marianne von Wallmoden, was the daughter of a Hanoverian general, Johann von Wendt, who held command in the 1740s; their son, Johann Ludwig von Wallmoden, became another Hanoverian general.

George II certainly knew more than his British or Hanoverian ministers about war, and was determined to control military patronage. Due to the nature of political exigencies, he had less control over both army and warmaking than Frederick William I of Prussia or his son Frederick the Great (r. 1740–86). Nevertheless, in 1744–6, George was able to keep Pitt from the Secretaryship-at-War, a post which he sought and which was very much the king's *commis* for military affairs.

In Britain, George II sought to end corrupt financial practices in the army and did his best to further merit as the basis for promotions. Like his father, George promoted the principle of long service as the main way to advancement, a theme that was also to be taken up by his grandson, George III, and did his best to counter the purchases of military commissions. Although his goal of ending corrupt financial practices and officers' pecuniary perquisites in particular was, like that of his father, only partially implemented, the traditional character of proprietary soldiering (private ownership) at troop and company level was fundamentally changed, and to the significant detriment of the incidental income of captains. Regimental entrepreneurship, however, largely escaped unchanged, and colonels maintained their private financial position until the reign of Queen Victoria. Thus, the interests of the king ran counter to those of the military establishment. When George asked Charles Churchill what had become of his hautboys (soldiers who played an oboe-type instrument), Churchill struck his hand on his breeches pocket, so as to make the money rattle, and answered 'Here they are, please Your Majesty, don't you hear them'.[35] This was not the best basis for an effective response to the French army when conflict with France began in 1743.

George's concern about the army, and his association of it with his own prestige, led him to insist that he approve new uniforms, which was a clear statement of his own role and, correspondingly, the subordination of that of colonels. In 1751, moreover, colonels were prohibited from using their own crests in regimental colours or clothing. The new uniforms were depicted in a series of paintings by the Swiss-born David Morier (1705–70) that were of interest to George. Morier also gained the patronage of Cumberland.

George's concern with the military, of which he was commander in chief, also ensured that he took a close interest in operations, pressing the ministers on military policy and intervening over command decisions.[36] Individual officers could expect the king to know of their conduct and to have views on it, and, if he did not, this was seen as affecting their chances for promotion and desirable commands. In 1731, Colonel John Campbell wrote to Charles, Lord Elphinstone making this clear, and also showing how the royal oversight of patronage worked for Scotland:

> I was at Court ... when Lord Ilay [later 3rd Duke of Argyll] went into the King's Closet to receive his commands in relation to the Peer [Scottish representative peer] to be chosen in poor Loudoun's place. Just before he went in he showed me a list of eleven or twelve, among which you were. He told me at the same time that he had put your name there that the King might be acquainted with it, and when he came out of the Closet he told me that the King said you were a young lord just come from your travels, upon which he set him right and told him who you was. I said he might have added what would have done you no harm was that you had been a considerable time in the service and had been wounded in it.[37]

In 1740, it was not surprising that Argyll's breach with the government, which led to his losing the post of Master-General of the Ordnance and the colonelcy of the Royal Horse Guards, should be attributed to the king's indignant refusal to accept the Duke's demand for the title of field marshal,[38] although a range of factors played a role.

George was also important on other occasions. In 1756, when the fall of the Mediterranean base and colony of Minorca to the French in the opening stages of the Seven Years' War reflected a multiple, indeed scandalous, failure in British warmaking, he was frank in his opinions about military conduct, harshly treating Lieutenant-General Thomas Fowke, the Governor of Gibraltar, who had refused to obey orders to send a battalion on Admiral Byng's fleet to help the besieged garrison of Minorca. Fowke was cashiered, losing his rank and his regiment, and George was reported as saying 'that if he was unfit to serve for one year, he certainly was so for ever',[39] which was a dismissal of any half-measures. Fowke (c. 1690–1765), had followed his father, a captain, into the army in 1702, in 1707 exchanging positions with the latter who died a year later. Fighting in Spain during the War of the Spanish Succession, Fowke managed to retain his commission during the peacetime low-period for military careers, although this meant he had to move regiments three times, becoming a major in 1716 and a lieutenant-colonel in 1722, but then holding that rank until the outbreak of war brought new regiments and promotion: to colonel in 1741 and brigadier-general in 1745. Court-martialled after the humiliating defeat at Jacobite hands at Prestonpans in 1745, Fowke was exonerated and served in the Low Countries in the War of Austrian Succession, becoming a major-general in 1747.

The Byng trial led to controversy over the quality of mercy, not least George's attitudes. The episode provided an opportunity for Henry Fox, who was trying to embarrass the ministry, to tell the House of Commons on 23 February 1757:

> That during the nine years that himself had been Secretary at War [1746–55], it had been his constant practice on all courts martial to acquaint the King with any favourable circumstances that had appeared. That he had always found His Majesty disposed to lenity, and when he said nothing, the King would ask, 'Have you nothing favourable to tell me?'

The pugnacious George, however, was determined to maintain his control of the army against all-comers, whether opposition politicians or, indeed, his own ministers, categories as he was aware between which individuals could move. In some respects, the king played a role akin to Marlborough and Cadogan in directing a military interest, although there was not the political pressure on him that they faced. Horatio Walpole recorded in 1740 that his Prime Ministerial brother, Robert, was snubbed by George:

> When he lets fall a word or two in favour of some officer, is told (that is between you and me) that he does not understand any thing of military matters, and by this means he has often the ill will of disappointments, which were not in his power to prevent ... Sir Robert has very little to do in the military promotions; he recommends friends and relations of members of Parliament to be ensigns and cornets, but his Majesty himself keeps an exact account of all the officers;

knows their characters, and their long services, and generally nominates, at his own time, the colonels to vacant regiments.[40]

'At his own time' meant that George would not be hurried to suit his minister and his political calculations in terms of parliamentary management. Nevertheless, George also helped Walpole with appointments to the army. Thus, in 1740, Sir James Lowther observed, 'Colonel Mordaunt has got a regiment, they give almost all of them to young colonels that are in the House [of Commons].'[41] John Mordaunt (1697–1780), a Walpole loyalist, had indeed received army promotion, but was also a protégé of the king. The grandson of a Viscount, he was an equerry to George from 1737 to 1760, and was promoted by him through the ranks of general (brigadier-general, 1745, major-general, 1747, lieutenant-general, 1754) and became a Knight of the Bath in 1749. Mordaunt was cleared at a court martial after his failure to capture Rochefort in 1757. Earlier in 1740, Sarah, Dowager-Duchess of Marlborough provided a more wholesale account of the role of Walpole:

> Upon the Duke of Montagu's being in a violent passion with him and saying he would go to the King, he has added in effect three places more to the Great Wardrobe, which, I am sure, as he makes it, is at least ten or twelve thousand pounds a year, that of the Master of the Ordnance, General Evans's Regiment and he was to have had the Band of Pensioners, but the Duke of Bolton having been promised to be Master of the Ordnance, Sir Robert compounded that business, to gratify the Duke of Montagu in the Ordnance, and gives him the Place of the Pensioners, and a pension [annual payment] to make up the disappointment, and another pension to the Duke of Montagu to pay to my Lord Cardigan for his disappointment in not having the Pensioners.[42]

Montagu lacked any competence. Appointments tended to reflect political factors and patronage: 17 of the 57 colonels in 1762 were MPs.

Government favour, family influence and personal links were all important factors in promotion. Sir Charles Hotham (1693–1758) received his first commission when only 13, and was promoted to lieutenant-colonel in 1720 and colonel in 1731 thanks to longstanding royal friendship and George's approval of his role on a diplomatic mission in 1730. This friendship was an important aspect of the emphasis on loyalty in appointment to positions of command, which reflected the key role of the army as the support of government, in the face of both a rival claim to the throne and a populace willing to use force to protest against unwelcome policies. This element of professionalism, the political dimension vital to the tasking of the military, did not, however, help ensure operational competence in the expansion of empire.

Family links were particularly significant with the succession of sons to paternal posts, which helped steep officers in military culture and regimental loyalty. Thus, James replaced Charles, Lord Tyrawley as colonel of the 7th Foot in 1713. Wellington's career owed much to the support of his eldest brother, Richard, Marquess Wellesley.[43] These were not the only links. Thomas Picton (1758–1815) was influenced by his uncle, lieutenant-colonel William Picton, who both told him tales of victory and secured him a commission in the 12th Foot with the rank of ensign at the age of thirteen. The uncle subsequently oversaw his military education, including his reading, and got him a transfer into a new regiment under his colonelcy. Similarly, Coote Manningham (c. 1765–1809), a second son, began as a subaltern under his uncle Sir Robert Boyd, colonel of the 39th Regiment, in the siege of Gibraltar. Boyd (1710–94) had entered the army in his father's profession of civilian storekeeper, and was commissary general in Germany in 1758–9.

Officer absenteeism could be a significant problem, for example for the garrison on Minorca in 1756, as could straightforward incompetence, not least as officers lacked training other than 'at the cannon's mouth.' These elements were more serious because of the extent to which officers, notably those without connection and patronage, were placed on half-pay in peacetime, and therefore became very much a second-class of military service. Nevertheless, officers who owed appointment and promotion in large part to political connections and social background could still be effective commanders, such as John, Marquess of Granby (1721–70), eldest son of the 3rd Duke of Rutland, who became a colonel in 1745 and a major-general in 1755. A brave and talented cavalry commander in Germany during the Seven Years' War, he went on to be Master-General of the Ordnance in 1763–70 and commander in chief in 1766–70; he was less successful in these roles, however, in part because he allowed himself to be manipulated by the regimental agents and the assorted business of army politics. The pressures of national politics and precarious personal finances also weighed on him.

The work of the Ordnance was then taken on by the Honourable Henry Seymour Conway (1719–95), the second son of a peer. Conway joined the army in 1737, served on the staffs of both Wade and Cumberland, was captured at Lawfeldt in 1747, served at Rochefort (1757) and as Granby's deputy in Westphalia (1761–2), and became a lieutenant-general in 1759. Conway worked very hard at the Ordnance, as Lieutenant-General of the Ordnance from 1767 to 1772, and mastered its administration. He was also a political figure. Bitterly attacking the War of American Independence in Parliament, Conway became commander in chief in 1782 with the change in government and the decision to bring the war to a close, resigning in December 1783 when there was another change of government. Another aristocrat, George, 4th Viscount Townshend (1724–1807), who had become a colonel in 1758 and a major-general in 1761, was Master-General of the Ordnance in 1772–82 and in 1783.

These appointments reflected the pressure and favouritism of personal and political links, but these were also a form of recommendation and a reflection of the degree to which social eminence and political connections helped ease the process of command in an aristocratic society. Ministers, for example Thomas, Duke of Newcastle, 1st Lord of the Treasury from 1754 to 1756 and 1757 to 1762, were very much continually put under pressure for military patronage, notably to colonelcies, and war brought no respite. George II and the captain general, Cumberland, both played a role in the response to this pressure, much to Newcastle's concern.[44] And so on at every level. Thus, in 1740, Upton Peacock, physician general to the army in Ireland in 1725–44, was recommended for an additional salary because a friend of his who was a government supporter was ready to back a piece of legislation.[45] Irish posts were less attractive to the English, which meant that they were seen as particularly advantageous by Irish-born officers seeking appointments.[46]

Military service under significant patrons could provide an opportunity for advancement based on merit. Thus, John Cope, commissioned into the Royal Regiment of Dragoons in 1707, served under James Stanhope, and that link subsequently helped him gain commissions in fashionable regiments in 1715 and 1720.

Aside from favouritism and corruption, which could reward both merit and its absence, the ability of the army to act as a campaigning force was also lessened by the number of separate and clashing relevant administrative departments and officials, including the Board of Ordnance, the paymaster general, the Secretary at War, and the Secretaries of State. Furthermore, problems could arise from civilian control. In 1782, Charles, 3rd Duke of Richmond, Master-General of the Ordnance and a frequent complainer, wrote to Major-General Charles Grey about how to repel a possible French attack on Plymouth, noting:

> I am sure you can have no idea of the many real difficulties that exist and prevent one's doing business with that dispatch that could be wished. I have many delays to surmount in my own office, but depending also upon others, upon the commander in chief who has his hands completely full and then upon a numerous Cabinet which is not the more expeditious for consisting of eleven persons who have each their own business to attend to.[47]

In practice, just after the formation of a new ministry under the Marquess of Rockingham was not the most sensible time to expect speed, but, writing in wartime, Richmond captured a central feature of the military organisation that arose from the nature of British politics: the ministers answered to civilian control, and were expected to do so in war as well as peace.

This was also true of the situation in India, with the East India Company in control of its forces; but British regular forces in the empire tended to find civilian control unwelcome and to be unresponsive to it. This created serious tensions, notably in North America. However, in the West Indies, fears of slave risings and of French intervention ensured a degree of enforced compliance by the local authorities with military needs.

A Range of Resources

A far smaller army than that of France was a consequence of a smaller population, political wariness about a large army, the urgent needs of manning the largest navy in the world, and the opportunities provided by an expanding economy. Ironically, the issues of population size and (to an extent) politics were also present for Hanover, which had an army far smaller than that of Prussia. Given the personal link between Britain and Hanover from 1714 to 1837, this was of direct consequence for the British Army as that of Hanover could only be of limited use to Britain, while there was also the issue of protecting Hanover. Rising to 22,000 men during the War of the Spanish Succession, the establishment was reduced in 1715 to a size of 14,500–15,000 and did not rise to about 19,000 until after 1727, when Prussia had an army over three times as big.[48] In 1775, 1783 and 1789, the Hanoverian army numbered only 15,503, 23,197 and 17,836 troops.

Although they could not be used for patronage as Irish commands could be, the Hanoverian forces were part of the range of resources that made up the British military, while also, like the *sepoys* in the army of the East India Company, having an identity very different to that of the British Regulars. Service overseas was very much linked to talent and energy; in Jane Austen's novel *Sense and Sensibility*, the 35-year-old Colonel Brandon, who has served 'in the East Indies', in other words India, is a positive character.[49] Preferring positions at home, those of great social position did not tend to serve in distant and disease-ridden India unless they were true professionals. Indeed, to focus solely on the regular army is mistaken if success in India is considered. Repeatedly, the regular army was the key force in winning success for Britain, but so also were other elements of this hybrid military. Meanwhile, commanders of ability rose by both merit and interest or patronage, and each was a factor in the fortunes of an army that, despite some very significant defeats, was generally successful.

CHAPTER 2

Fighting the French on the Continent, 1689–1748

Huns, Goths or Vandals never proved themselves such barbarians as we have done. Neither saint, nun, church, or convent were spared.

HENRY ST JOHN MP (LATER VISCOUNT BOLINGBROKE) OF ENGLISH ATTACK ON CADIZ, 1702.[1]

I had my right and left hand men killed twice by my side, and was myself shot through the hat, which I thank God was all I suffered.

ANONYMOUS, INFANTRY PARTICIPANT AT BATTLE OF DETTINGEN, 1743.[2]

An army that could operate as far as Bavaria and Madrid in the 1700s was scarcely one confined to the Low Countries and northern France. These had been the main field of operations for English armies for centuries, although Richard I and Edward I were the most prominent (but not only) English leaders on the Crusades to the Holy Land, while English forces had been successfully sent to Portugal in the 1140s, 1380s and 1660s. From the long-term perspective of the army's contribution to empire, there were a number of important consequences of the army's role in conflicts in Europe in 1689–1748, successively in the Nine Years' War (1689–97), the War of the Spanish Succession (1702–13), the War of the Quadruple Alliance (1718–20), and the War of the Austrian Succession, in which Britain was involved from 1743 to 1748.

A consequence was the fixing of most Bourbon (French and Spanish) resources to war in Europe, which greatly helped lessen the Bourbon effort at sea and in the colonies, and notably so with the French failure to sustain naval expenditure from the mid-1690s. On the other hand, the

Bourbons would have done this anyway, because of both their European-centred goals and their army-dominated military-political culture.

Secondly, having done so earlier, not least in the 1560s, 1585–1604, and in the late 1650s, the army became used anew in Europe to acting as an expeditionary force, and, despite the political legacy critical of armies at home, the politics that enabled this action became established. Such a strategy meant a relatively small land force that relied on local support for force augmentation and as force-multipliers, notably from allies, subsidised troops, *sepoys* and colonial forces. Moreover, this strategy required naval support, and carried the risks of a dependence on allies (as in the War of Spanish Succession), of the difficulties of moving from littoral force projection to inland operations (as in the American War of Independence), and of the difficulties as a whole of adjusting to the practicalities of wars as they existed, rather than as they were desired. This was more the standard problem of the 'friction of war.'

Thirdly, there was the buildup of empire in Europe itself, in the shape of the stabilisation of control over the British Isles discussed in the last chapter, the acquisition of Gibraltar (1704), Minorca (1708), and the naval presence that these bases facilitated. The subsequent sieges faced by these positions indicated their importance to France and Spain, while their importance to Britain can be seen in the garrisons deployed and fortifications built. In combination, Gibraltar and Malta became a major and costly part of army activity.

In contrast, the British did not pursue gains in France or the Low Countries. In 1726, when war with Austria appeared a prospect, there was consideration of gaining Bruges, Nieuport, and Ostend, 'with a territory annexed to them sufficient to maintain the garrisons in those places, as part of a partitioning of the Austrian Netherlands (Belgium) between Britain, the United Provinces and France, with Britain providing a peacetime garrison for its share of between 8,000 and 10,000 troops. However, Horatio Walpole, the envoy in France, pointed out that this plan would be unwelcome to France, the Dutch and Parliament, the last not wanting the cost or an additional force that might be used to overthrow the political system in Britain.[3] The idea was not pursued and there was no war. Ostend was discussed anew as a possible acquisition in 1748,[4] but this did not proceed; moreover, although Britain won agreement in 1713 to place a commissioner in Dunkirk to ensure that the harbour was not able to act as a naval base, the English annexation of the town seen in 1659–62 was not resumed.

The Nine Years' War

The Nine Years' War of 1689–97 left a difficult legacy, with complete success over the Jacobites in the British Isles not matched by comparable, or even much, success in the Low Countries, where English troops were deployed from 1689 and, in greater number after the lessening of the Jacobite challenge in 1692. The size of the British corps in the Spanish Netherlands (Belgium) rose from 10,972 in 1689 to 29,100 (plus 27,209 foreign troops in British pay) in 1694–7.

Under the pressure of this war, British fighting effectiveness increased and both officers and troops acquired valuable experience. The similarity in weapons and tactics between British and French forces did not make sweeping victory in battle impossible. However, such victories were not due to distinctive weaponry or unique tactics, but instead to numbers of troops and good generalship: especially in terms of the retention and employment of reserves and the exploitation of terrain, as well as the experience and motivation of the soldiers, and the chance factors of battle. Under the talented Marshal Luxembourg, who prefigured the role of Marshal Saxe in the 1740s, the French inflicted defeats on Allied armies at Steinkirk (1692) and Neerwinden (1693); these hard-fought battles saw the Allies fight with determination to avoid collapse, however. British losses were heavy, especially for the infantry at Steinkirk, where five regiments were largely destroyed and General Hugh Mackay, a keen proponent of the socket bayonet, was killed.

Changing Weaponry

Relatively small regular forces (by the standards of the French) made it easier to keep the British Army trained and equipped, and thus to respond to significant changes in the methods of fighting. These were important because weaponry and the nature of land battle changed fundamentally at the start of this period. In the battles of the mid-17th century, such as the major Parliamentary victory over the Royalists at Naseby (1645), the key battle in leading to final Parliamentary victory in the First Civil War, the infantry had been divided between the musketeers, who provided firepower, and the pikemen. Their long pikes offered defensive strength, protecting both them and the musketeers from cavalry and pike attack, and also provided the opportunity for advancing forward. The squares of pikemen helped structure battlefield formations, while the pike was the last of the major weapons that focused on stabbing or slashing, rather than firepower.

This system was swept away in the 1690s, thanks to the (earlier) invention and dissemination of an effective socket bayonet, an important and underrated innovation in military technology. Whereas, with the plug bayonets used earlier in the 17th century that were inserted in the barrel of the musket, it had been necessary to remove the bayonet before firing the musket, the socket bayonet enabled firing with the bayonet in place. All infantrymen were thus armed with a weapon that combined firepower and steel. However, this did not greatly encourage attacks, because bayonet drills were, for a long time, based on pike drills, with the weapon held high and an emphasis on receiving advances. It was not until the 1750s that a new bayonet drill, with the weapon held waist-high and therefore easier to carry, made it easier to mount attacks. As pikes were succeeded by muskets equipped by socket bayonets, so matchlock muskets were replaced by flintlocks. In connection with the demise of pikemen, body armour ceased to be worn by infantry, although heavy cavalry continued to have it for the protection it provided against blows from sabres (heavy swords).

Moreover, all the new British regiments raised from 1689 were equipped with flintlocks, a costly requirement. The new Land Pattern Musket could be fired at least twice a minute by well-drilled troops in good conditions and, at 11 pounds, weighed one pound less than the matchlock previously used, an important difference given the need to hold it level and steady. In the flintlock musket, powder was ignited by a spark produced through the action of flint on steel. There were, however, serious problems with the musket. Its fire could readily be disrupted by poor weather, especially rain and, to a lesser extent, wind. Damp powder caused misfires.

Even in perfect conditions, effective range for an individually aimed musket shot was limited, while it was unusual to exceed three shots a minute. Accuracy was compromised by the nature of the barrel, which was unrifled, and, in order to avoid fouling by powder and recoil, generally a loose fit for the shot. The shot, as a result of the significant windage (gap between barrel and shot), 'bounded' down the bore, and might then leave the barrel in any direction, a process known as balloting. Moreover, the rough-cast shot was often elliptical and thus unlikely to travel as designed, and particularly so if fired at range. In addition, the ramrods used to drive down the shot often bent and jammed in the musket, broke, or went rusty; and frequent use of the ramrod distorted the barrel into an oval shape. The need for rapid reloading during battle increased the risk of the mistaken use of ramrods, including leaving them in the barrels. Furthermore, muskets had poor sights, while worn flints and blocked touch-holes caused misfiring, and reloading became more difficult as the bore fouled with powder.

The problems created by short-range muskets, which had a low rate of fire and had to be re-sighted for each individual shot, were exacerbated by the cumulative impact of poor sights, eccentric bullets, heavy musket droops, recoil, overheating, and misfiring in wet weather. As muskets were smoothbore and there was no rifling, or grooves, in the barrel, the speed of the shot was not high and its direction was uncertain which greatly compromised accuracy. Non-standardised manufacture of muskets and balls, and wide windage, meant that, unless held in place, the ball could roll out if the barrel was pointed towards the ground, while, at best, the musket was difficult to aim or to hold steady. Balls were rough cast, and the spherical bullets maximised air resistance which, again, ensured a need to fire at short range.[5] The accuracy of muskets and cannon were therefore limited, and training, unsurprisingly, stressed rapidity of fire, and thus drill and discipline. Musket fire was usually delivered at close range and in volleys, as impact and accuracy markedly diminished thereafter.

There was no 'Take Aim' command in the British drill. It was simply, once the musket was primed and loaded and at the left shoulder, 'Make Ready!' (shoulder to the poise position in front of the soldier with lock at about eye level and then cock), 'Present!' (bring butt to right shoulder and point down range at the enemy), and 'Give Fire!' (pull the trigger, then immediately lower to the loading position with right hand on the cartridge box at the hip). In a rapid fire scenario, the only commands were 'Prime and Load' and, once the officer saw that the line was ready and the muskets at the shoulder, then the three command firing sequence. The full drill, about sixteen steps/commands, was only used for formal and ceremonial volley fires.

It was difficult in any case to aim in the noise and smoke of a battlefield, while the heavy weight of muskets led to musket droop: firing short. Another reason for poor aim was the bruising to the shoulder produced by the recoil if the firing was heavy, and if mistakes were made during firing. Just holding and firing the musket required considerable effort and led to discomfort if not pain. Volume firepower, instead, was achieved by arranging the infantry in closely packed, shoulder-to-shoulder, linear formations, and training them to fire as fast as possible, a measure that further inhibited individual aiming. Soldiers fired by volley in a process designed to maximise the continuity, impact and rate of fire, rather than employing individually aimed shot.[6] Training through drill was also the best way to use soldiers whose lack of experience resulted from the continual infusions of new recruits, and to familiarise them with battle.

The speed of fire was enhanced by the use of paper cartridges, with the ball, the correct amount of powder, and wadding all in a single package, which made reloading easier and also allowed each soldier to carry more ammunition. This usage was typical of the improvement in capability taking place around an existing technology, rather than by means of changing to a new one. In contrast, the 1740s saw developments in breech-loaded rifles, such as the Ferguson Rifle, which, as they did not need to have the shot rammed down the barrel, could be fired six times a minute. Such guns, however, proved unsuited to frequent use, the loading mechanism being susceptible to clogging by powder.

The exchange of fire at close quarters between lines of closely packed troops could lead to high casualty rates, and for both sides. Low muzzle velocity, moreover, resulted in dreadful wounds as the shot bounced off bones and internal organs. Infantry was also vulnerable to artillery, notably grape and canister shot: a bag or canister of tin with small balls inside which scattered as a result of the charge, causing considerable numbers of casualties at short-range, both deaths and, even more, wounds. Major John Norton described how at the battle of Queenston Hights in 1812, the American grapeshot 'rattled around'.[7]

Siege warfare, moreover, could be very costly, and notably so if a position was firmly defended, as in the Peninsular War for the British faced by French defenders at Badajoz, Ciudad Rodrigo, Burgos and San Sebastian. John Deane of the Foot Guards wrote of the successful, but lengthy, siege of French-held Lille in 1708, a victory for Marlborough which, however, cost the besiegers 14,000 casualties:

> This murdering siege, it is thought, has destroyed more than [the 1695 siege of] Namur did last war, and those that were the flower of the army: for what was not killed or drowned were spoiled by their hellish inventions of throwing of bombs, boiling pitch, tar, oil and brimstone with scalding water and such like combustibles, upon our men, from the outworks, and when our men made any attack. Especially the English Grenadiers have scarce 6 sound men in a company; likewise many other inventions enough to puzzle the Devil to contrive.[8]

The grenadiers had the risky task of approaching enemy fortifications and throwing in lighted grenades, a role that exposed them to defensive fire. The horrific nature of the casualties was compounded by the limitations of medicine, surgery and after-care, but major efforts were made to help men survive, not least by amputation.[9] Fortifications, on which the French had invested much time and cost, notably with the works built or improved by Vauban, gave the French a strategic depth that posed a major problem for the British and other attackers.

In battle and siege, the combination of earlier methods with the weaponry of the gunpowder age thus made the experience of war very unpleasant. Moreover, Marlborough's battlefield tactics, with their emphasis on the initial struggles on the flanks and the reliance on the bayonet in the infantry attack, entailed an acceptance of heavy casualties.

Infantry had hitherto been divided between musketeers and pikemen, although the proportion of the latter fell during the 17th century. The combination of pikemen and musketeers was complex to manage, and led to a degree of tactical inflexibility as well as a density of formation that prevented linear deployment over the extensive front necessary in order to maximise firepower. The introduction of the socket bayonet and flintlock musket at the close of the 17th century contributed to a major change in tactics, training, and the face of the Western battlefield; and the British Army was not to experience a comparable change in weaponry until the introduction of rifled guns in the 19th century, a situation that led to a necessary focus on proficiency in the given technology.

In contrast, bayonets provided protection, again against infantry and cavalry, but without lessening or compromising firepower, and in the 1700s the pike disappeared, leading to an increase in tactical flexibility. Halberds (spontoons, half-pikes) were retained by non-commissioned officers, but largely for ceremonial purposes to keep troops in line and for signalling command rather than as real weapons, while swords were used by officers and cavalry.

Standardised infantry weaponry permitted more effective drill; and drill and discipline were essential to firepower. Without pikemen, more linear and thinner formations were employed on the battlefield with the infantry close-packed and deployed over an extended front in order to maximise firepower. Battalions were drawn up generally only three ranks deep (two in the American War of Independence of 1775–83), and firings were by groups of platoons, in a process designed to maximise the continuity of fire and fire-control. Linear formations operating across a more extended front, however, accentuated the serious problems of command and control posed by the limitations of information and communication on the battlefield, and this situation put a premium on the availability of sufficient officers and on their skill.

Despite the bayonets, hand-to-hand fighting on the battlefield was relatively uncommon, and most casualties, both fatalities and wounds, were caused by shot; in part because few units would stand up to a well-delivered and aggressive bayonet charge, instead often breaking in the face of one. Thus, for those French troops wounded in the British victory at the battle of Oudenaarde in 1708 and admitted into the *Hôtel des Invalides* in Paris, 65 per cent of the wounds were inflicted by musket shot.[10]

Infantry was flanked by cavalry units, but the proportion of cavalry in Western armies declined during the 18th century as a result of the heavier emphasis on firepower and the greater cost of cavalry, which was also troublesome to transport overseas. Cavalry was principally used on the Western battlefield to fight cavalry, and, in contrast, cavalry advances against unbroken infantry and their firepower were relatively uncommon. However, due to its linear formations and the difficulties of regrouping rapidly during combat, infantry, as the British discovered at French hands at Albuera in the Peninsular War in 1811, was very vulnerable to such attacks in flank and rear, as well as on the move.[11]

The War of the Spanish Succession

The British Army reached a height during the War of the Spanish Succession in part because the main field force was well commanded by the talented, experienced, energetic and personable John, Duke of Marlborough (1650–1722). The French army was no longer at the peak of its capability that it reached in the early 1690s, which helped Marlborough, as did solid support from the Dutch that was not sufficiently appreciated by British public opinion, and cooperation from the Austrians, whose army had also much improved, notably under Prince Eugene. Captain general of the British forces in the Netherlands from 1701 until 1711, and also, as Master-General of the Ordnance, in control of the artillery, Marlborough rapidly gained the initiative from France and displayed an effective boldness, notably in the Blenheim campaign in 1704, which was a successful combination of the strategic, operational and tactical offensives. Cavalry played a crucial role in the British victory at Blenheim on 13 August where, having drawn the French reserves into resisting attacks on the French flanks, the British broke through the centre of their position.

This victory showed the importance of being able to control the flow of a battle, the need to impose on, and profit from, opponents' decision-making, and, specifically, the value of cavalry-infantry coordination, or at least combination. Marlborough chose his subordinates well and knew how to get the best from them. Alongside stand-off firepower, there could be close-quarter fighting. Jean Martin de La Colonie recalled of the successful British storming under Marlborough of the Schellenberg heights on 2 July 1704:

> We were all fighting hand to hand, hurling them back as they clutched at the parapet; men were slaying, or tearing at the muzzles of guns and the bayonets which pierced their entrails; crushing under their feet their own wounded comrades, and even gouging out their opponents' eyes with their nails, when the grip was so close that neither could use their weapons.[12]

In this victory, the British and their Dutch allies still suffered about 1,500 dead and 4,000 wounded.

Two years later, at Ramillies on 23 May, Marlborough again obtained a victory by the use of well-timed concentrated force. In a six-hour battle, he broke the French centre after it had been weakened in order to support action on the flanks, the method employed at Blenheim. At both, he showed the characteristic features of his generalship. Cool and composed under fire, brave to the point of rashness, Marlborough was a master of the shape and details of conflict. Keeping control of his own forces, and of the flow of the battle, he was able to move and commit his troops decisively at the most appropriate moment.

After a failure to achieve much in 1707, the battle of Oudenaarde on 11 July 1708 was another victory which led to Marlborough regaining the initiative in the Low Countries anew. After several hours fighting, during which both sides moved units into combat as they arrived on the battlefield and the French pressed hard, the French position was nearly enveloped when Marlborough sent the cavalry on his left around the French right flank and into their rear, leading the French to retreat with heavier casualties. Marlborough was contrasted with the less successful British commanders in Spain, notably the volatile Charles, 3rd Earl of Peterborough in 1705–7 and Henri, Earl of Galway, a Huguenot defeated in 1707 and 1709.

Made more conspicuous by this failure of the contemporary Allied campaigning in Spain, Marlborough's campaigns were the highpoint of British success in Europe on land during the period, but also illustrate the problems of assessing success. He engaged the main French field army, a task Wellington did not take on until Waterloo, when he faced a scratch army compared to that deployed by Napoleon against the Austrians at Austerlitz (1805) or Aspern-Essling (1809). Moreover, Wellington's fame can in part be attributed to his later longevity, to politics, to the absence of his being smeared by corruption, as Marlborough was to be, and to the lack for Britain of any subsequent victory comparable to Waterloo, and, indeed, any major war until 1914. Yet, there was also a significant difference, as Waterloo did lead to the fall of Napoleon, while none of Marlborough's victories had the same effect on Louis XIV, or, more modestly, served to offset French successes elsewhere, notably in Spain. However, the skillset shown by the British Army in Europe under Marlborough helped provide a good basis for subsequent military activity, and even if the link to the conquest of empire was somewhat indirect, it was important.

Under Marlborough, the army had reached a peak of success that it was not to repeat in Europe for another century. With Marlborough also much helped by his allies and by a relatively good administrative system, this was largely a matter of basic fighting quality. The pay and conditions of the troops were very poor, although better than the norm for many British working men or for other armies. However, the combat effectiveness of British units, especially the fire discipline and bayonet skill of the infantry, and the ability of the cavalry to mount successful charges relying on cold steel, was clear. It owed much to their extensive experience of campaigning and battles in the 1690s and 1700s, and these also played a vital role in training the officers and accustoming the troops to immediate manoeuvre and execution. Experienced men provided a critical steadying influence on the new men in their first conflict. This was the most battle-experienced British Army since those of the Civil War, and the latter did not take part in battles that were as extensive, nor sieges of positions that were anywhere near as well fortified, as those that faced Marlborough's forces. The infantry, drawn up in three ranks, were organised into three firings, ensuring that continuous fire was maintained. British infantry fire was more effective than French fire, so that the pressure of battlefield conflict with the British was high. The inaccuracy of muskets was countered by the proximity of the opposing lines, and their close-packed nature.

The cavalry was made to act like a shock force, charging fast, rather than as mounted infantry relying on pistol firepower, and Marlborough used a massed cavalry charge at the climax of Blenheim, Ramillies, and Malplaquet. The artillery were well positioned on the field of battle, and were then re-sited and moved forward to influence its development. Marlborough was also effective in siegecraft, as shown in 1708 in the successful (although very costly in terms of casualties) siege of Lille, a major French fortified position. Marlborough benefited from the extensive experience the Anglo-Dutch forces had gained from campaigning in the area in the 1690s, as well as from impressive staff work, excellent artillery, and an effective logistical strength, based on good public finances, that helped in sustaining operations.[13]

It is important, however, to note that the war also revealed deficiencies in the British military system, and notably so in Spain where there were serious defeats, as well as other problems. Major-General John Richards, an Irish Catholic who, because of his Catholicism, had served Austria and Venice, but, in this war was paid by the British as part of the Allied forces in Spain, recorded in May 1705, 'our mortars could not be worst served … slow … they shot as ill as could be … the fuses were so ill made that … great many of them never burnt at.'[14] The repeated deficiencies of the British forces in Spain were in part due to the difficulties of fighting there, but were also a comment on Marlborough's more skilful direction of operations.

Like Wellington's battles, Marlborough's were fought on a more extended front than those of the 1690s, let alone the 1650s, and thus placed a premium on mobility, planning, and the ability of commanders both to respond rapidly to developments over a wide front, and to integrate and influence what might otherwise have been in practice a number of separate conflicts. Clarity in command under fire was a key element. Marlborough was especially adept and successful in coordinating the deployment and use of infantry, cavalry and artillery. At Malplaquet on 11 September 1709, however, Marlborough won, but only at great cost, as the French had learned how to oppose his tactics, thus lessening their effectiveness and the resulting capability gap.

Malplaquet, and the slow progress in capturing French fortresses that followed, helped move the political dynamic away from Britain and, within it, from the Whig government to their Tory rivals. Marlborough had turned an army and system of operations developed for position warfare, or at least forced into it in the context of the circumstances of war with the French in the Low Countries, into a means to make war mobile. Nevertheless, France's combination of fortifications and field armies ensured that hopes of breaking into that country to any depth were not plausible. Short of doing that, it was not clear how a large British Continental commitment could best be a success on the offensive; this strategy was not successful until 1814, and only after heavy defeats for France in 1813. This issue was to recur with Wellington's campaigning into Spain. Separately, he found the Portuguese (but not the Spaniards) more dependable allies than Marlborough had the Dutch.

The strategic dilemma was an aspect of the equation. There is a tendency to think automatically of armies in terms of improvement and, at the least, development, but it is difficult for an army to sustain a state of proficiency through time. Had the army maintained this proficiency, and in particular an ability to inflict defeat on the French in the Low Countries in the 1740s and 1790s, this would have transformed the wars of the period, and the military and political history of Britain might well have been different as a consequence.

1714–41: Years of Peace

However, there was a marked reduction in the effectiveness of the army after the War of the Spanish Succession; this challenges systemic accounts that, due to the structure of the British state and notably its public finances, it was uniquely, or at least particularly, impressive. In practice, there was a marked regress after the war, as also (but to a lesser extent) in the navy. Numbers were heavily cut, which was a habitual pattern in British military history reflecting the relative weakness of the military interest. This was a pattern that helped to give the army a start-stop character. Hostility on the part of the opposition to a substantial army, or, in many cases, any army, combined with the desire of Sir Robert Walpole, First Lord of the Treasury from 1721 to 1742, to contain, if not cut government expenditure and therefore taxation, and his reluctance to become embroiled in European power politics. As a result, little was spent on the army. Furthermore, far from training for battle, the army was divided, as a result of its modest size, into units that were too small for such training.[15]

This situation was not the best basis for an effective response to the larger French army, but Britain was allied with France from 1716 to 1731. In the 1720s, there were confrontations in European international relations but no conflict, while Britain relied on allies in order to protect its Continental interest, as in 1723 when Charles, 2nd Viscount Townshend, the Secretary of State for the Northern Department, praised alliance with Prussia:

> Which in effect puts into the scale with His Majesty [George I] the whole force and strength of Prussia, at least three score [60,000] men, excellent troops. Before this the power of Great Britain lay only in its fleet. ... But now this strict union is made with the King of Prussia [Frederick William I], and his Majesty is become master as it were of so mighty a land force, he will not only be more secure, but also more respected both in the North and the South, and have it in his power to act more independently from the Houses both of Austria and Bourbon, and preserve the Peace of Europe with less submission to the terms of either.[16]

In addition, the reluctance to increase the size of the army helped lead to an emphasis on raising troops by subsidy treaties with foreign rulers. Thus, under a treaty of 1726, that was a response to an international crisis that began the previous year, £125,000 was paid as an annual retainer to the Landgrave of Hesse-Cassel in order to ensure the first called on the services of 12,000 troops. These payments were a major source of contention, not least as they were clearly paid at that time for the defence of Hanover against Austria and Prussia. German politics was the rationale in every respect. The expenditure brought no benefit to the British Army, while, as the private instructions to the envoy to Cassel made clear, it was appreciated that the Landgrave had his own reasons for maintaining good relations with Austria. The Hessians were asked in 1727 if they could deploy 15,000 troops.[17] After the Hessians were paid off in 1732, the land tax then fell to one shilling in the pound. They were to be employed in later wars, but, because the Hessians were hired under specific subsidy treaties, their fixed costs were not borne by Britain.

Meanwhile, Marlborough's victories proved a continuing reference point, as in November 1730 when, at a time of deteriorating relations with France, the *Political State of Great Britain* reflected 'there are yet some Frenchmen alive who saw the English at the battles of Hochstadt [Blenheim], Ramillies, Oudenaarde and Malplaquet, and it is to be hoped the Count of France will take their advice.' In the 1730s, the government faced repeated opposition pressure to cut the size of the army, as in 1733 when it defeated a motion to reduce it to 12,000 men. Charles Delafaye, Under Secretary in the Southern Department, noted the remark of William Pulteney, the opposition leader in the Commons, that this issue was that of passing the Rubicon, the key occasion in a session. In opposing the motion that year, Walpole had emphasised the threat from Jacobitism.[18]

Subsequently, Britain remained neutral in the War of the Polish Succession (1733–5), a far-flung struggle, including conflict in Italy and the Rhineland; whereas France, at war with Austria, gained military success, training on the job, and combat efficiency. The French had discussed an invasion of Britain and there was a plan to recapture the Channel Isles,[19] but, helped by the French not invading the Austrian Netherlands (Belgium), there was no conflict between the two powers. George II followed the war with interest,[20] but in Hanover in 1735 only reviewed his troops. Peace helped keep the land tax down, but also ensured that the British Army was no longer at the cutting edge in tactical practice, let alone debate or innovation. Indeed, in 1743, when conflict resumed with France, the army lacked both numbers and particular effectiveness.

The War of the Austrian Succession

The renewed need for the army in 1742–3 reflected the political situation, not so much France attacking Austria from 1741, but the fall of the pacific Walpole in February 1742 and the rise of the belligerent John, Lord Carteret. In 1742, an army under John, 2nd Earl of Stair was sent to Belgium, the basis for the force that was to move into Germany in 1743. Stair (1673–1747), a veteran of the Nine Years' and Spanish Succession wars, who had served at Steinkirk, Ramillies, Oudenaarde, Lille and Malplaquet, was made a field marshal in March 1742.

A step planned by the new ministry from the outset,[21] this army was seen as a protection for Belgium against French attack,[22] one made more necessary by good intelligence on the deficiencies[23] of the defences there and signs that France would act.[24] As there was no such French attack until 1744, it was unclear, however, what the army could or should do. Marshal Belle-Île, the leading French general, noted the limited size of the British Army and the cost of its operating as reasons why it was ordinarily good for France if Britain campaigned on land in Europe, but, in the context of 1742, he was worried that a large force of British and Allied troops could be built up in Belgium and then attack France.[25] Such ideas were indeed advanced, but were not pursued, in large part in order not to compromise the neutrality of Belgium, but also due to bad weather.

The first time British troops had been in this area for three decades, there was the need to make new supply[26] (and other) arrangements. In order to supplement the British forces, Carteret sought to offer subsidy treaties to friendly German rulers, only for the payment of Hanoverians to arouse criticism, notably from Pitt, who remained in opposition until 1744. In the event, in December 1742, the Commons agreed to hire 16,000 Hanoverian troops, and subsequently defeated an opposition motion to stop the hire. Pitt was willing in January 1744 to support the maintenance of British troops on the Continent, and the following month, in the face of French invasions preparations, backed an increase in the army. Others, however, remained critical, an opposition ballad of 1744 claiming:

Abroad our gallant army fights
In Austria's cause, for German rights
By English treasure fed
Hessians and Hanoverians too
The gainful trade of war pursue
With Carteret at their head.

Meanwhile, on 27 June 1743, at Dettingen near Mainz in Germany, superior British musketry in rolling fire helped bring victory over the French, although it initially proved difficult to prevent the soldiers from firing at too great a range to inflict heavy casualties. George II commanded the British Army, but became unpopular due to his favour for the Hanoverians who made up part of the force.[27] Dettingen, moreover, could not be exploited, in part due to political and military indecision, as well as serious differences of opinion, combined with the effects of poor weather and disease and the lack of an adequate artillery train. There was nothing to match the determination and unity of command that Marlborough had offered. Lieutenant-General Charles, 2nd Duke of Richmond, wrote to a leading British minister, Henry Pelham:

> You ask me what we have been doing since Dettingen [British victory]. The answer is easy, nothing, then you'll say why nothing, to which I will answer…. Nothing was prepared such as bread, forage, hospitals etc to go on with.[28]

As after Blenheim, so after Dettingen, the following year saw a shift of focus to the Low Countries. In this case, war formally broke out in 1744 and the neutrality that had hitherto protected the Low Countries ended. This was a strategic problem for a British government fearful of the risk of invasion and anxious about British interests in the region; but also a political opportunity as the deployment of troops there could be seen as a national interest, whereas their dispatch into Germany was regarded as serving Hanoverian interests.

The Low Countries, however, were also an area where France could readily deploy forces. Field Marshal Wade, now the British commander there, who had served in the region in the 1690s and 1700s, was expected to advance into France in 1744. However, he had to report that the opposing French army was at least twice the size, writing, 'if we could have all opportunity of engaging them with an equal front, I think we ought not to decline the combat. But to attack them at disadvantage, would be rash, since the loss of a battle would be attended with the loss of the country', adding, ten days later, that the prospect of reinforcements would, he hoped, in a letter that reflected his interest in cavalry and his concern with the surface cover:

> Induce us to be careful to avoid as much as possible coming to a general action, but to keep upon the defensive, until the arrival of those succours … which, if they come in time, will not only put us on an equality with the enemy as to our foot, but enable us to follow them into those open parts of the country where our horse may be of more service to us than they can be in this inclosed country.

In the event, it was to be the French who took the initiative. The other battles on the Continent during these years involving British troops as part of Allied armies – Fontenoy (11 May 1745), Rocoux (11 October 1746), and Lawfeldt (2 July 1747) – were French victories, reflecting the skilful generalship of Marshal Saxe, who had served under Marlborough at Malplaquet.[29] The dogged fighting quality of the British troops helped to ensure orderly retreats, notably at Fontenoy, where a participant recorded that 'there were batteries constantly playing upon our front and both flanks',[30] and Rocoux. Fontenoy arose as a result of Cumberland's attempt to relieve besieged Tournai. In attacking the hastily prepared French positions around the village of Fontenoy his infantry displayed anew their discipline and fighting determination, but the battle demonstrated the strength of a defensive force (in this case the French) relying on firepower and supported by a strong reserve. The different result to Dettingen reflected in part better French generalship, but also the degree to which British steadiness and firepower were more effective in defence. The battle signalled the failure of attempts to prevent French gains in the Austrian Netherlands (Belgium).

This conquest was eased by the withdrawal of troops to fight the Jacobites. Treating subjects separately helps bring out the development of particular themes, but there are also the elements arising from both the interaction and the simultaneity of these themes. In particular, directing troops, other resources, and attention, to specific challenges meant that they were not available elsewhere, points that recur with successive conflicts. Thus, in late 1745, the French army on the Channel coast exercised a powerful influence on the British ministry, greatly influencing the instructions sent to Cumberland. This helped explain why the Hanoverians, enjoying clear military superiority, did not succeed in bringing Charles Edward to battle in England in 1745, a failure that had enormous influence on the course of the war as it ensured that troops could not be moved back to Flanders until later in the war.

Thus, the Jacobites served French strategic interests, and that in part due to the relatively small size of the army and trade-off between home defence and focus on the Low Countries. In response to the '45, Andrew Stone, the Duke of Newcastle's private secretary, thought the attempt 'desperate: But I cannot think it is altogether to be despised. We are so naked of troops, that, if a body of men [French troops] were to be flung over, no one can say what may be the consequences.' Noting 'hardly any regular force between Berwick and London', Newcastle was anxious. Robert Trevor, envoy at The Hague, wrote of the despatch of Dutch troops to Britain: 'My private letters represent their presence as but too necessary.'[31]

The British fought well on the continent, but did not win victories. At Roucoux in 1746, although the Anglo-Dutch troops fired more rapid volleys than French, Saxe advanced in columns rather than an extended firing line, and, after a lengthy artillery duel, his columns, benefiting from an Allied deployment on a line that was too long, prevailed.[32] At Lawfeldt in 1747, the British infantry inflicted heavy losses on the attacking French in a four-hour defence of the village, only surrendering their position on the fifth attack.

William, Duke of Cumberland (1721–65), the second son of George II, became colonel of the First Regiment of Foot Guards in 1741 and a major-general in 1742. Wounded at Dettingen, he became a lieutenant-general immediately after, and in 1745 was made commander in chief of the Allied forces in the Low Countries, and, as such, was in command at Fontenoy and Lawfeldt.

Allied fighting determination and quality was not enough: the French, who in the 1746 campaign outnumbered the Allies by about 180,000 men to 90,000, captured Ostend (1745), Brussels (1746), Antwerp (1746), and the major Dutch fortresses of Bergen-op-Zoom (1747) and Maastricht (1748). French successes exposed both Britain and the Dutch heartland to the risk of invasion.[33] The war in the Low Countries was very expensive – not only due to the need to support the British forces, but also to pay for Allied forces, including items such as winter forage for Hessians in November 1746 and an account for extraordinary expenses for the Hanoverians for the 1746 campaign that even Cumberland found questionable.[34]

The war proved disappointing on a number of levels, with allies letting Britain down by not providing the promised forces,[35] but the French also deployed an effective and well-commanded army. The resulting sense of concern can be gauged in a letter sent to Cumberland in 1748:

> I have by the King's order given a hint of the necessary attention to preserve your army. I am sure your Royal Highness will not on any account or from any expectation run a risk which if it should happen must prove the ruin of the whole, for upon the preservation of your Royal Highness' army, weak as it is, depends the safety of this country, the Republic of Holland, and indeed the whole alliance.[36]

Aside from battle, there were hard terms of service. Although the Dutch (allies) and the French (enemies) were similarly affected,[37] that did not lessen the difficult circumstances faced by the British troops, those in the Low Countries dying from fevers in August 1748 thanks to the 'wetness of this country, the bad stagnated ditch water we drink, the bad food ... we lie in barns and open cowhouses with little or no straw.'

The net effect of the disappointment in the Low Countries was to undermine the British quest for empire; in the peace treaty that ended the war, that of Aix-la-Chapelle (1748), Britain returned Louisbourg and Cape Breton Isle (see next chapter) to France, and thus in turn receiving back Madras (Chennai) and obtaining the French withdrawal from the Low Countries. This was very much not the military strategy that would obtain imperial success. Indeed, the failure of the British Army in the Low Countries in 1744–8, while not total, as that in the Low Countries in 1793–6 was to be, was subject to criticism that helped to strengthen the already strong political focus on the idea of Britain as a naval power with a trans-oceanic destiny. However, as the following chapters make clear, that destiny itself required success from the army, both across oceans, in Europe, and in the British Isles.

The Cumberland Years

As part both of efforts during the War of the Austrian Succession and of a postwar reform drive, there was an attempt to improve the army's effectiveness. A key player, Cumberland had already in 1744 played a role in the improvement of training at the Academy at Woolwich.[38] With the support of his father, he, as commander in chief, pressed the importance of merit in promotions and the responsibilities of commanders. His ally, Henry Fox, was Secretary at War, and a considerable number of MPs looked to Cumberland, who very much led an important group of officers; although other officers fearing his reforms looked to his elder brother and rival, Frederick, Prince of Wales.

More generally, Cumberland's controversial political position, alleged political ambitions, partisanship, and reputation as a martinet limited his influence. After the death of Frederick in 1751 left Cumberland as a possible regent for his nephew (the future George III) should George II die soon, there were frequent references to the example of Richard III supplanting his nephew Edward V in 1483. Separately, on 25 November 1752, *Old England*, a London opposition newspaper, warned about the danger of Britain becoming a military power, a clear reference to Cumberland.

However, the post-war restructuring seen in the Austrian and Russian armies after 1748 was not matched, in part due to the anti-military ethos of British politics and the related support for an emphasis, instead, on the militia. There were also specific suspicions about Cumberland, the difficulties of enforcing discipline and diligence on aristocratic officers – notably, if they owned their positions – and the more general absence of a bureaucratic ethos. As a result, the ability of the army to respond in a united and planned fashion to new developments was limited, and, indeed, there was an absence of a unified military command structure able to devise and sustain coherent peacetime programmes of planning and improvement. This reflected the continuance of existing bureaucratic systems and, in particular, a failure to emulate the more unified naval structure.

There is no automatic equation of reform and improvement, and no simple contrast between change and failure. Nevertheless, despite the serious defeats of the army in the latter part of the recent war, there was only limited success in improving its capability in the subsequent peace years. This failure exacerbated the problems created by the small size of the peacetime army and, therefore, the need to expand, equip, train and deploy it rapidly at the outset of each war.

Peace brought the disbanding of some units and the neglect of others, as well as a preference for spending elsewhere – usually, but not always, on the navy. Thus, Pitt pressed Newcastle in a private meeting in 1753 on the need 'to make some savings in the army in Scotland and Gibraltar in order to provide for the expense of this subsidy ... without savings made, the new expense with Russia may be difficult, if not impracticable.'[39] George II and Cumberland were scarcely going to accept this, but there was strong opposition to sending British troops to the Continent, one pamphleteer in 1755 declaring: 'There can be no manner of doubt that Great Britain never maintained an army upon the Continent but at three times the price at which she might have hired an equal body of auxiliary troops.'[40] Such politics was important to the context of military activity.

CHAPTER 3

Fighting for Empire, 1689–1753

Nine Years' War and War of the Spanish Succession

By 1713, when the War of Spanish Succession ended for Britain (it continued between the German states and France until 1714), its forces were already in the West Indies, North America, Gibraltar, Minorca, West Africa and India, and the army was clearly a major aspect of what might otherwise have been only a naval power. Nevertheless, army units often principally operated in concert with naval counterparts, as in the capture of Gibraltar in 1704 and Minorca in 1708. So also very much in the West Indies, North America, West Africa, and, for the British at this stage, India, as most settlements they sought to control were coastal, and warships were the key means of access and the source of artillery both against fortifications and with reference to opposing warships.

The largest transoceanic attack in the warfare of 1689–1713 by any European power was that in 1711 during the War of the Spanish Succession on Québec, France's major position in Canada. Brigadier-General John Hill was sent with 5,300 troops in 30 transports escorted by ten ships of the line, a formidable force. This was intended as a knock-out blow, and was very different in scale to the attacks on French Canada mounted in 1704–10, attacks that had brought control over Nova Scotia.

The expedition illustrated the political character of strategy and, notably, the degree to which tasking, which was set by politics, created challenges for effectiveness, including in viable targets and in command choices. Intended to improve Britain's position in negotiations with France, the expedition was designed to distract attention from Marlborough and his campaigning in the Low Countries and to vindicate the 'blue water' policies advocated by the Tories who had recently gained power. Hill, the brother of Abigail Hill, the Tory favourite of Queen Anne, owed his promotion to connections rather than ability, and his career hitherto had been singularly void of achievement. He was a demonstration of the drawbacks of patronage divorced from real merit.

Separately, there was no experience (for any power) of sending an expedition of this size to North America, and the execution of the plans displayed the improvisation that can so often prove the reason for failure. On the other hand, coping with chaos was (and remains) a key aspect of military activity, and the balance between success and failure is often a very fine one. Preparations were hasty and, as part of the cooperative character of the imperial military, the government relied on over-optimistic assumptions of logistical support from New England. The British, nevertheless, were able to get their force to the St. Lawrence estuary, but, once there, eight transport ships and nearly 900 men were lost on rocks near the *Ile aux Oeufs*. Even though more than 6,000 troops and most of the fleet had survived, this failure led to the abandonment by the irresolute Hill both of that expedition and of the supporting landward advance from Albany on Montréal.[1] Hill, nevertheless, became Lieutenant-General of the Ordnance and was promoted major-general; although, in a reversal of the situation for Marlborough, Cadogan and Stair, his career ended when George I and the Whigs came to power in 1714.

Canada, which then meant essentially the French dominance of the St. Lawrence valley, had not yet fallen, but the Peace of Utrecht of 1713 left Britain with territorial gains: notably Newfoundland, Hudson's Bay and Nova Scotia, where the leading base Port Royal had been captured in 1710 after a failure to do so in 1707. These successes were important as they lessened the strategic depth of French Canada and provided Britain with closer-in bases for action in subsequent conflicts. Given the frequency of previous wars with the Dutch (three conflicts between 1652 and 1674) and the French (two in 1689–1713), it was reasonable to assume that the army would soon be called on anew. This was not least the case because the Tories, who negotiated the Peace of Utrecht in 1713, lost office in 1714 following the accession of George I; while their successors, the Whigs, had opposed the peace terms and, notably, broken from some of Britain's allies.

The fighting in 1689–1713 had shown that the North American colonies were capable of mounting attacks on their French counterparts, but these colonies did not develop the governmental structures that the ministry in London thought would strengthen the military situation. This wish had led James II to create a Dominion of New England (1686–9), only for it to be overthrown in 1689 as part of the Glorious Revolution. In the 1690s, to make administration more effective and to encourage a united military response, the government sensibly wanted a unified military command in New York and New England, a measure, however, abandoned in 1701 in the face of colonial opposition. In addition, Connecticut successfully saw off pressure to provide military support.

The Nine Years' War had not been a success for the British in North America or the Caribbean, not least with a failed attack on the island of Guadeloupe in 1691, and the situation in the War of the Spanish Succession remained difficult. The problems encountered by the British continued to be grouped in three categories: those that were exogenous, notably the environment; secondly, those that were rival, that is relating to the French and Spaniards; and thirdly, those that were integral, in the sense of their own deficiencies on land. The first very much included disease. In 1703, Lieutenant-Colonel James Rivers wrote of his wish to leave Jamaica: 'to get out of this unhealthy climate as soon as possible which diminishes the forces both sea and land very considerably every day … for fear of this service several of the officers quitted their commission.'[2] Disease was also a major problem in North America, as with the British advance on Lake Champlain in 1709.

The French were adept opponents in the West Indies, both able to operate in the North American interior and developing impressive fortifications, particularly in Québec in the 1690s,[3] but also at Montréal (1688), Michilimackinac (1700), and Detroit (1701). Anchoring the French presence, these forts drove up the burden of war for both sides, requiring garrisons in defence but the obstacle of stronger forts, notably cannon, and the delay forced on attackers. The weaknesses of the British forces included the difficulty of coordinating land and sea operations, as against Québec in 1690 and 1693, and Guadeloupe in 1691[4]; and the problems of sustaining operations in the face of disease.

The British Army, indeed, would not have been especially well-prepared for further trans-oceanic operations to expand empire, had war resumed after 1714 – not least because, in a change that had fundamental strategic implications, a Bourbon, Philip V (r. 1700–46), was now on the throne of Spain and could hope to ally with France.

The War of the Quadruple Alliance

Unexpectedly, Britain under the Whigs was, alongside France, its ally from 1716 to 1731, to fight Spain in 1718–20. In that war, the Spanish colonial base that fell, Pensacola, the capital of West Florida, did so to a French force, and not a British one. The British commitment in the war was partly naval, but the army was involved with about 4,000 troops in a successful amphibious expedition in 1719 to attack the potential invasion base-area in Galicia. An expedition under Lieutenant-General Richard, Viscount Cobham was ordered to attack Corunna, but, judging it too strong, he captured Vigo and its shipping. A force from Vigo under Wade pressed on in 1719 to capture Pontevedra, destroying the arsenal.

Cobham (1675–1749), the Eton-educated son of a baronet, became a captain in 1689, fighting in Ireland and Belgium in the 1690s, and under Marlborough in the 1700s, being promoted to lieutenant-general in 1710. Stripped of his Colonelcy in 1713 for voting against the Treaty of Utrecht, he was restored to favour under George I, only to lose his Colonelcy in 1733 for attacking the Walpole government, being restored in 1742 when it fell. A mentor of William Pitt, Cobham provided continuity from earlier military circumstances.

Looking forward to future fame, John Ligonier (1680–1770), already a brave veteran of the battles of the 1700s, led the Grenadiers who stormed the fort in Pontevedra. He went on to be knighted at Dettingen, command the infantry at Fontenoy, be captured at Lawfeldt, and become commander in chief (1757–9), field marshal (1757), and Master-General of the Ordnance (1759–63).

1721–38

Little real experience was gained in the 1710s, 1720s and 1730s in overcoming the problems of imperial warfare. There was conflict with French-backed Native Americans, notably the Abenaki in the 1720s in modern Maine, with other Native Americans, particularly the Tuscaroras and Yamasee in the 1710s, and also an unsuccessful attempt in 1728 by a small force of Carolinians and Native allies to take St. Augustine, the main Spanish base in East Florida. In practical terms, however, the deployment of regular forces in North America was limited, while the colonial population was understandably most concerned about Native opponents if local and particularly so when the latter were on the attack. In 1715, the Yamasee raided to within twelve miles of Charleston and the initial military response was unsuccessful. South Carolina was obliged to increase expenditure on defence, but more value was obtained from the support of fellow colonists, notably Virginia, and from the splintering of Native opposition, with the Cherokee coming round to help the Carolinians in 1716 and the Creek deserting the Yamasee in 1717.[5] Such a splintering was also seen on a very different scale with the rivalry between the European powers in North America.

There were more regular troops in the West Indies where rival colonies were closer and the threat of a slave rising greater. Either of these factors can be cited at the expense of the other, but, in practice, the number of troops was a matter of both elements. Jamaica was the largest British colony, and the challenge there was the Maroons, runaway slaves who controlled much of the sparsely populated and mountainous interior. The need to prepare for different military circumstances was emphasised in 1738 by Edward Trelawny, the talented Governor from 1738 to 1752 who had served as a volunteer in the Austrian army in 1734 during the War of the Polish Succession:

The service here is not like that in Flanders [Belgium] or any part of Europe. Here the great difficulty is not to beat, but to see the enemy... in short, nothing can be done in strict conformity to usual military preparations, and according to a regular manner; bushfighting as they call it being a thing peculiar by itself.

The Maroons were finally granted land and autonomy in treaties in 1738 and 1740 that ended the First Maroon War, which had begun in 1728. British forces had been successfully ambushed in 1730 and 1733, and the Maroons had gained and won the initiative, launching an attack on a barracks in 1735, and attacking estates with greater frequency from 1736. The construction of new barracks in Jamaica in 1737 was a cause of unwelcome expense to the settlers.[6] The campaigning and costs revealed the problems of counter-insurgency warfare. Neither the colonial militia nor the Regulars, whose numbers were increased by two regiments in 1731, could prevail. Trelawny broke the impasse with his negotiations, and conflict with the Maroons did not revive until the Second Maroon War of 1795–6. He remained determined to strengthen Jamaica against the Bourbons, and the British were fortunate that the crises posed by French opposition and Maroon resistance were kept separate, unlike in 1795–6.

In West Africa and India, the British were heavily dependent on fortifications and local forces. In West Africa, the source of slaves, the minor factory [fortified base] at Sekondi fell in 1694, but the leading base at Cape Coast Castle was never taken. British cannon drove off Dahomey forces that attacked the fort at Glehue in 1728.[7] In India, there had been defeat at the hands of the Mughal Emperor, Aurangzeb, in the 1680s, while, in 1717–21, joint land-sea attacks on the Konkan Coast forts of the piratical Maratha naval commander, Kanhoji Angria, failed. Instead, after he died, emphasis shifted to exploiting the rivalries between his sons and seeking local allies.[8]

The army therefore was but little involved in the Walpole years in imperial conflict. British interests, instead, were largely dependent on local forces, and these were focused essentially on defence. It was not, however, that the army concentrated on developing its competence in European warfare, for the major emphasis, as in the confrontation with Spain in 1726–7, was on naval activity. There were plans for war with

Austria in 1726–7 and Spain in 1730, but in neither case did confrontation and plans for attack lead to actual war.

Wars with Spain and France, 1739–48

The situation was more complex during the next period of full-scale conflict: with Spain in the War of Jenkins' Ear, from 1739 to 1748, with France from 1743 to 1748 (although this war was not declared until 1744). British land operations in the colonies were again heavily reliant on naval support and were divided between regular and militia forces. The most significant of the former was the attack on Cartagena, on the coast of modern Colombia, in 1741. Its supporting fortresses were captured that March and the fall of the city appeared imminent. However, an assault on the well-defended hill fort which dominated Cartagena failed, and, after disagreements about the best way to launch another attack in the face of heavy losses through disease, the troops re-embarked in April. A major flaw had been the lack of support by the fleet for the land operations, and notably a refusal to land seamen in order to provide greater numbers.[9] The expedition included 3,700 American recruits as well as 5,800 British troops. The Americans, under William Gooch, Virginia's Governor, encompassed vagrants drafted in Virginia and Pennsylvanians fleeing indentured service, but most were volunteers. Due to disease, however, only about 10 per cent of the Americans returned home.

Subsequent operations by this expedition were also unsuccessful, troops landing in Cuba and Panama being affected by disease and, due to poor command decisions, unable to attack either Santiago or Panama City. In the former, a base called Georgestadt was established near Guantanamo Bay, but landing over eighty miles from Santiago exposed the troops to a long and dangerous (due to disease) advance through woody terrain ideal for Spanish guerrilla action, and the troops withdrew before reaching their goal.

There was no other trans-oceanic expedition on this scale during the war, although it continued until 1748. A large-scale attack on Canada was planned for late in the war, but was not pursued due to the pressure on European commitments; as a result, the emphasis was on local forces. While understandable given the commitments in 1746–8, this compromised the experience that could be gained and put to use by the regular army. The local forces achieved one major success, the capture in 1745 of Louisbourg, the French base on Cape Breton Island. The Massachusetts militia under William Pepperell landed safely before bombarding the land defences, although inexperience led to casualties among the artillerymen. With the walls breached and the naval squadron able to reduce the food available to the defenders and eventually to force its way into the harbour, Louisbourg surrendered. As was necessary given the target, the Massachusetts militia acted tactically like European regulars and not as wilderness warriors.

Pepperel had next suggested an invasion of Canada proper. The British government agreed in April 1746 and planned to send six regiments of troops to sail up the St. Lawrence, with two more coming from American units stationed at Louisbourg. Other colonial troops would advance north from Albany. The colonies raised about 7,000 men, the largest contingent from Massachusetts, but there were a series of delays. The St. Lawrence expedition was postponed until 1747, and then cancelled. Instead, the Breton port of Lorient (to the British L'Orient), the main base of the French East India Company, was attacked in 1746. That year, the French sent a fleet plus 3,000 troops as a counterattack to regain Louisbourg, but it was wrecked by disease and bad weather. Their policy, a parallel to that of the British at Cartagena in 1741, underlined the organisational and operational problems of amphibious attacks, and the degree to which local bases and forces could be very important in their success. The loss of Louisbourg meant that the French lacked a local base.

At a smaller scale, there was British failure in the attack on Florida, with the campaign in 1740 against St. Augustine unsuccessful. Having earlier, in the absence of a declaration of war, written to Walpole that 'the best measures here would be only to turn the Indians loose',[10] Colonel James Oglethorpe, the bellicose Governor of Georgia, now planned a methodical siege of St. Augustine, only to be thwarted by the South Carolina Assembly's insistence on a short campaign. The Spaniards resisted bravely, mounting an effective night sortie, the naval blockade failed to prevent the arrival of supply ships, the well-fortified position resisted bombardment, and, once the momentum of advance and success was lost, Oglethorpe's force was struck by desertion, especially on the part of his Native American allies and troops from South Carolina. The effects of disease exacerbated the situation, and Oglethorpe retreated.[11] There was no equivalent to the success against Louisbourg. Separately, in India, Fort St. George at Madras (Chennai) fell in 1746 to French attack, while a British expedition in 1748, having decided that Mauritius would be too difficult to take, failed to capture the major French position in India at Pondicherry.

The regular army had served more as a force for Home and European conflict in the 1740s than one for defending the empire. After France joined the war, the latter task was largely left to local forces, and Britain was fortunate that France and Spain focused on European warfare. With the exception of the unsuccessful 1746 expedition against Louisbourg, French amphibious plans against Britain centred on its invasion, which was tried, unsuccessfully, in 1744 and prepared for, again unsuccessfully, in the winter of 1745–6. This threat obliged the British to focus efforts in Europe, which was one of the reasons for the 1746 expedition being sent against Lorient: the British troops sent there would speedily return to Britain.

However, that functional interpretation of British policy, while significant, underplays the politics of strategy, a key element throughout – as in the Québec expedition in 1711, and notably so when the monarch was directly interested. Issues of honour and prestige, as well as politics, then took on a particular energy. Although George II had been forced in 1744 to part with his Continentalist minister and foreign policy expert, John, Lord Carteret (Earl Granville), and failed in a political crisis to bring him back in February 1746, the king remained the key political heavyweight. This role helped ensure a commitment of British troops to the Continent. So did the ministry, being a Whig group brought up in the idea of the necessity of the 'Old Alliance' that had fought France in 1689–1713. Due to these politics, the army remained a major component of Britain's military structure and its attention was focused on Europe.

A Wide-Ranging Force

The unpopularity of the Peace of Aix-la-Chapelle in 1748 centred on the return of Louisbourg to France. Its capture had indicated the strength and range of British military power for warships and New England militia were responsible for a success that in 1758 was to be secured only by a far larger force. The combination of units from different geographical areas helped give British military power an impressive range, flexibility and versatility. This crucial means served to ensure that a state with a relatively small army could supplement its forces and, in doing so, use empire itself as a force-multiplier. Thus, in 1741, when Britain was at war with Spain, Colonel John Stewart, part of the Scottish military diaspora, wrote from Jamaica:

> If ever Britain strikes any considerable stroke in this part of the world, the blow must come from the North American colonies not by bringing new men from ... [Britain], but by sending officers of experience and good corps to incorporate with and discipline the men to be raised there, these troops as the passage from thence is much shorter might be transported directly to any part of the Spanish West Indies and arrive there with the health and vigour necessary for action, whereas troops sent from home as our own experience has taught us, are by the length of the passage one half disabled with the scurvy and the other half laid up with diseases contracted by confinement and the feeding of salt provisions.[12]

The terms of military combination changed greatly during the period, but the potential of combination remained crucial. Moreover, as in this case, correspondence could serve to spread the message. Stewart's recipient, a Scottish aristocrat whose military service linked Marlborough's campaigns to that of the War of Austrian Succession, never served outside Europe, but such correspondence helped keep him and others informed.

Individual careers often reflected a great geographical range of service. Thus, Lieutenant-Colonel Justly Watson (c. 1710–57) became a cadet gunner in about 1726, served during the siege of Gibraltar (1727), in the Caribbean (1741–4), being promoted to be Engineer-Extraordinary in 1741, in the expedition to Lorient (1746), in North America (1754–5, 1756–7) and West Africa (1755–6), improving the fortifications of British positions in the West Indies, North America and West Africa. His father, Lieutenant-General Jonas Watson (1663–1741), served in the campaigns of

William III in Ireland and the Low Countries, and under Marlborough, commanded the artillery at Gibraltar (1727) and was killed at the siege of Cartagena. Justly Watson's daughter, Miriam, married General Sir William Green (1725–1811), who had been appointed a practitioner engineer in 1743, making his name as chief engineer during the 1779–1783 siege of Gibraltar, where he had earlier worked as engineer from 1761. Greene had earlier served at Fontenoy, Lorient, Bergen-op-Zoom, Newfoundland, Nova Scotia and Québec, while his son became a colonel. These were the family webs that helped hold the army, like the navy, together.

Compared to the glorious successes of the Seven Years' War, notably the years of repeated victories in 1759 and 1762, the earlier imperial struggles appear less impressive and distinguished; judging them in this hindsight is not helpful, however. Looking forward instead of backward, the trans-oceanic successes of the period 1689–1748 compare favourably with the situation over the previous sixty years, or, indeed, century. If Cartagena in 1741 was a failure, the Western Design under Oliver Cromwell against Hispaniola was an even bigger one, while the track-record of successful raids on the Spanish New World proved difficult to replicate. The three Anglo-Dutch wars in 1652–74 had seen successes as well as failures in West Africa and the New World. As far as non-Western powers were concerned, the English had not sustained a presence in Hormuz, they had abandoned Tangier in 1684 as a result of the pressure from Moroccan attacks,[13] and the East India Company was obliged to plead for a pardon from the Mughal Emperor Aurangzeb in 1690 after a conflict that had begun in 1685 turned increasingly against the Company.

Compared to this previous events, the situation in 1689–1748 was one of a stronger presence in the West Indies and North America, and the avoidance of disaster in India until the loss of Madras to the French in 1746. That loss is instructive, as the dynamic from the late 17th century did not appear to be one of British growth, but rather of the greater strength of the French empire, a strength that left Britain vulnerable. Indeed, the biggest prize, the Spanish Habsburg empire, had been largely won for a branch of the Bourbon dynasty ruling France, and this left Britain in a more vulnerable position. This vulnerability was in part avoided as a result of poor Franco-Spanish relations from 1716 to 1733 and 1747 to 1758, but also because French policymakers, and certainly those outside the Ministry of the Marine, did not focus on a trans-oceanic struggle with Britain, let alone with conquering Britain's colonies. This marginality of Britain to most French policymakers, certainly as compared to control over the lands bordering France, provided a vital help to Britain.

This situation was replicated, albeit in a different way outside Europe. None of the major non-Western powers were interested in trans-oceanic power projection. Manchu China, the other great expansionist power on the world scale, focused on landward conquest in Tibet and Xinjiang, and not on reviving Mongol or Ming naval capabilities. Japan and Korea were in isolation, and there was no Mughal or Maratha naval force of major significance. All of this provided Britain with opportunities not to have to fight. In India, the British were particularly marginal, and the major conflicts in the first four decades of the 18th century involved the Mughals, the Marathas, and the successfully invading Nader Shah of Persia. Thus, rather than seeing the question for this period as being focused on British success or failure, with, indeed, failure apparent in light of what was to come later, the situation was one of (limited) success in North America, effort without victory in the Caribbean, and marginality in India. The strengths and weaknesses of the British Army were not of key consequence in these results.

CHAPTER 4

The Seven Years' War, 1754–63

The military force maintained by the Crown on the continent of North America, consists of seven independent companies, usually stationed in South Carolina, Virginia and New York, and each company, when complete, consists of one hundred men, but, as neither the officers or private men have ever seen any service and the companies are generally at a great distance upon separate duty, they can not be thought as they are now employed to be of any general service.

CHARLES TOWNSHEND MP.[1]

The French lined the bushes in their front with one thousand five hundred Indians and Canadians where they also placed their best marksmen, who kept up a very galling, though irregular, fire upon the whole British line, who bore it with the greatest patience and good order, reserving their fire for the main body of the French, now advancing ... The general exhorted his troops to reserve their fire, and at forty yards distance they gave it, which took place in its full extent, and made terrible havoc amongst the French. It was supported with as much vivacity as it was begun and the enemy everywhere yielded to it.

RICHARD HUMPHRYS, 28TH FOOT, BATTLE OUTSIDE QUÉBEC, 1759.[2]

Crisis

The threat was very much felt in Britain, prior to the large-scale French invasion preparations in 1759. Crisis and alarm were seen in December 1757, with an express from Bridport, a coastal port, bringing the news to nearby Dorchester that French troops had landed there and were marching inland. In fact, a French privateer had driven a British coaster ashore and had sent some of its hands to pillage the ship. Similarly, in April 1755, Dublin 'was alarmed' by (false) reports that the French had invaded western Ireland.[3]

Conventionally dated to 1756 when Britain's ally Frederick II 'the Great' of Prussia invaded Saxony and the French successfully attacked the British base at Minorca, the Seven Years' War is like World War Two in that its beginning can be differently dated. Just as the latter began to a degree in 1937, with the outbreak of full-scale war between China and Japan, so the earlier conflict really began in 1754 with fighting in the Ohio Valley, fighting that led in 1755 to unsuccessful British attacks on French bases in North America. Indeed, in a repetition of Britain's delayed entry into the War of the Austrian Succession, in 1742–3 it was not until 1758 that the British Army made a significant intervention in European power-politics, and the forces sent to Germany that year did not begin fighting the French until 1759.

This ensured that the war for empire was to the fore earlier in the Seven Years' War, although the commitment to Germany was also to be conceptualised in terms of winning America in Germany, by means of the distraction of French forces. At the same time, the subsequent reading back of strategic assessment in order to vindicate or castigate policy choices requires correction in terms of the particular issues, problems and discussions of the time. This is notably so of the 'slowing down' of past analysis arising from the need to address specific conundrums in terms of the prioritisation of resources in a context of limited information and uncertain performance. This situation was accentuated by the geographical scale of commitments, and the consequent timescale of deployment.

Fighting had broken out in the extensive Ohio Valley area, where Britain and France had competing territorial claims and supporters among the rival Native groups. The French offensive against Natives trading with British merchants began in 1752, and was intensified in 1753–4 as the French moved in troops and built forts, which threatened to exclude Britain from the entire interior of the Continent. The issue was exacerbated by the failure of diplomatic efforts to settle disputes. Each power also developed their rival interest in the Maritimes, the French at Louisbourg, and British founding the fortified naval base of Halifax to that end in 1749. This led to the deportation of Acadians, inhabitants of Nova Scotia who would not convert to Protestantism, and to localised conflict with Mi'kmaq Native Americans. War was waged from 1749 with the latter, who largely fought by means of ambushes and raids, and on whose behalf the French played a part. As part of the crisis, British troops in 1753 also suppressed a rebellion by new German immigrants in the village of Lunenburg. What was known, with reference to the Acadians, as Father Le Loutre's War was to lead into the Seven Years' War.[4]

In the event, it was to be the Ohio Country that was the basis of wider conflict. In London, on 21 August 1753, with Ligonier present, the Council decided:

> That, with regard to the settlement said to be intended to be made by the French on the River Ohio, general orders should be sent to the several governors in North America, to do their utmost, to prevent, by force, those, and any such attempts, that may be made, by the French, or by the Indians in the French interest.[5]

Neither power wanted war, but the earlier failure of negotiations over the contested frontier dictated the course of conflict in a way that could not be finessed. A colonial garrison of forty men in Fort Prince George (near modern Pittsburgh) was forced to surrender by a larger French force on 17 April 1754, leading George Washington to advance at the head of a small force of militia into the contested area. He defeated a smaller French detachment on 28 May at the battle of Jumonville-Glen, only for a larger French force to force him to surrender at Fort Necessity on 3 July. Washington's choice for a fort was poor, but he thought he would be reinforced, and that there would be no siege.

In the aftermath, French-supported Native Americans raided widely, and the British confronted the situation that was to redefine their response to North America's status within the empire: the lack of troops (fewer than 900 Regulars) made it vulnerable and obliged Britain to send more troops in turn, with Newcastle warning that, otherwise, all North America would be lost.[6] The short-term consequences in terms of the risk envisaged ensured the need for a response. This response was both immediate and long-term, the consequences of the latter in the 1760s helping to exacerbate relations with the American colonists.

Already cited in part, the memorandum sent by Townshend was more significant because he was, as a Lord of the Admiralty, a member of the government. Proposing that the troops already there be gathered together and placed under a commander who had 'served in America, where there are so many peculiar circumstances attending the manner of carrying on war', Townshend backed a strategy of taking the offensive using men raised locally:

> If a regiment should be sent from hence, the transportation will be extremely expensive, and the men both new to the service and strangers to the climate. But if a regiment should be raised there, the expense will be much less, and the men not only accustomed to the climate, but in a degree to the service.

Rather than resting on the defensive, and offering inadequate protection, the memorandum proposed an advance to cut the forward French positions and their Native supporters off from Montréal. It was claimed that only offensive operations would deter the French from future attacks.[7]

Townshend's response was a sensible one in light of the cost-structure of British military imperialism in 1754, but the regular army was in fact to be given a far bigger role due to the rapidly changing politics of the situation. Tasking, rather than existing in some abstract realm of strategy, was heavily politicised. The anxiety of the Newcastle ministry about its domestic political strength had a major impact,[8] just as was to happen in 1756 in the aftermath of the failure to maintain control of Minorca.

Feeling obliged to adopt a firm attitude under pressure from Cumberland, Henry Fox, and George, 2nd Earl of Halifax, president of the Board of Trade, the ministry dispatched two regiments to North America in September 1754 in order to mount wide-ranging attacks the following year, rather than the more limited goal of simply driving the French from the Ohio Valley. The assumption was that the British forces would be able to deliver results; nevertheless, the political context remained significant as Britain and France were not formally at war, and neither ministry sought a full-scale conflict. That ruled out attacks on the major French bases of Louisbourg and Québec, which may well have been a sensible choice, as they were well-fortified, but also ensured a dissipation of effort. That the attacks in 1755 only achieved mixed success was secondary to the strategic failure of failing to use the initiative taken in order substantially to reduce the opposing French threat.

The headline event in the resulting campaign was the total defeat of the British force sent to attack Fort Duquesne near Pittsburgh, but the range of possibilities in 1755 was far better displayed by the attack on the French forts that threatened Nova Scotia, targets made more vulnerable by the possibility of using British naval strength. Fort Beauséjour fell on 16 June 1755 to a force of 250 Regulars and 2,000 New England militia, and Fort Gaspereau surrendered two days later.[9] As a result, the threat to Nova Scotia was blocked unless there was to be a commitment of French forces from further afield.

The situation in the interior was far less happy. A force, largely of Regulars fresh from Britain, under Major-General Edward Braddock, an arrogant protégé of Cumberland, was defeated on 9 July near Fort Duquesne by the French and their Native allies, who made excellent use of tree cover. The unprepared column's response to the ambush was inadequate. Instead of attacking the ambushers, they held their ground, offering excellent targets and taking heavy casualties before breaking.[10] The lack of light infantry and sufficient Native American auxiliaries caused particular problems in the battle, but also reflected an attitude that assumed that the conflict would be a conventional matter of sieges, as Lord George Sackville had confidently anticipated:

> If Braddock gets his cannon over the mountains and through the marshes I do not doubt of his success, but I apprehend great difficulties in Crown Point, because that is the strongest fort, and is the nearest at hand to be reinforced from Montreal and Quebec. If they force that, Canada is open to us.[11]

The reality instead was one of French and Native allies in the ascendant, a process accentuated on 8 September when a militia force advancing from Albany towards Fort St. Frédéric was ambushed near Lake George and fled. In 1756, when war was declared on 17 May, the French captured Forts Ontario, George and Oswego. They also took Minorca, where Fort St. Philip fell to a far larger amphibious force after a siege.

The British Army had to be rapidly expanded at the start of the war. Calling on Hanoverian troops, who landed on 20 May, to help prevent a threatened French invasion proved contentious. Their arrival led to a *cause célèbre* centred on a Hanoverian soldier arrested at Maidstone on suspicion of theft, but released from the custody of the civil authorities by a Secretary of State in accordance with George's wishes.[12] This issue helped fire demands for the buildup of the militia.

Moreover, the new British commander in North America, John, 4th Earl of Loudoun, another difficult Cumberland protégé, whose campaign experience was restricted to serving in Scotland in 1746, was unwilling to search for a compromise on the reimbursement and control of colonial troops; as a result, there was scant cooperation.[13] In this, Loudoun was expressing Cumberland's views on the need for military direction for the war effort. This was an aspect of Cumberland's linkage with a militarisation of empire, one already seen with his conduct in Scotland.[14] Far from being inflexible in military matters, Cumberland was keen to develop light infantry and for units in North America to acquire experience by scouting expeditions in woodland.

In 1757, the government's desire for a vigorous campaign leading to the capture of Louisbourg and Québec[15] was thwarted by fears about a larger French fleet in North American waters. Instead, the French attacked anew, capturing Fort William Henry at the head of Lake George after isolating its outnumbered garrison and, more generally, pushing the British onto a defensive in which they were vulnerable. Fort William Henry itself was a product of the changing British presence. Built in late 1755 as an aspect of the forward policy adopted that year, Fort William Henry was not the typical colonial fort of a picketed structure of locally hewn logs, relatively inexpensive and easy to equip (and abandon), but, rather, an artillery fort on a more standard European model, albeit adapted to North American circumstances.[16]

As a reminder of the problems of organizing effective operations, the talented and decisive French commander Louis-Joseph, Marquis de Montcalm, faced the difficulty of managing Native American allies (themselves highly diverse) and was also critical of the Canadian troops under his command on account of tensions similar to those between British Regulars and colonial militia. Montcalm (1712–59) was an example of a commander with extensive experience of European conflict – in his case, the Wars of the Polish and Austrian Successions – who only visited Canada for the first time as commander in chief there. The tensions of cooperation seen with both sides were different in scale and context to those in India, but, as there, were a crucial aspect of warfare and notably so when advancing into the interior. Montcalm had arrived with 3,000 Regulars, thus changing the French military profile and alliance in North America.[17]

At this stage, British politicians, especially Pitt, were opposed to sending troops to the Army of Observation, a German force partly financed by Britain, formed to protect Hanover. Cumberland, the commander, complained to Fox that July: 'I hear you send two thousand men more to North America, what for God knows. Here I am sure you'll send none, though perhaps they would be more necessary than anywhere England can employ them.'[18] Once units had been dispatched to a particular location then they were 'fixed', first in transit, and then in location. To a degree, that element is underrated if the focus instead is on the relative ease of fungibility suggested by reference to Germany or America, as if there was a strategic fluidity and geopolitical outcome for the asking.

In the event, the heavily outnumbered Cumberland was defeated by a French invading force at Hastenbeck on 26 July 1757 and forced into retreat; he then signed a neutrality agreement for Hanover, which a furious George II disavowed. Rather than helping Cumberland, Pitt had been readier to attack the French naval base at Rochefort in another version of the Lorient attack of 1746, presented as likely to 'cause a considerable diversion'[19] to the benefit of Cumberland and Frederick II. However, against a background of extravagant hopes, a combination of poor intelligence, inadequate cooperation between naval and army commanders and indifferent generalship led to a failure to attack the port, and instead to an expedition that was widely criticised as amounting only to 'robbing a few orchards and vineyards.'[20] Pitt then evaded blame by setting up a Commission of Enquiry into the conduct of the generals, and also played an active role in the court martial of Sir John Mordaunt, the army commander, appearing before it in order to criticise the generals. He also told the Sardinian envoy, Count Viry, that failure at Rochefort was due to Cumberland's hostility to the scheme and his influence in the army – probably an example of his paranoia, but a view that Newcastle appeared to share.[21] Cumberland espoused the cause of the generals, while Mordaunt's acquittal reflected the court martial's view that the expedition had been misconceived. Politics was frequently the prism through which operations were perceived: the choices of where to campaign, of the commanders, and the response to what happened. The political character of reputation underlined this perception. Thus, the failed attempt on St. Malo in September 1758 was brought home on those commanders responsible, who were protégés of the court of George, Prince of Wales, and their treatment helped seriously to damage relations with Pitt.

The *Monitor*, a pro-Pitt newspaper, had declared its hostility to sending troops to the Continent in its issue of 24 December 1757:

> To pretend to measure swords with the common enemy of Europe in pitched battles on the Continent is making the remedy worse than the disease …to contend with her by a continental war is to give her an opportunity, by spinning out one campaign after another, to reduce us to beggary.

The paper proposed not 'expensive campaigns' but a fleet and a militia: 'people, properly disciplined and officered, are the best defenders of their own territories and privileges.'[22] Meanwhile, the British ministry had urged George, as Elector, to keep Cumberland's force together and active against the French.[23]

The Campaigns of 1758

In 1758, there was to be change in Britain's European policy, while the initiative was taken in North America. As Robert, 4th Earl of Holdernesse, the Secretary of State for the Northern Department, pointed out: 'the efforts made in America exceed in magnitude anything that has ever been attempted in that part of the world. Twenty-seven thousand men, regular troops, are actually employed there.'[24] However, the largest force, that under Major-General James Abercromby, the British commander in chief in North America, directed against French-held Fort Carillon (the precursor of Fort Ticonderoga) was a total failure. An 'unlucky ill conducted'[25] frontal assault on 8 July, without artillery preparation, led to heavy casualties, especially among the 42nd Foot (The Black Watch),[26] and to the abandonment of the operation, prefiguring the defeat at New Orleans in 1815. Abercromby (1706–81), the eldest son of a MP and army officer who had been ADC to Marlborough in 1711, was appointed an ensign in 1717, promoted to captain in 1736, purchased a major's commission in 1742, became a colonel in 1746, the year he served in the attack on Lorient, and fought in the Low Countries, being wounded in 1747. Loudoun's second-in-command in 1757, Abercromby was a good organiser, but he proved totally unsuccessful as a battlefield commander in 1758.

It would be easy to juxtapose failure at Carillon in 1758 with success that year against Louisbourg in order to suggest that the army was likely to succeed only if cooperating with the navy; but, while warships did provide valuable mobility and firepower, there was also the need to focus on the specific contingencies of individual campaigns, notably command skills. Thus, alongside success at Louisbourg, which surrendered on 26 July, there was a carefully prepared advance on Fort Duquesne by an army of 7,000, mostly American provincials, whose success indicated the value of experience and being trained for woodland conflict. In an advance from one fortified position to another, Braddock's mistakes were avoided and, crucially, Native American support was secured, the latter helping to make the military environment safer. However, as with the failure to capture Louisbourg in 1757, that at Carillon in 1758 was very serious because the window of wartime opportunity was not limitless: the financial credit essential to the war effort was one time-sensitive factor, but so were international and domestic politics.

Whatever the target, there was danger. In his journal, Richard Humphrys of the 28th Regiment described the landing on Cape Breton Island on 8 June 1758, prior to the attack on Louisbourg:

> About three in the morning the men of war began to play against their batteries and breastworks, and the troops being in their boats two hours before day …. About six the signal was made to land, when the whole set off with the greatest eagerness and a terrible fire began on both sides, that nothing was seen or heard for one hour but the thundering of cannon and flashes of lightning, where the never daunted spirits of British soldiers landed and forced their way through the batteries and breastworks. As soon as the enemy found that we had landed,

and that they could not make any farther resistance, they gave way and began to retreat in great disorder leaving us to take possession of all their works. The attackers on the right behaved gallantly and forced their way through the rocks, but unfortunately as one of the boats was making for the shore a wave took her and she overset, being loaded with grenadiers.

All bar one died.[27] Their heavy loads would have put them very much at risk, but the vast majority of people did not know how to swim anyway. The landing itself was dangerous due to heavy French fire on the vulnerable, slow-moving boats, where there was no cover, but the British, who had trained at Halifax for this landing, succeeded in part by landing on the right behind the cover of rocks, and in part by subsequent assaults using the bayonet. The latter, moreover, proved significant in the resulting siege of Louisbourg. So also did digging trenches and the use of cannon in a five-week bombardment. With the assistance of the fleet, the cannon were brought forward successfully, and sited and managed well.[28]

The campaigning in 1758 demonstrated the complexity of evaluating overall success. Although the British Army was adapting to the multiple challenges of fighting in North America,[29] the war could not go on for ever, and another year in which the British enjoyed superiority in numbers in North America had not led to the capture of Québec that Pitt had hoped for.[30] Moreover, there had been a failure on the part of three very separate offensives to provide mutual support, and the French had been able to focus their efforts against Abercromby. The sense of frustration was clear when James Wolfe wrote from Louisbourg on 9 August:

> I don't well know what we are doing here – with the harbour full of men of war and transports – and the fine season stealing away, unenjoyed – I call it so because we should use it for the purposes of war. We have enemies close at hand, and others at a greater distance, that should in my mind be sought after ... Our fleet, it seems wants anchors, and cables, and provisions and pilots, pretty essential articles you will say ... I am sure Abercromby wants assistance – we have it to spare.[31]

Yet, while the British exploitation of success was limited, the process of incrementalism in achieving objectives at the end of 1758 was such that the French were now in a more vulnerable position, and this was exploited in 1759 with the expedition to Québec. Meanwhile, the government had changed its policy on sending British troops to Germany, in order to keep Hanover and Prussia in the war. In addition, in order to meet expectations of 'blue water' policies, as well as Frederick the Great's request that Britain distract France,[32] attacks were also mounted on Cherbourg (successfully) and St. Malo (unsuccessfully), the latter reflecting the danger that the French would be able to assemble in sufficient numbers to wreck the siege necessary to capture a fortified position.[33]

Success in 1759

The 1759 expedition to Québec saw successful coordination with the navy, but, as for the French at Carillon in 1758, depended on the move by the opponent. In the case of 1759 for the British, the key move was the French coming out to fight, rather than remaining in Québec and letting the British, late in the season, bear the burdens of a siege in the context of a countryside they did not control. Leaving Louisbourg on 6 June, Wolfe had arrived near Québec on 26 June, but his operations along the Beauport shore were initially unsuccessful. On 31 July, an attack on French positions was repelled by Montcalm's larger army, with the British suffering 440 casualties to the French 60. As winter approached, it had seemed increasingly likely that the British would fail to capture the city, which had formidable natural and man-made defences.

Wolfe risked a bold move. James Cook, later famous as the explorer of the Pacific, had thoroughly surveyed the St. Lawrence, charting its rocks, and British warships had passed beyond Québec making upriver raids. The army was to follow. On 1–3 September, British troops left their camp and moved along the southern bank of the river, opposite Québec, before, after delays due to the weather, landing in the early hours of 13 September on the northern bank, west of the city. Some 200 light infantry scaled the cliffs and successfully attacked a French camp of 100 men. The remainder of the British force then landed, climbed the cliffs, and advanced to the Plains of Abraham near the city.

The French could have remained within Québec's fortifications waiting both for a siege and the onset of winter to exhaust the British and for nearby French forces to concentrate, thus greatly outnumbering the British; in 1775–6, the British successfully remained within the fortifications when Québec was fruitlessly besieged and assaulted by American forces. Instead, the French came out to fight, and their battle tactics worked to the advantage of the British. A French column assault was received by regular volley fire, the muskets loaded with two balls, that inflicted losses before the French broke in the face of a bayonet charge, the 78th Highlanders using the broad sword:

> About 9 o'clock, the French army had drawn up under the walls of the town, and advanced towards us briskly and in good order. We stood to receive them; they began their fire at a distance, we reserved ours, and as they came nearer fired on them by divisions, this did execution and seemed to check them a little, however they still advanced pretty quick, we increased our fire without altering our position, and, when they were within less than a hundred yards, gave them a full fire, fixed our bayonets, and under cover of the smoke the whole line charged.[34]

In scale, this victory on 13 September 1759 was very different to that of the British at Minden in Germany on 1 August, but there was a common theme of impressive fighting quality able to defeat French attacks, with both effective platoon firepower[35] and bayonet fighting playing a role. In Britain, bell ringers were paid for celebrating both victories.[36] Québec had surrendered on 18 September. This was not the sole triumph on land in 1759, as a force of Regulars, American provincials, and Native Americans under Colonel William Massey advanced from Albany to Lake Ontario with the French, in turn, moving out of Fort Niagara only to be defeated by defensive British fire at La Belle-Famille on 24 July, the fort surrendering two days later. At the same time, the French abandoned Ticonderoga without resisting attack because the British attack on Québec led them to focus their forces there.

This did not mean that the British invariably won. Indeed, on 28 April 1760, at the battle of Sainte-Foy outside Québec, a French force attacked and defeated the thin and greatly outnumbered British line, with the British then retreating into the city with heavier casualties. It was besieged until a British relief force arrived by river when the ice of the St. Lawrence melted.

Helped by the experience of recent conflict in the 1740s, the long-term reliance on a firepower ensured by drill and discipline provided the fire discipline of the professional, long-service British troops who could fire more volleys a minute than Continental counterparts. At the typical firing distance of 40 to 100 yards, this weight of volley really told, and provided a strong preliminary to a bayonet charge also at close range; although, as at Cowpens in 1781 in the American War of Independence, there, in turn, were serious consequences when the opponent stood their ground and fired a volley that could inflict serious casualties.

In the Seven Years' War there was an improvement in British generalship compared to the War of the Austrian Succession, with Granby and Wolfe being especially impressive; the British troops showed continued quality, notably the infantry with their alternate fire system, particularly impressive at the short range they sought, a range that was both deadly and an easier prelude to a bayonet assault.

Victory in 1760

The North American campaign of 1760 was also a striking achievement. Troops advanced from Québec, Crown Point and, in largest numbers, Lake Ontario under Brigadier James Murray, Colonel William Haviland, and General Jeffrey Amherst respectively, the three forces moving on Montréal, the last passing hazardous rapids on the St. Lawrence. In the face of this pressure, the French surrendered on 8 September. Humphrys noted:

> History can hardly produce a more striking instance of excellent military conduct in three separate expeditions against one place, by different routes, without any communication with each other, and through such a dangerous and difficult country, meeting almost at the same time, at the destined rendezvous.[37]

The British Army, methodically effective at the operational and strategic level in 1760, had proved a force capable of operating in the New World, and the contrast with the problems and limitations of 1755–7 was readily apparent. Less positively, a relatively small French force had absorbed much of the British Army. Moreover, the dispatch of British troops to the New World would have looked less sensible if French plans to invade Britain had proved successful, and there was speculation as to whether the French intention was to deter the British from sending troops abroad.[38] The government was well aware of the French preparations and of their scale, including for example the French wish to purchase 400 Swedish cannon to that end.[39] John, 4th Duke of Bedford, the Lord Lieutenant of Ireland, warned that transferring troops from there to Bengal (in India) risked France exploiting discontent in Ireland, not least if the British fleet was shut up in the English Channel by adverse winds.[40] Other Lord Lieutenants of Ireland, such as William, 3rd Duke of Devonshire in 1740, raised similar fears.[41]

Operations in Europe

Given both the significance of Wolfe's success at Québec in 1759, and that the next major war was to be fought in North America, it is not surprising that attention focuses on Wolfe. In practice, British units proved able to combine effectively in Germany in the Anglo-German army under Duke Ferdinand of Brunswick from 1758, and to operate successfully in the New World, although amphibious attacks on the French coast in 1757–61 did not serve to gain a major strategic advantage. The army was divided in subsequent decades between 'Germans' and 'Americans' with reference to where they had served. There were indeed contrasts, but also fewer differences than might be imagined, as Continental warfare was less hidebound, rigid and limited than often believed, and 'woodcraft' and dispersed tactics were found there as well as in North America. However, Ferdinand of Brunswick and Granby are in danger of being forgotten, as is the tradition of British conflict on the Continent during that war. The 'Germans' were to be portrayed as inflexible, but Minden was a great victory, one where the disciplined retention of formation and the related ability to combine firepower and mobility were crucial:

> The ardour of the English battalions and Hanoverian Guards carried them into the midst of the enemy, and though they found themselves raked by the cannon, attacked on their flanks and rear by cavalry, they made so brave and so glorious

a resistance, and so often renewed their attacks, that the enemy soon began to give way, and the whole affair was over in two hours.[42]

The British artillery was also impressive that day, notably on the left: 'The destruction our cannon made on that side was prodigious, and kept the enemy in such respect, that the battalions had no recourse to their small arms.'[43] However, the British cavalry failed to cement the victory by charging, which led to the court-martial of the commander of the British contingent of the army, Lieutenant-General Lord George Sackville (1716–85), later as Lord George Germain, Secretary of State for America during the American War of Independence.[44]

Granby, like Marlborough, benefited from his determination to gain and retain the initiative, and, like him, was expert at coordinating infantry, cavalry and artillery. Victorious at Warburg (1760), where the French suffered 3,500 casualties, Granby, Sackville's successor as the British commander in the combined force under Ferdinand, fought off a French attack at Fellinghausen (1761), and was successful at Gravenstein (1762) and Wilhelmstahl (1762). The last, in which the French force was outflanked and nearly encircled, helped protect Hanover from attack. Yet, although many officers of subsequent importance in the army served under Granby, the war in Westphalia did not engage British interest. Moreover, it seemed inconsequential compared to the campaigning in North America and that of Frederick the Great, with his development of the method of the oblique attack.

In practice, however, these Westphalian victories were crucial, as the French hoped to win back in Hanover what they had lost in North America. As with the British force successfully sent to protect Portugal against Bourbon invasion in 1762, failure would have counteracted colonial gains,[45] repeating the experience of 1748. In contrast, ensuring the absence of this factor was to be a key element of the strategy of the War of American Independence: France then had to defeat Britain overseas, as there was no British vulnerability in Continental Europe arising from the weaknesses of Hanover or Britain's allies.[46]

The serious operating difficulties for the British in both Westphalia and Portugal reflected the problems of a strategy reliant on a Continental commitment by the army. Thus, moving south from the landing port of Emden in 1758, the 7,000 strong British force found East Friesland (Frisia), a territory of their ally Prussia, bare of supplies; the commissionary responsible for supplies, Michael Hatton, complained:

> No contractors, no regular magazines … a continued rain [therefore] the roads are become so bad … the major part of the baggage is behind … the bread for want of covered waggons is dissolved, though I bought the best coverings I could, as is the two days of bread the men had in their knapsacks, and I am afraid there is not a dry cartridge in the army. We have bread at Gesfield … but that can't be got to us, nor we can't get to that. There has not been a pot boiled these two days, the rain put out the fires … there are potatoes … which the men will get if the waters fall a little.

When he reached Coesfeld, Hatton found the available supplies inadequate and too expensive.[47] The bleakness of the situation for wealthy Britain can also be seen in the case of the expeditionary force sent to Allied Portugal in 1762 in a successful attempt to thwart a Spanish invasion.[48] That July, Colonel Marescoe Frederick of the 75th Foot provided a depressing account of the logistical problems he faced on the march to Santarem, problems that in part arose from the poverty of the region. Arriving at Porto de Mugen, Frederick had found no beef or bread prepared for his troops and it proved impossible to obtain adequate supplies:

> All the bread that the magistrate said he could possibly get before they marched was two hundred small loaves which was so small a quantity it was impossible to divide amongst the men. I ordered the regiment to march the next morning at half an hour past three, but the carriages for the baggage not coming at the proper time it was past six before they began their march. It was late in the day before they got to Santarem…. the magistrates had provided no quarters for them neither was there beef or bread for the men, and … they were fainting with the heat and want of food.

If food was one area of shortage, there were also complaints in Portugal about the lack of shelter, beds and straw.[49] Linked to supply problems, and again imposing strain on troops, were the more widespread problems of communications. Rivers could be used as supply routes but were often inadequate due to drought, floods, ice, or, as with the Weser in Germany in 1761, a slow flow.[50] The following year, in Westphalia, 'the heavy rains had so spoilt the roads and the whole country that the artillery could not possibly get on.'[51] Alternatively, as Captain Fraser Folliott found in Portugal, a supposed ford over the River Tagus was five feet deep and the current very rapid, while the roads nearby were impassable for wheeled vehicles.[52]

The difficulties of operating can be underplayed due to emphasis on battle, but they were serious. Moreover, these difficulties were accentuated if troops were sent to distant targets where, aside from being close-packed in the ships, a lack of immunity to disease was a problem. This was particularly an issue in the Caribbean, notably with malaria and yellow fever. About a third of the British force sent to capture Havana in 1762 died as a result: landing on 7 June, the British took the surrender on 13 August.

In addition, such expeditions were made more unpredictable by the weather both on land and at sea. Storms prevented French invasions planned for March 1744 and January 1746. In turn, Charles, 3rd Duke of Marlborough, wrote from the English Channel off Cherbourg in June 1758:

> We had been excessive unlucky in our winds as I was prevented three days ago from landing on the coast of Normandy by a gale of wind … last night I had everything ready to attack the forts of this place, just before we stepped into the boats the wind blew so excessive hard that we were forced to desist, and have had great difficulty in preventing some of the transports form being blown on shore.[53]

Major-General Studholme Hodgson, commander of the expedition to Belle-Île in 1761, reported at one stage: 'we could get nothing landed yesterday, it blew so excessively hard.'[54] Yet, as a sign of a successful military infrastructure, the British in their siege of the citadel at Le Palais on the island fired 17,000 shot and 12,000 shells from a battery of 30 cannon and 30 mortars.[55] Alongside the use of mines as a prelude to infantry assault, the artillery also played a key role at the siege of Havana in 1762:

> Our new batteries against the town being perfected (which consisted of forty-four pieces of cannon) we all at once, by a signal, opened them and did prodigious execution. Our artillery was so well served and the fire so excessively heavy and incessant … that the Spaniards could not possibly stand up to their guns.[56]

Hodgson (1708–98), the son of a merchant, joined the Foot Guards in 1728, fighting under Cumberland at Fontenoy and Culloden, and under Mordaunt on the Rochefort expedition. Belle-Île was his last command in the field, but, in accordance with the practice of the period, he continued to win promotion in the army, ultimately to Field-Marshal in 1796.

There was bravery, especially in battle, and not least in light of the limited medical provisions for the wounded. Yet, operations were also far from heroic. Major-General George Townshend reported from Westphalia in September 1761:

> This exhausted, pillaged, infected country where nothing but chicanes in war, and misery and despair to the inhabitants remains. Our army is really a scene of indiscipline, weakness and almost despondency. I never saw so much pillage and desertion; it is general.[57]

Captain William Fawcett, who will return in chapter eight, had revealed his sympathies the previous year, noting, with reference to Westphalia, that 'the poor soldiers lying upon the damp, and without straw, occasions great sickness in the army.'[58] In the spring of 1761, there were over 3,000 British troops sick in hospital in Westphalia, enough to cause a shortage of men.[59] While concerned about the wounded, Granby was able to do little about the limitations of the medical care available. Fawcett's correspondence reflected the range of behaviour. In 1759, noting that the advanced posts of the two forces were very close, he wrote of:

> A sight extraordinary enough, to those who are not acquainted with the formalities of war. The French, to do them justice, are a very generous enemy and above taking little advantages: I myself am an instance of it, amongst many that happen almost daily. Being out a coursing a few days ago, I was galloping at full speed after a hare ... into a thicket, where they had a post of infantry, and must infallibly have been taken prisoner, if the officer commanding it had not shown himself; and very genteelly call out to stop me. We frequently discourse together.[60]

In turn, in 1758, Sackville wrote from Germany:

> Our sentinels and advanced posts are in perfect harmony and good humour with each other, they converse frequently together and have not yet fired though officers go out of curiosity much nearer than there is any occasion for.[61]

Sackville was to go on to be Secretary of State for America in 1775–82. Episodes of restraint and courtesy have tended to characterise the image of conflict in the era, with particular attention devoted to the British and French at the battle of Fontenoy in 1745 and their initial willingness there to let the other side fire first, if firing prematurely and/or if the troops were less well-disciplined and therefore had to receive the heavier fire of a better-disciplined force. Moreover, the treatment of prisoners had improved since the mid-17th century.[62] Yet, at Fontenoy, this conduct in part was due to the disadvantage that could accrue from firing first. There was also often much brutality in the treatment of the soldiers, as well as civilians. Thus, at Dettingen, British soldiers plundered and stripped their dead and wounded compatriots.[63] Fighting included the use of case-shot against close-packed rows of soldiers and the slaughter of fleeing infantry by cavalry. Fawcett, in 1760, captured the commonplace nature of death:

> The destruction of two or three hundred poor wretches, is looked upon as a mere trifle here, whenever there is any point to be carried which is thought of consequence … 500 or 1000 fine fellows, in full bloom and vigour ordered to march up, to possess themselves of an eminence, an old house, or windmill, or other particular piece of ground, with a certainty of one half of them at least, being, at the same time, exposed to certain death in the doing of it. Nevertheless, this does and must happen almost daily, so long as the war lasts.[64]

Much conflict was a matter of the *petite guerre* (irregular warfare), such as small-scale clashes around outposts, described by Conway in Westphalia in 1761 as 'small skirmishes, and almost daily marches and counter-marches.' The following year, he referred to such fighting as heavy: 'the French fought quite close to the point of bayonet.' In such clashes, light troops were at a premium, for example in driving the French back over the River Lahn in 1762.[65] Yet outpost conflict could also be of a different scale, Granby reporting from Westphalia that year on:

> An affair which lasted from five in the morning till dark night without intermission. It was an attack upon my advanced post which I supported with my whole reserve; the cannonade on both sides was as severe as ever was known. It began at five, continued till dark night with the utmost fury … our

artillery consisted of 18 heavy 12, 8 heavy 6, 2 light 12 pounders, and 8 or 9 howitzers, the enemy's artillery and ours were very equally matched ... our loss in killed and wounded ... near eight hundred.[66]

Although victories such as Minden could be, and frequently were, attributed to God,[67] the Seven Years' War indicated the multiple capabilities of Britain as a military system, as well as the resilience that enabled recovery from serious initial failures. In terms of weaponry, the army was in an acceptable position. In 1715, the Board of Ordnance had instituted a system of supply in which it contracted among different manufacturers for the parts of firearms which were stored by the government and, when required, sent to private gunsmiths for assembly, ensuring both necessary supplies and the enforcement of patterns.[68]

More significantly, the British infantry proved more than satisfactory at Minden and Québec, while the artillery had played an important role at the former. The army was not noted for tactical innovation, unlike that of Frederick the Great, but the far smaller forces the British deployed in battle proved able to cope with the different battlefield scenarios they had encountered. In part, this was a matter of the effectiveness and fighting quality already demonstrated, albeit in difficult circumstances during the War of the Austrian Succession. The army fulfilled both defensive and offensive tasks more successfully in this war than had initially seemed likely, and was therefore able to bring the advantages brought by naval strength and victory to fruition.

Crucially, the British spent far more on the struggle in Canada and had a larger army there than the French: in 1758, 24,000 Regulars and 22,500 provincial troops compared to 6,600 *troupes de terre*, 2,900 *compagnies franches de la marine*, and about 15,000 militia. This posed a logistical burden, and in order to minimise risk, the British focused on securing lines of communications and creating a flexible support system to assist the advance.[69]

The Militia

Alongside the presence in North America, there was strength in the British Isles. This was politicised and contentious, notably with the calls for a militia, which was seen as an expression of a robust and purposeful masculinity. The weakness of the existing system was apparent during the '45. Thus, the Secretary of State for Scotland was informed from Dumfries that 'the body of the people' were 'extremely hearty in the common cause, but without arms, without officers, and without any advice of any kind from any of the officers of the crown.'[70] The alternatives subsequently presented by the opposition were of a militia 'all interested in the general weal, rather than ... a rabble of mercenaries, either natives or foreigners.'[71] Indeed, Pitt pointed out that the Tories, who in this prefigured Thomas Jefferson, wanted 'to make us depend upon the militia only',[72] whereas he argued for a complementary system of militia and Regulars. However, the militia system established in England and Wales was adopted only with some difficulty, including major riots in Bedfordshire, Hertfordshire, Lincolnshire and Yorkshire against the new obligations. In 1759, during a panic about a potential French invasion, Sir Richard Bampfylde MP, a militia officer, reported from Plymouth:

> The uncertainty of our pay since we arrived at this place, has been the occasion of those disorders amongst the private men [ordinary troops] ... I am under great apprehensions of a future insurrection on that account.[73]

George Fortescue was more optimistic:

> ... the great spirit and unanimity with which the officers act; the expertness of the men in their exercises; their great diligence in their present duty; and remarkable sobriety, and decency in their quarters, have put these troops in the opinion of every unprejudiced person, in the most respectable, and useful footing .... I have no doubt, but the uniting so many gentlemen of fortune in the present service of their country will in this country particularly, be attended with very happy consequences.[74]

In considering invasion, the French were more impressed by the British Regulars than the militia, and also, despite their pressure to act, by Jacobite weakness.[75]

The militia survived the war and, under legislation of 1762, was obliged to drill for four weeks in peacetime each year. This focused on the response to anticipated conflicts and threats of invasion. Britain gained the capability to defend with depth. Meanwhile, disputes over the militia, and other political tensions, had interacted with the dispatch of troops abroad. In late 1759 and 1760, Pitt took an active role in supporting the dispatch of more troops to Ferdinand's army, where the British contingent rose to 22,000. This was a matter of the quelling of worries about French invasion of Hanover, concern over French resilience in Westphalia (where more French troops had been sent after the blocking of invasion schemes), and the need to hold onto America in Germany in terms of subsequent peace negotiations.

Whatever the strategic context, the circumstances for troops were frequent difficulties. Following heavy rain in northern Germany in August 1758, Charles, 3rd Duke of Marlborough, who earlier in the year had faced storms in the Channel thwarting a landing, wrote, 'the foot [infantry] have marched the last day almost up to their middle in water the whole way.'[76] And yet, it is the repeated success in responding to circumstances that emerges most clearly. The multiple failures of the army and the wider military and governmental systems in the early stages of war[77] had been overcome.

CHAPTER 5

Fighting for America, 1763–83

It was not fair to shoot at us from behind trees;
If they had stand open as they ought before our great
guns we should have beat them with ease

....

Of their firing from behind fences, he makes a great pother,
Ev'ry fence has two sides; they [the Americans] made
use of one, and we only forgot to use the other.

THE KING'S OWN REGULARS,
AMERICAN REVOLUTIONARIES' SONG OF 1775.

The 1760s

Failure to hold onto the Thirteen Colonies that became the United States was to create a lasting idea of the obsolescence of the British Army, one that is particularly significant because it is strongly held in the United States. The validity of this approach as an overall judgment of the army, however, is questionable, not least because it leads to an underplaying of the need to consider effectiveness in particular contexts. To expect a military to face all its tasks with proficiency and success is unrealistic, and notably so for imperial powers that had wide-ranging commitments, such as, for this period, Manchu China, Mughal India, Ottoman Turkey, Russia and Britain. That was even more the case if the challenge was in a new environment, as, for the British, with the political dimension of the war in North America in 1775–83 compared to their earlier conflicts there.

These conflicts were both with France and with Native Americans, and, in the 1760s (in a parallel with the situation in India from the mid-1750s), the latter involved regular British forces to a degree not hitherto seen. Sequential fighting was a key element, with the surrender of New France in 1760 making it easier to focus on the Cherokee in 1761, whereas the effort against them in 1760, already hit by serious logistical problems and effective guerrilla resistance, had had to be cut short to the benefit of the campaign in Canada. Governor William Bull of South Carolina reported in 1761 that Anglo-American prisoners released by the Cherokee claimed that:

> Their young men from their past observations express no very respectable opinion of our manner of fighting them, as, by our close order, we present a large object to their fire, and our platoons do little execution as the Indians are thinly scattered, and concealed behind bushes or trees; though they acknowledged our troops thereby show they are not afraid, and that our numbers would be formidable in open ground, where they will never give us an opportunity of engaging them.[1]

In turn, the force of regular troops, Carolina Rangers and Allied Native Americans deployed under Lieutenant-Colonel James Grant in 1761, indicated the variety of units that commanders had to learn to command and combine. A scorched-earth policy, in which settlements and crops were burned, was countered by Cherokee resistance based on highland hideouts; but food and ammunition shortages, disease and despair engendered by the scorched earth policy led the Cherokee to agree terms.[2]

Grant (1720–1806) himself was typical as an officer in his Scottish background and wide-ranging career. Born the second son of a Scottish landowner, he became an ensign in 1741 and purchased a captaincy in 1744. Serving on the Continent from 1743 and fighting at Fontenoy, he was thwarted by the cancellation of the Canada expedition, serving instead on the Lorient expedition of 1746. As a major in a newly formed Highland regiment in 1757, Grant recruited men from his clan; he took part in the expedition against Fort Duquesne in 1758, but was captured and held in Montreal until November 1759. Quarrelling in 1758 and the early 1760s with American colonial officers, Grant served in the force that captured Martinique and Guadeloupe in 1762, before becoming Governor of East Florida from 1763 to 1773. Sent to North America in 1775, he played an active role, notably at the Battle of Long Island, going on to capture St. Lucia from the French in 1778. Returning to Britain in 1779, ill with fever and gout, he praised the quality of the Patriot troops. Grant was commanding general of the army in Scotland from 1789, retiring from the army in 1805 as a general.[3]

There was effective resistance to regular and colonial forces in Pontiac's War in 1763–4, with the Native Americans, angered by colonial expansionism, driving them from the Ohio Valley, and, in doing so, demonstrating the adaptability of their way of war, specifically in displaying the new skills appropriate for fighting Europeans.[4] However, the capacity of the Regulars and colonials to respond to Native American successes and to mount fresh efforts was indicative of the manpower resources they enjoyed, resources that were far greater than those of the Native Americans. Conflict with the latter tested both Regulars and colonials and encouraged the development of experience with what was termed 'small war'.

With space at a premium and with the benefit of hindsight, it is easy to treat Pontiac's War as a minor epilogue to the Seven Years' War or an inconsequential prelude to that of American Independence. However, that approach neglects the variety of tasks facing the army and underplays the significance of the Native Americans to the control of trans-Appalachia at this point, while elements of the War of Independence can be seen in Pontiac's War, notably the contrast between control of the interior and that of key sites within and outside it. That the campaigning was simultaneous to the bitter struggle that ensured British control of Bengal in India against far more numerous opponents adds to the interest in considering multiple challenges and multi-faceted imperial capability.

The large number of forts lost or abandoned in May–June 1763 in the initial stages of Pontiac's War, represented influence over a substantial area, but the garrisons of most of these small forts were tiny: 16 in Fort Sandusky, 12 in Fort Miami, 21 in Fort Ouiatenon, 28 in Fort Michilimackinac. A series of Native American ambush victories prevented relief attempts and demonstrated that the British were less effective at fighting in the woodlands of the frontier zones than their opponents, especially when acting offensively. Moreover, British dependence on supply routes made them further vulnerable to ambushes.

Apparently prefiguring defeat in the War of Independence, the war, like the French Revolutionary, Crimean, Boer, and two world wars, also showed strengths alongside weaknesses, and not least an ability to recover and improve. Even in the initial attacks, the major forts, Pitt, Lignonier, Bedford, Niagara, Oswego, London, Carlisle, Lancaster, and Detroit, did not fall or were not attacked. In part this was because Native American methods and force structure were not appropriate to methodical siegecraft, but the quality of the defence was also a factor. The British were therefore well placed to mount a response, and in doing so, benefited from their opponents' shortage of firearms and ammunition, as well as from Native American divisions. The British had the room for manoeuvre provided by the region of cultivation and settlement nearer the coast, just as in 1775–83 they were to have that offered by the Atlantic.

The war ended with a series of treaties in 1764 in which the Native Americans returned all prisoners, but ceded no land. The stabilisation of relations with the Native Americans in 1764 had entailed the British accepting the limitations of the use of force. Instead, they turned back to diplomacy. Although the British authorities assured themselves that their terms were imposed, the settlement was in practice a compromise. Indeed, Native American resistance encouraged the British government to oppose colonial settlement west of the Alleghenies, which greatly helped to increase colonial anger with British control. However, the Native American issue was much less prominent for the British in the early 1770s than it had been a decade earlier. In place of the extended network of forts, defended portages, and roads created earlier by British troops, there were few military posts in the interior, in large part due to concern about Massachusetts.[5] These posts suffered from the pressures of the climate on both fortifications and troops.

In turn, the breakdown of colonial peace in 1775 led to a broadening-out of conflict between settlers and Native Americans.

The next conflict with Natives, Lord Dunmore's war with the Shawnee in 1774 over settler expansionism, saw the governor of Virginia, the 4th Earl of Dunmore, reliant on militia who were able to deploy in strength and, benefiting from the Shawnee not receiving Iroquois help, to drive them to terms. At the same time, competition between the Pennsylvania and Virginia militias proved part of the frontier equation, with each province also building forts.[6]

The colonial militia had not been adequately used in Pontiac's War, but its ability to deploy in numbers and win success had been amply demonstrated in conflict in North America, notably with the successful advance on Fort Duquesne in 1758, although tensions with the British had increased as a result of Braddock's 1755 campaign.[7] Some British officers indeed loathed the American troops during the Seven Years' War and thought them incompetent, a judgment that the war did not bear out. This view reflected not so much a hostile response to an American proto-nationalism as the negative perception that many regulars held of militia and, indeed, of civil society, whether British or colonial.[8] There was to be a comparable failure on the part of British ministers when considering American colonial civil society.

The warmaking of the 1750s was more generally a significant preparation for the War of Independence, which was very much a civil war within the British military system, as was indicated by the career of George Washington. Indeed, the composition and operation of the American army during the War of Independence was in many respects part of the tradition of British military practice.

The size of the regular force to be allocated to North America after the Seven Years' War had been a matter for debate in Britain even before that conflict had ended. Although Pitt told the House of Commons that the Peace of Paris of 1763 was only an armed truce with France and that the number was inadequate, George III (r. 1760–1820) argued that February that 10,000 troops should be stationed in North America to protect it in the event of a new war with France. George made no reference to the use of troops to overawe the older colonies, but he came to support his ministers' views that the colonists should pay for their security, thus lessening the burden on a heavily indebted Britain. Yet, George and his key adviser, John, 3rd Earl of Bute, who, as First Lord of the Treasury, headed the ministry from 1762 to 1763, failed to appreciate the likely risks of this legislation in North America, and also ignored the views of experienced British ministers: Bute's predecessor, Newcastle, claiming that the planned force was too large, and therefore overly expensive.[9] The overall establishment was set at 45,500 men.

George himself took an interest in military matters, as well as fulfilling his political responsibilities. He did not find personal resolution or glory in war, being the first king since James I (r. 1603–25) not to lead troops into battle. As a young man, George had followed his father, Frederick, Prince of Wales, in neither being trained for war, nor being given opportunities to serve, despite his firmly pressed request to do so in 1759, which was rejected by George II. Particularly active in controlling promotions, and jealous of his authority in the army, George III followed the royal norm in reviewing his troops. Indeed, in June 1771, the Danish Secretary of Legation reported that it was almost superfluous to note that George reviewed troops twice or thrice weekly, as was his normal occupation each June. George was also interested in weaponry and, in 1786, Sir William Fawcett, the adjutant general, returned two guns the king had sent him, 'the bayonet of that which is intended for the use of the Light Infantry having been made to fix, agreeably to your Majesty's directions.'[10]

Whereas American colonists initially lauded the British soldiers during the Seven Years' War, their postwar mood quickly changed, and notably so when the ministry appeared to be positioning troops to enforce new taxes.[11] Although the provision of barracks as a result of the Quartering Act of 1765 proved acceptable,[12] the imposition of a series of fiscal duties, notably the Stamp Act of 1765 and the Townshend Duties of 1767, led to mob action that wrecked the measure, and the lack of troops in the East Coast cities, as compared to on the frontier facing the Native Americans, removed the capacity for a firm response. In turn, the government sent troops in the face of disturbances in Boston in 1768, but the troops had no clear duties and their presence increased tension, leading, on 5 March 1770, to the 'Boston Massacre', in which five Bostonians were killed by troops acting in self-defence. Although seen by many Americans as proof of the militarisation of authority, in practice this action accorded with conventional conduct during crises.

War with the Colonists

In 1774, Major-General Thomas Gage, the commander in chief in North America, was also appointed Governor of Massachusetts, arriving in May, but, in September, his attempt to remove gunpowder from a provincial magazine led to a show of force by militia that to a degree intimidated Gage, who accurately pointed out that only large numbers of troops could prevail. In January 1775, Pitt, now Earl of Chatham and an opposition figure, pressed in the House of Lords for conciliation, especially for the withdrawal of the troops, but his motion was defeated. Conflict was on the way.

To turn to war in North America in 1775–83, the image is clear, and the message obvious. Across a sun-kissed meadow, dappled with shade, lines of British soldiers, resplendent in red, move slowly forward, while brave American Patriots crouch behind trees and stone walls ready to shoot them down. Frequently repeated on page and screen, the image has one central message: one side, the American, represented the future in warfare, and one side, the American, was bound to prevail. Thus, the War of American Independence is readily located in both political and military terms. In both, it apparently represents the triumph of modernity and the start of a new age: of democracy and popular warfare. Before these forces, the *ancien régime*, the old order, was seemingly bound to crumble and its troops, the British, were doomed to lose.

The apparent contrast between John Burgoyne, the British commander at the battle of Saratoga (1777), and his victorious American opponent, Horatio Gates, was therefore apt. Burgoyne (1722–92) was the son of an army officer, but his real father may have been his godfather, Robert, 1st Lord Bingley. In 1737, having attended Westminster School, jointly with Eton the most fashionable in the country (many other officers, including Thomas Gage, attended Westminster), the young Burgoyne purchased a commission in the fashionable Horse Guards. In 1751, he eloped with Lady Charlotte Stanley, the daughter of Edward, 11th Earl of Derby, who eventually became another patron. In contrast, Horatio Gates (1727–1806) was born in England, his parents a customs official and the housekeeper to Peregrine, 2nd Duke of Leeds. His mother moved on to work for Charles, 3rd Duke of Bolton, who helped the young Horatio gain a commission in the army, in which he served from

1745 to 1754, before purchasing a captaincy in one of the New York Independent Companies in which he served until 1769.[13] Before too much is made of inherited incompetence versus egalitarian merit, Gates' role in Patriot success in the Saratoga campaign was a matter for debate, while he was to be heavily defeated by Charles, 2nd Earl Cornwallis, an old Etonian, at Camden in 1780.

Indeed, a reminder of the complexity of background and of the strands in British military history was provided by Major-General Charles Lee (1732–82), the second-ranking officer of the Continental Army. Son of a colonel and grandson of a baronet, Lee joined the regiment in which his father was colonel and served as an officer in North America in 1754–60 before serving successfully in Portugal as a major under Burgoyne in 1762. With his regiment disbanded at the end of the Seven Years' War, he was placed on the half-pay list, and served in the Polish army, finding his drift into opposition politics blocking his chances of getting a post. Like several other former officers, Lee travelled to North America, in his case in 1773, and eventually joined the Revolution. A difficult man but thoughtful commander, not least in his support for irregular warfare, Lee is a reminder of the diversity of views in the British Army and military tradition.[14] As an additional study in contrasts, Anthony Wayne was the grandson of a Captain Anthony Wayne who had served at the Boyne in 1690 and moved to Pennsylvania in 1722, their son Isaac serving in the Pennsylvania militia in 1755–8, and the younger Anthony (1745–96) raising a Pennsylvania militia unit in 1775 and becoming a general in the War of American Independence.

The generally asserted political location of the struggle is that of the defining fight for freedom that supposedly ushered in the modern world. This approach helps place the conflict as the start of modern warfare. Moreover, considering the war in the latter light supposedly fixes our understanding of the political dimension. Defining the conflict in terms of modernity also explains Patriot success and British failure, as most people adopt a teleological perspective (arguing that the course of developments was inevitable) and assume that the future is bound to prevail over the past. These views are overly simplistic, although there were serious difficulties for the British, as captured by Captain William Evelyn, part of the relief force sent to help the column retreat from Concord and Lexington in April 1775:

> They [the British column] were attacked from the woods and houses on each side of the road and an increasing fire kept up on both sides for several hours, they [the Americans] still retiring through the wood whenever our men advanced upon them ... we were attacked on all sides from woods, orchards, stone walls, and from every house on the road side...

He later added 'some other mode must be adopted than gaining every little hill at the expense of a thousand Englishmen', a reference to the battle of Bunker Hill outside Boston on 17 June 1775, where 228 had been killed and 826 wounded – 42 per cent of the force engaged – compared to 100 and 271 Patriots.[15] Indeed, as a result of Bunker Hill, where the Patriot position had only fallen in the third assault, British tactical and operational capabilities were now in question, Gage writing to the Secretary at War:

> These people show a spirit and conduct against us they never showed against the French, and everybody has judged of them from their former appearance and behaviour when joined with the King's forces in the last war [Seven Years' War] ... They are now spirited up by a rage and enthusiasm as great as ever people were possessed of and you must proceed in earnest or give the business up. A small body acting in one spot will not avail, you must have large armies making diversions on different sides, to divide their force. The loss we have sustained is greater than we can bear. Small armies cannot afford such losses, especially when the advantage gained tends to little more than the gaining of a post.[16]

Imagining the war as an apparently foregone conclusion has several misleading consequences. First, it allows historians of the period to devote insufficient attention to the fighting and, instead, to focus on other aspects of the Revolution, underplaying, even neglecting, the central point: no victory, no independence, no constitution, no new society. Secondly, thinking British defeat inevitable gravely underrates the Patriot achievement in thwarting Britain. Thirdly, any appearance of inevitability removes the sense of total uncertainty in which contemporaries made choices and risked their life and those of others.

The war, instead, benefits from being centrally located in military history and has to be understood as a formidable challenge for the Patriots. Britain in 1775 was the strongest empire in the world. Other states, especially, but not only, China, Russia, Austria and France, had larger armies, but no other state had Britain's capacity for force projection. Britain not only had the largest navy in the world, but also a navy that had soundly beaten the second largest navy, that of France, as recently as 1759. In a confrontation in 1770 with Spain and her ally, France, over the Falkland Islands, it was the Bourbon powers that had backed down. Supporting its navy's capacity to operate at a distance and thus to project and support the army, Britain had a network of overseas bases, especially around the North Atlantic. Halifax was a particularly important one, guarding the Gulf of the St. Lawrence and enabling Britain to project its naval power down the Atlantic seaboard of North America.[17] There were also bases in the West Indies.

The war effort rested on the best system of public finances in the world, and necessarily so given the cost of the massive logistical burden. The National Debt, guaranteed by Parliament, enjoyed international confidence to an extent unmatched among Britain's rivals, and the British could therefore borrow easily, borrow large amounts and go on borrowing. Indeed, in a marked contrast to the situation facing the Patriots, the War of Independence was to be waged without a serious financial crisis. In part, this reflected the buoyancy of government customs revenues, based as they were on Britain's central role in Europe's global trading system.

Rich, Britain was also politically stable until 1782, and certainly so in comparison with 1754–7 or 1761–70. The ministry of Frederick, Lord North, the First Lord of the Treasury from 1770 to 1782 and a politician without military experience, had just won the general election of 1774. Under the Septennial Act, it did not have to fight another election until 1781, but, perfectly legally, it was to hold and win the next election in 1780, just as wartime elections had been won in 1747 and 1761. The parliamentary opposition criticized the war in America, but the government was in control of Parliament, and this position was not lost until a collapse in parliamentary confidence after defeat at Yorktown led to North's resignation in March 1782. The war divided the political élite, and some officers, including very senior ones, refused to serve in North America, but there was no serious breakdown in discipline within the army.

The British Army had plenty of experience in fighting in North America, notably, but not only, as a result of conquering Canada from France in 1758–60. Moreover, the British commanders were selected on the basis of merit and adapted rapidly to the conditions they were to face.[18] Some suggestions showed excessive adaptability, as in 1779 when a proposal to raise a regiment composed of smugglers was rejected as being too dangerous.[19]

Compared to Havana and Manila, which the British had captured from Spain in 1762, the eastern seaboard of North America was a relatively benign area for operations. In particular, the killer diseases of the Tropics were absent. It was also an area especially vulnerable to amphibious operations, in which the British were potent and skilled. In 1775, about 75 per cent of the population of the Thirteen Colonies lived within 75 miles of the coast, and this included most of the white colonists who counted politically. Their vulnerability to sea-power was accentuated by the weak and limited state of roads and bridges, which led to an emphasis on coastal traffic, and because inland towns, such as Philadelphia and Albany, were also ports reachable up rivers. All the major towns could be reached by water, while the eastern seaboard of North America is sectioned by waterways that aid maritime penetration: round Charleston, further north the Chesapeake, the Delaware and Long Island Sound, and, countering any American invasion of Canada, the St. Lawrence. The last, for example, enabled a British squadron to relieve Québec from Patriot siege in May 1776 as soon as the ice melted, as had also happened with the French siege in 1760. The potential impact of amphibious attack was noted by Captain William Leslie of the 17th Foot when describing the landing at Kips Bay, near the site of the modern United Nations, on 14 September 1776:

> We landed under cover of the shipping, without opposition, although the Rebels [mostly Connecticut militia] might have made a very great defence as they had high grounds, woods, and strong breastworks to cover them, but they scoured off in thousands when the ships began to fire.[20]

Leslie, a son of the Earl of Leven and nephew of Brigadier-General Alexander Leslie, was, however, mortally wounded at the battle of Princeton in the following January, an instance of the difficulties of moving to inland operations.

Once ashore, the British on the whole, despite their experience on the retreat from Concord and Lexington, did not have to face a new type of foe. Pressed by Washington to adopt the form of a conventional European army, the Patriots trained and deployed the Continental Army, which relied on the volley fire and linear formations with which the British were familiar. Captain William Congreve recorded of the battle of Long Island on 27 August 1776, a battle the British won:

> I found the enemy numerous and supported by 6-pounders [cannon]. However, by plying them smartly with grapeshot their guns were soon drawn off but the riflemen being covered by trees and large stones had very much the advantage of us, who were upon the open ground ... [had] not the light infantry of the Guards ... come up in time I believe we should all have been cut off.[21]

The major difference to conflict in Europe was that the general absence of cavalry from the battlefield[22] ensured that troops fought in a more open order. However, heavily encumbered British regular units found that thickly wooded and hilly terrain posed problems, as did entrenched positions. The troops also faced a difficult environment. Brigadier-General Henry Percy, wrote from Boston in 1774: 'We have days here full as hot as Spain, I am at this instant writing to you sweating without clothes. But our climate is horribly inconstant, for we have it sometimes very cold.'[23] Temperatures of 90–100°F during the day, with sudden drops to around 60°F, are not unusual in a New England summer. The troops who attacked the Patriot defences in the battle of Bunker Hill advanced uphill carrying 70lb packs in a scorching 90°F heat, while, advancing from the St. Lawrence toward Lake Champlain in June 1776, Lieutenant William Digby of the 53rd Regiment complained of 'the great heat', adding in July:

> The weather was intensely hot, scarce bearable in a camp, where the tents rather increased than diminished it, and the great number of men in so small a space, made it very disagreeable, though we all went as thinly clothed as possible, wearing large loose trousers, to prevent the bite of the mosquito.[24]

General Alexander wrote to his brother from Staten Island in July 1777 after his return from

> Our marching and counter-marching in the Jerseys ... the weather was much against us, for we had it very hot and a good deal of rain, and no tents... We embark tomorrow... I hope it is north, for the climate will be our enemy if we go southward.[25]

Heatstroke was a problem for soldiers at the battle of Monmouth Courthouse, New Jersey, on 28 June 1778.

These were difficult circumstances, but there were no new weapons that might make British war-making redundant. One was tried and, had it worked, it would have changed the war, neutralizing British naval power; but, as yet, the submarine could not fulfil its potential: the dependence on human energy for movement, and on staying partially above the surface for oxygen, made it only an intimation of the submarine of the future. On land, the Patriot rifle was very useful in sniping, as at Saratoga. Percy, the commander of the relief column, reported to Gage the day after the advance to Lexington and Concord on 19 April 1775. Having met the retreating troops at Lexington, Percy ordered his two cannon to fire on the pursuers, and then sought to cover the retreat:

> Sending out very strong flanking parties which were absolutely necessary, as there was not a stone wall or house, though before in appearance evacuated, from whence the rebels did not fire upon us. As soon as they saw us begin to retire, they pressed very much upon our rear guard.... we retired for 15 miles under an incessant fire all round us ... losing a good many men in the retreat.... behaved with their usual intrepidity and spirit.[26]

Wounded on the retreat, Jeremy Lister wrote of 'a general firing upon us from all quarters, from behind hedges and walls.'[27] The damaging impact of Patriot riflemen later was recorded by Captain William Leslie who was on the left of the British line at the battle of Long Island in 1776, and thus part of the force designed to engage the Patriot front while its left flank was turned. He had already, in his letter to his father, noted a truth borne out by contradictory accounts of most battles:

> A private officer has so little opportunity of knowing the particulars of any action that does not happen under his own eye that I shall mention nothing but what I

saw… At 5 o'clock we began our march again, and about 7 perceived the Rebels within musket shot drawn up to a great extent at the top of a rising ground with every advantage they could wish; their right extended to a marsh over which they could retreat under some cannon, their left was covered with a very thick wood in which were innumerable riflemen; it is supposed there were two lines in the rear to support their main body; in their front were two field pieces, and all the bushes, hedges, trees and hollows were lined with riflers. Our disposition was very soon made … some grape shot dislodged them from the bushes near our front and from which they fired at our regiment at a few yards distance … the advanced guard, who were much incommoded by riflers from behind the hedges; during all this time showers of grape were tumbling among us which wounded some of our men … A few minutes after I joined the advance guard I was told Sir Alexander Murray was killed and Lieutenant Morgan wounded, my two most intimate friends! I was never so shocked in my life … a little after poor Murray's fate the fire ceased by degrees and the Rebels began to retreat in pretty good order across the marsh on their right, at last a company of grenadiers appearing in their rear a panic seized them and they took to a precipitate retreat without the least order.[28]

However, the rifle's slow rate of fire and inability to carry a bayonet gravely reduced its value as a battlefield weapon, unless firing from cover. Rather than assuming that rifles were necessarily better than muskets, it is worth noting the comments in 1849 of Sir Charles Napier, the commander in chief in India: 'As an old rifleman myself I cannot be supposed to have any prejudice against the rifle, but as a weapon of war … it is inferior to the musket.' His reasons included the rifle taking longer to load and being heavier, the musket/bayonet combination being more effective than the rifle at close quarters, and the rifle fouling more than muskets after firing.[29]

Patriot firepower could be lessened, even countered, by a number of techniques. These included outflanking, closing, and the use of artillery, and the deployment of riflemen in the British forces, notably Hessian *Jägers*. Moreover, the British and the Loyalists proved effective in some of the skirmishing warfare, for example near New York, in 1778.[30]

On the British side in the War of Independence, there was consideration of innovation in weaponry, but no significant change. Ferguson's breech-loading rifle was accurate but seen as likely to use ammunition too rapidly. In 1779, Major-General Charles Rainsford submitted a plan for a mixed cavalry-light infantry force with arms 'rifled, or otherwise well made, with sights like the German rifled barrel, and bayonets like the infantry',[31] but that proved only an idea, and the standard British deployment remained close-order, the regulations for the First Battalion of the Norfolk Regiment in 1780 stating: 'In firing great care to be taken that the battalion is in close order, that the men level well, and ram down their cartridges, as a slow well-directed fire is far preferable to an hasty irregular straggling one.'[32] In contrast, Lieutenant-General Thomas Desaguliers, Colonel Commandant of the Royal Artillery from 1762 until 1780 and Chief Firemaster (Superintendent) of the Woolwich arsenal from 1748 until 1780, made advances in the science of gunnery, the manufacture of cannon, the capabilities of mortars, and horse artillery. In 1773, a new horizontal boring machine was introduced at Woolwich, improving the manufacture of cannon there.

Moreover, it would be misleading to see the British as tactically hidebound. Based on the Seven Years' War, they had implemented from 1770 a light infantry system whereby one of the companies of each regiment was designated as a light company. These were the most agile men who were the best shots. They could fight as either skirmishers in an extended line, as a regular two or three line unit, or as flankers; but this form of war was in its infancy, and, given the weaponry of the day, concentrated volley fire from a linear formation remained the best way to inflict significant damage on an opposing force in battle.

The major role of the Patriot militia created a problem for the British, not due to rifles but both in operational terms, for example by restricting the range of the British supply-gatherers, and in the political context of the conflict, especially in harrying Loyalists. At the outset of the Revolution, militia units overcame royal governors, and defeated supporting Loyalists. In December 1775, Dunmore, the last royal Governor of Virginia, was defeated by Virginia militia at Great Bridge, with his North Carolina counterpart Josiah Martin following two months later at the battle of Moore's Creek Bridge. The British failure to crush the rebellion in 1775 gave the Americans time to organize themselves politically and militarily, to extend the rebellion greatly, and to weaken the Loyalists. These successes helped give the Patriots strategic depth, lessening the importance of British operations first in New England and subsequently in the Middle Colonies: British victory in either would not ensure automatic compliance further south. Furthermore, the militia could provide at least temporary reinforcements for the Continental Army. It helped also to ensure that the British were outnumbered and thus limited their effectiveness as an occupation force.

Lastly, the political context was crucial. Had all the colonies in the Western Hemisphere rebelled, then the British would not have stood a chance, but the economically most crucial ones (the West Indian sugar islands, such as Jamaica and Barbados), and the strategically vital ones, those with the naval bases (Nova Scotia, Jamaica, Antigua), did not rebel. As a result, the British had safe bases – to both north and south of the entire Thirteen Colonies, from which to mount operations. When, in March 1776, General Sir William Howe withdrew from Boston, leaving the Patriots, whose artillery now dominated the harbour, victoriously in control of the Thirteen Colonies, he did not have to retreat to Britain. Instead, he sailed to Halifax and rebuilt his force, so that, that summer, the Empire could strike back, Howe landing on Staten Island at the start of the New York campaign, beginning the war the Patriots had not wanted.

The eventually successful British defence of Canada against American attack in 1775–6 ensured that, as with East Florida (modern Florida minus the Panhandle), there were also land frontiers across which the Patriots could be attacked. Digby left an account of the last clash in Canada, an American attack on the British camp at Trois Rivières on 8 June 1776:

> About 4 in the morning an alarm was given by an outpiquet of the approach of a strong body of the enemy ... soon after the alarm was given a few shots were heard from one of our armed vessels that was stationed a small way above the village who fired on part of the enemy advancing between the skirts of the wood and the river. In the meantime the troops on shore were ordered to line every avenue from the village to the wood, and take post in the best manner possible ... About 5 o'clock strong advanced parties were sent towards the wood, where they discovered the enemy marching down in three columns, who immediately began a heavy fire with small arms, which was instantly returned. In the meantime, a strong reinforcement of our troops with some field pieces arrived, which soon

swept the woods, and broke their columns, the remains of which were pursued by us, as far as was prudent. The enemy from that time did nothing regular, but broken and dispersed, fired a few scattered shots, which did little execution.[33]

Although definitely not helped by flawed instructions and inadequate prior planning in Canada, General John Burgoyne mishandled the subsequent invasion south from Canada in 1777. He had an insufficiently flexible approach to forest operations, with the heavy baggage train a particular mistake. The army had too few light infantry. It was as if the lessons of the Seven Years' War had not been learned by the British, although the Patriots, who also hit hard with their riflemen,[34] had resources in defence of such terrain greater than those of the French. Burgoyne eventually surrendered 5,895 men at Saratoga on 17 October 1777, but Canada was now safe, Patriot schemes to invade it were not pursued, and British forces there posed a strategic challenge that would have been more apparent had Sir Guy Carleton in 1776 or Burgoyne in 1777 been more successful. After Saratoga, the northern frontier remained disturbed, not least with conflict between Loyalists and Patriots,[35] but there was no British Army-size advance southward anew until that of 1814 which only got to Lake Champlain.

More serious from the Patriot perspective were the Loyalists, for this was a civil conflict, the first major Patriot civil war. Loyalists fought and died for their vision of America, just as indeed Patriots did, and in some areas, especially Georgia, the Floridas, coastal South Carolina, North Carolina, the eastern shore of the Chesapeake, and parts of New Jersey and New York, Loyalists were particularly numerous, while the boundaries between Patriots and noncommitted, and between noncommitted and Loyalists were porous, and not fixed. Politically, the British had to move as many Americans as possible across these boundaries; and Patriot strategy interacted with their opportunity to do so. The Patriot emphasis on position warfare in order to protect their major cities (New York in 1776, Philadelphia in 1777, Charleston in 1780), or to capture those in British hands (Boston in 1775, Philadelphia in 1777, Newport in 1778, Savannah in 1779), gave the British opportunities to defeat their opponents and, by thereby creating an impression of failure, to affect opinion within America. In doing so, they were greatly helped by the many problems facing the Patriots. All military matters entail responding to difficulties, often in a crisis situation, but to create and sustain an effective army was no easy task, and the Patriots encountered many setbacks in doing both. Money and supplies were serious issues, and much of Washington's correspondence is an account of organisation and improvisation under great and persistent pressure. The anti-authoritarian character of the American Revolution, and the absence of national institutions, made it difficult to create a viable national military system for land – and, even more so, sea – power. Initial enlistments for one year did not amount to a standing army.

The Patriots also faced a central strategic dilemma, as they could not defeat the British, other than in the limited (but important) sense of denying them victory and hoping that this would lead them to abandon the struggle. As John Paul Jones showed, the Patriots had privateers able to operate in British waters, but they lacked a fleet, let alone the amphibious capacity and strike force to take the war to the British Isles. Indeed they still did not possess this during the subsequent War of 1812, and did not gain such a potential until the 20th century.

France and Spain, which entered the war as the Patriots' allies in 1778 and 1779 respectively, possessed such a capability. Furthermore, unlike in the other wars in 1688–1815, in which they were at war with Britain, they were not fighting any other power. However, their joint invasion attempt on southern England in 1779 was, partly due to disease amongst the invasion fleet but also thanks to the problems of coordination, as unsuccessful as the others separately mounted by them during the century; this meant that Britain could stay in the struggle, and, thereby, choose when to attack. Moreover, although there was sympathy for the Patriot cause in Britain, there was no movement of civil disobedience, and this sympathy anyway ebbed when France, the traditional enemy, entered the war as an ally of the Patriots. The major outbreak of violence in Britain, the Gordon Riots in London in 1780, obliged the government, directed by the angry George III, to use troops to restore order, and with success; these riots were however directed against legislation favourable to Catholics, and not against the war.

The ability of Britain to stay in the struggle, was a real problem for the Americans, as only a brief conflict had been envisaged in 1775.

Instead of their willingness to fight overawing George and forcing him to negotiate, as they had hoped, thereby avoiding the high-risk outcome of independence, the British in 1776 sent a major army to defeat the Revolution. Thus, the British Army rested on a depth of resilience that provided a crucial persistence. The struggle, in which at that stage Britain faced no other enemies, then became more sustained and bitter than had at first seemed likely, and, as later with the American Civil War (1861–5), the political differences between the two sides were accentuated as the war continued.

Even worse, in 1778, the British government, re-evaluating their strategy but not their goals,[36] displayed a determination to continue the struggle on land in America despite French intervention. This was against the advice of the British parliamentary opposition and despite the fact that the British now faced serious threats in home waters, the Mediterranean, the West Indies, West Africa and India, challenges that greatly expanded when the war widened to include Spain in 1779 and the Dutch in 1780. These multiple threats had serious consequences for troop numbers, both overall and in particular areas. In 1778, Sir Henry Clinton, the British commander, with reference to the units sent to the West Indies, complained:

> All the world are witness how mortifying this command has been to me. I was promised an army complete, and a reinforcement of 12,000 British and 2,000 Germans; instead of which 9,000 are taken from me.

The following February, Clinton commented on the possibility that the fall of Georgia to the British might affect South Carolina: 'there was a time when this operation must have been attended with every success, but that time is no more. Instead of near 36,000 men ... I am reduced to little more than 18,000.'[37] That September, the rank-and-file present and fit for duty were 16,184 men based in New York, 3,781 in Rhode Island, 3,587 in the South, 1,750 in Halifax and 1,241 in West Florida. Overall numbers might sound considerable, but many troops were committed to garrison duties and others were operating in hostile terrain.

Did any of this matter? After all, the British, at one stage or another, held all the major towns in North America, and they won a series of major battles, including Long Island (1776), Brandywine (1777), and Camden (1780), the last of which became a total rout as the British forces fired as they advanced. Yet, the Patriots were willing to continue fighting. There was a basic strategic problem for both sides: neither could knock out their opponent, however many battles they won. As a result, the war would have to end, as indeed it did, with a compromise peace. Even after Yorktown (1781), there was little assumption that the British defeat there necessarily meant the end of the war:[38] the British still held on to New York City and Charleston. Indeed, the eventual peace settlement partitioned British North America, leading to the creation of what eventually became Canada as well as what became the United States. Similarly, the War of 1812 resulted in a compromise by which Canada remained part of the British empire.

Whether this outcome in 1783 could have been changed by more British victories depended on how far Patriot resilience would have survived serious defeat. The willingness of Charleston, which had seen off weaker British attacks in 1776 and 1779,[39] to accept the consequences of British victory in South Carolina in 1780 was instructive, and poses a question mark against the bombastic claims of liberty or death made by some Patriots. On 5 June, over 200 of the more prominent citizens of Charleston, which had surrendered on 12 May, congratulated the British commanders on the restoration of the political connection with the Crown. A loyal address came from Georgetown the following month, while several of the leading politicians of the state returned to Charleston to accept British rule.

This appeared to be a vindication of the British policy of combining military force with a conciliatory stance, offering a new imperial relationship that granted most of the American demands made at the outbreak of the war. Cornwallis was optimistic about the situation in South Carolina. It is scarcely surprising that some northern politicians came to doubt the determination of their southern counterparts, and it is important to underline the extent to which British military operations were intended to improve the chances of successful negotiations.

More generally, the voluntaristic character of American military service was also a serious problem for the Patriots, and, in 1776, the British had nearly succeeded in turning it against them. As the British, having landed on Staten Island on 3 July, scored one victory after another in the New York campaign between August and December 1776, Washington's army, which had initially fought on resolutely, all but disintegrated. Men laid down their arms and returned home. At the same time, covered by the British advance, Loyalists came forward in numbers in New Jersey. The failure of the meeting on 11 September 1776 between the representatives of both sides, with independence a fundamental stumbling block, encouraged the dramatic step of advancing on Philadelphia, the capital of the Revolution. As a result, Washington's counter-attack in the Trenton campaign, launched at the close of the year, was, to a great extent, a make-or-break operation, and indeed a risky counterpart to the Jacobite attack at Culloden. Richard Henry Lee wrote to Washington on 27 February 1777:

> I really think that when the history of this winter's campaign comes to be understood, the world will wonder at its success on our part. With a force rather inferior to the enemy in point of numbers, and chiefly militia too, opposed to the best disciplined troops of Europe; to keep these latter pent up, harassed, and distressed. But more surprising still, to lessen their numbers some thousands by the sword and captivity![40]

Victory at Trenton also revitalized resistance and permitted Congress to raise a new army, including many men who agreed to serve for three years, a luxury Washington had never enjoyed before. Yet it had been a gamble, a dangerous operation that was dependent on surprise and, anyway, partly miscarried. It is worth asking what would have happened if Washington had failed to surprise the Hessians at Trenton, so that they had driven him back to Pennsylvania and the British had continued to garrison New Jersey; or if he had been no more successful at Trenton than he was to be at Germantown the following year, when, although he pushed them hard, he failed to defeat the British in a counter-attack near Philadelphia. Not only is it unclear that Congress would have been able to raise a new army for 1777, but also uncertain that the Patriots, who were anyway to be defeated at Brandywine (11 September 1777) in the prelude to their loss of Philadelphia, could have put up a better effort earlier in the year had it been in the aftermath of defeat in battle.

Stemming the tide of success at Trenton, instead, led the British to abandon much of New Jersey in early 1777, which had disastrous political and military consequences. The local Loyalists were hit hard, compromising future chances of winning Loyalist support in the Middle Colonies. Nevertheless, the British government continued to be helpful, Germain writing to Sir William Howe in May 1777 expressing the hope that that year's campaign would end the war:

> I am extremely concerned to find that you do not imagine your force to be as suitable to the operations of the ensuing campaign as you confess it was to those of the last: My concern is however in a great degree diminished by the intelligence which we daily receive of the rebels finding the utmost difficulty in raising an army.

Germain continued by envisaging a multilayered military. He anticipated that Howe's success 'will enable you to raise from among them such a force as may be sufficient for the interior defense of the province, and leave the army at liberty to proceed to offensive operations.'[41] Howe (1729–1814), the son of a Viscount, had joined the army in 1746, buying a commission, served in Belgium during the War of the Austrian Succession, commanded a regiment at the siege of Louisbourg (1758), played a key role in Québec (1759), served at Belle-Île (1761) and Havana (1762), and was promoted to major-general in 1772. His elder brother George, 3rd Viscount Howe, who had helped make the uniform and tactics of the army more suited to forest operations in North America, had been killed in the Ticonderoga expedition of 1758 the day before the battle of Carillon.

In the event, the British advance in 1777 on Philadelphia, the key goal that year, was mounted, not rapidly by land from Trenton, but, instead, slowly, by sea, via the Chesapeake. Howe and his surviving brother, the naval commander Admiral Lord Howe, were both of the opinion that a demonstration of British power and the capability to destroy the rebellion by defeating the Continental Army and capturing New York and Philadelphia would cause the populace to come to their senses and negotiate a settlement. This analysis, however, proved flawed.

Philadelphia, moreover, did not fall to Howe, a general whom it is not easy to evaluate conclusively, until 26 September.[42] By then Burgoyne's force had marched south from Canada and was very exposed in the Hudson Valley near Saratoga. It was to surrender on 17 October. A speedier victory near Philadelphia in 1777 might have put Howe in a better position to mount operations that would have made it harder for the Americans to concentrate against Burgoyne. This could also have given substance to the plan of cutting the Thirteen Colonies in half along the Hudson Valley, a move that would have dramatically reduced the articulation and thus use of American power and made it more a series of local forces, which the British could try to fight and/or negotiate with separately. However, Alexander Hamilton, one of Washington's aides, sensibly commented on British prospects on 5 April:

> As to the notion of forming a junction with the northern army, and cutting off the communication between the Northern and Southern states, I apprehend it will do better in speculation than in practice … would require a chain of posts and such a number of men at each as would never be practicable or maintainable but to an immense army.[43]

At the same time, the mishandling of British military activity was a matter in part of the difficulty of cooperation between two armies operating independently. Even had they cooperated, advances south from Ticonderoga and north through the Highlands would have been difficult. Yet, had Burgoyne been certain of a major advance coming from New York, he might have held on for a few days more at Saratoga before surrendering. In addition to the question of coordination, the very situation challenged Eurocentric military thinking: in North America, the terrain and supply situation were different to Western Europe, while the conflict was a war without fronts.

Late 1776 was not the only low ebb for the Americans. By 1780, they faced growing exhaustion and war-weariness. Already in 1779, Major Robert Rogers had written from New York to Amherst, who was in practice the British commander in chief: 'The face of affairs becomes every day more agreeable to our wishes. The dissensions among the rebels and the great depreciation of their paper, promises the happiest effects. If Great Britain will persevere, America must soon be conquered.'[44] Born in Massachusetts to Ulster-Scots setters, Rogers (1731–95) served in the New Hampshire militia in the 1740s and, in 1756, raised a unit of rangers who fought French-Native American forces. He raised ranger units anew in the War of American Independence.

The absence of major engagements in the Middle Colonies in 1779 and 1780 did not indicate a disinclination to fight. However, the manpower situation in both armies was a testimony to the strains from which they were suffering. The British had lost one army at Saratoga, and now had other pressing commitments, while the Patriots were finding it increasingly difficult to sustain a major army.

As a result, both sides sought new support: the British looked to the Loyalists, especially in the South, as a major military and political resource, as they had not done in the first stage of the war; while the Patriots sought to persuade the French to intervene in America, rather than fighting the British in the West Indies. The war, therefore, became a curious interplay of cautious moves and bold aspirations, as increasingly exhausted participants moved around the vast area in contention and played for stakes that had been raised as a consequence of the new factor of the intervention of French naval power, in an atmosphere that the changing arithmetic of naval strength helped to make volatile for both sides.

Hyper-inflation had wrecked the American economy, and the war indeed reduced median household wealth by more than 45 per cent. Furthermore, the resources that existed were mismanaged. The limited creditworthiness of Congress, and the reluctance of the states to subordinate their priorities and resources to Congress, meant that the army had to live from hand to mouth. Much of the supplying of the Continental Army relied on the issue of largely worthless certificates. In January 1781, short of pay, food and clothes, and seeking discharge, both the Pennsylvania line and three New Jersey regiments were to mutiny. The Pennsylvania mutiny was to be ended only by concession, including the discharge of five-sixths of the men. This episode is a reminder of the militarily precarious nature of the Revolution, and the extent to which the situation did not improve as the Revolution continued. This provides an instructive perspective on the war: both sides faced serious difficulties and had major drawbacks. Militarily, this meant both that there was everything to play for, and that managing limitations was as important as grasping opportunities. Politically, in a related process, these drawbacks also ensured not only that there was everything to play for, but also that whichever side was better able to respond to its weaknesses and persist was likely to win the struggle of will.

In 1780, this was still unclear, as it was a year of disappointment for Britain's opponents. Despite the anxieties expressed in 1778, French entry had not obliged the British to abandon New York, nor had it led to another Patriot attack on Canada, nor to the permanent postponement of British operations in the South. The French expeditionary force that arrived in Newport achieved nothing in 1780, while Washington was unable to shake British control of New York, and his troops were increasingly demoralized. The British were still powerful at sea, and, if their impact in the interior was limited, they revealed at Charleston and around the Chesapeake in 1780 an ability to use their amphibious forces to considerable effect, taking the initiative, harrying their opponents and disrupting the American economy. That year, the British strategy in the South was largely successful – at least until Patrick Ferguson's total defeat at King's Mountain on 7 October.

The close of 1780 saw the central themes of the 1781 campaign in America already clear: the need for Franco-Patriot cooperation if a major blow was to be struck against the British; Cornwallis's problems in the South;[45] the rising importance of the Chesapeake; and the crucial role of naval power. The contrasting results of the campaigns of 1780 and 1781 indicate, however, that these circumstances and problems made nothing inevitable.

Although King's Mountain, and the defeat of the impulsive Banastre Tarleton at Cowpens on 17 January 1781 did not involve the main field armies in the South, they ended the impression of Britain successfully gaining the initiative, tarnished the Southern strategy, and indicated that it had not had any significant consequences for the British in the Middle Colonies. Moreover, the Patriot use of partisan bands in the South led to a civil war in which neither side was in control, but British commanders were left frustrated and unable to gain significant advantage from success in battle.[46] It had been hoped that Loyalist militias would tamp down any violence and root out Patriots, thus restoring local security and royal government, but the militia in western North Carolina was defeated at Ramsour's Mill on 20 June 1780 by Patriot militia, while many of the Loyalists felt too intimidated to supply food to the army, and many neutrals moved toward the Patriots, at least in terms of not actively supporting the British and Loyalists.

Until early 1781, the odds of winning the war on the ground, at least in so far as battle was concerned, were still not too bad for Britain. After then, it was unclear that the British could have won in North America, and the Patriots' strategy of avoiding battle appeared increasingly valid.[47] Cornwallis found out the detrimental impact of the loss of public support in his campaign in North Carolina, a formerly heavily Loyalist colony, in 1781. Moreover, his march into Virginia meant that the British position in the South was not consolidated with all the discouragement that might have brought to the Patriots.

More British warships available might have led to a successful British withdrawal from Yorktown in September or October 1781, repeating that from New Jersey after Monmouth Court House in 1778, but this would not have resulted in victory. Instead, having fought their way to impasse in the Middle Colonies and the South, the British would have had to evacuate Virginia. Flawed naval command decisions made that impossible and led to the temporary and localized superiority the French enjoyed, with crucial results, in the Chesapeake that autumn. Although this superiority was neither the consequence, nor the cause, of a climactic battle in which one fleet destroyed the other, and there was no decisive shift in naval advantage against Britain, Cornwallis, besieged from 28 September by larger American and French forces totalling about 16,000 men, was obliged to surrender under heavy artillery fire in his very exposed position at Yorktown on 19 October. He had just over 6,000 rank and file, but only 3,273 remained fit for duty when he decided to surrender. Two days earlier, Johann Conrad Döhla, a member of the Ansbach-Bayreuth forces in Cornwallis's army, had recorded:

> At daybreak, the enemy bombardment resumed, more terribly strong than ever before. They fired from all positions without let-up. Our command, which was in the Hornwork, could hardly tolerate the enemy bombs, howitzers and cannonballs any longer. There was nothing to be seen but bombs and cannonballs raining down on our entire line.

Yorktown did not end the war, but it did bring its strategic conundrum to the fore. Lieutenant-General James Robertson, the Governor of New York and a veteran of Louisbourg (1758), Martinique (1762) and Long Island (1776), wrote that there were nearly 13,000 men in the garrison, compared to the just over 7,000 troops surrendered at Yorktown (about 840 sailors also surrendered). He added:

> ... we can arm four thousand very well disposed militia, this force I should think able to beat any Washington can collect, as he has now only 4,000 French. But an army confined to a defensive in posts is not only useless but ruinous, an army without the hope of getting back America should not stay in it – a reinforcement of at least of 4,000 well conducted might revive the hopes of our friends and turn the tide of opinion, and people's actions are governed by their belief about what government is to take place – the assistance or resistance we are to meet with depends on this opinion, and that on the measures His Majesty may be pleased to direct. If the war is to be carried on, even an assurance of this will prevent the growth of the rebel army, which the most sanguine hopes cannot collect – nor bring against the place till the middle of May – an army cannot lie on the ground – or horses find pasture sooner – our succours in place of arriving in August should be by the first of May.[48]

That, however, was not viable politically, either in Britain or in the United States.

World War

Nevertheless, more generally, for the British, the war was a defensive achievement. This was paradoxically so, as this was a global struggle in which they were alone. Aside from France, Spain and the Dutch, Britain was also at war with India's two leading military powers: the Marathas from 1778 to 1782, and Mysore from 1780 to 1784. There were serious defeats and blows during the conflict, not only the loss of the Thirteen Colonies, but those of West Florida (from the Florida Panhandle to the Mississippi) to well-led Spanish forces (1779–81), the Mediterranean island of Minorca to French and Spanish forces (1782), and the Caribbean islands of Dominica (1778), Grenada (1779), St. Vincent (1779), Tobago (1781) and Nevis, St. Kitts and Montserrat (1782) to the French; as well as serious defeats in India at the hands of the Marathas at Wadgaon (1779), and by Mysore at Perumbakam in 1780 and near the Coleroon river (1782).

Yet, the bulk of the empire was held. The Patriot attempt to gain Canada, defeated in 1776, was not repeated, despite discussion in 1778 of a joint Patriot-French attempt; the French and Spanish invasion attempt on Britain in 1779 was totally unsuccessful, Gibraltar withstood a long siege from 1779 to 1783, and the British were able to hold their key positions in India against both the Marathas and Mysore – and, despite French intervention, to end up with peace treaties that left these Indian powers with no gains at Britain's expense. Crucially, the French fleet was defeated by Admiral Rodney off the Îles des Saintes south of Guadeloupe on 12 April 1782. Thereafter, the Bourbon fleets remained on the defensive in the Caribbean. Britain had failed in the Thirteen Colonies, but the crisis of empire had been overcome. This was no mean achievement.

In what was, from 1778 to 1783, a war across a significant part of the world, the range of conflicts throws light on British military capabilities, notably the problems posed by the absence of a large-enough army. During the conflict, there was a major expansion in the size of British land forces and in the East India Company's forces in India, while German units were hired for service across the empire, from North America (where the Hessians were defeated at Trenton) to India. However, troops were spread thin, which ensured that casualty levels were a particular problem. Moreover, the limited forces at their disposal repeatedly affected the strategic options, operational plans, and tactical moves, of British generals. In 1780, the force of 6,000 men on St. Lucia under Major-General Vaughan alone requested from the Ordnance Office stores that included 1,800 spades, 600,000 musket cartridges, 200,000 flints, 50 tons of musket balls, 2,400 cannon shot, and 2,000 barrels of powder.[49] Such a capability was a key basis for British military activity, but, of course, it did not make success inevitable.

The initial stages of the war with France also highlighted serious issues of naval preparedness, although by the end of the conflict the British were outbuilding their Bourbon rivals. Furthermore, the need to confront a number of challenges around the world placed considerable burdens on the ability to control and allocate naval (as well as army) resources, and also raised issues of strategic understanding and of the accurate assessment of threats. The nature of communications prevented the exercise of close control and made it difficult to respond to developments adequately. This accentuated problems in cooperation between army and navy.

Poor operational decisions were indeed responsible for specific failures on land and sea, most obviously in the Yorktown campaign. However, only so much weight should be placed on poor leadership. After all, the British did enjoy important successes, there had been many failures in command in conflicts that had eventually been successful for the British, including the Seven Years' War (which is a pointed reminder of the fine divide between success and failure), and poor leadership in the War of American Independence was not restricted to the British.

Instead, it is worth noting the formidable nature of the tasks facing British commanders in a war that appeared, from 1778, to be getting out of control. When there was rebellion in Scotland in 1745 and in Ireland in 1798, Britain was also at war with France, but, despite later mythmaking, both these rebellions were weak, not least due to limited support, while neither posed the military challenge of the rebellion in the Thirteen Colonies. Furthermore, from 1778, Britain lacked the initiative overall. There were individual advances, such as the invasion of first North Carolina and then Virginia in 1781; or the expedition the previous year against Fort San Juan in modern Nicaragua, which was intended to push through to the Pacific, but instead fell victim to yellow fever. However, on the whole, Britain's opponents were able to take the initiative in North America, the West Indies and the Indian Ocean, and this caused major problems for British force-availability, and thus for individual army campaigns: for example, the unsuccessful defence of Pensacola against Spanish attacks in 1781.

Without naval dominance or the initiative, the British found that troops had to be spread out on defensive duties, and it was therefore difficult to take units from garrisons in order to assemble an expeditionary force, which was, for example, to be the pattern with attacks on French colonial positions during the Napoleonic War. Furthermore, losing the initiative exposed the weaknesses of British preparations. Being pushed onto the defensive did not necessarily lead to failure: Québec and Gibraltar both defied attack during the War of American Independence; but, in these cases, British forces benefited from defending well-fortified positions and from eventual naval relief, whereas, on other occasions, the situation was less favourable.

Despite the crisis of a civil war in the empire, the army itself had continued its usual practices of recruitment and promotion, each of which showed how far it was broadly embedded in British society. Moreover, whereas the Jacobite crisis of 1745–6 had led to the deployment of Hessians in Britain, in 1778–83 the equivalent 'Home Front' was in part in America, with the front in Britain left as the responsibility of national forces, principally militia. There was not yet the pressure of failure sufficient to demand reform, and the ability to deliver victory until 1781 suggested that the major problems were diplomatic, not military. That was mistaken, but the challenge in 1775–83 was certainly different to that which was to be faced during the French Revolutionary and Napoleonic Wars, not least in terms of scale, range and length. At the same time, the British, fighting alone, sustained a formidable effort during the earlier conflict.

CHAPTER 6

Winning Another Empire: India, 1746–1815

The enemy now brought three field pieces against us from which, as well as with their musketry and rockets ... our loss soon became serious ... the want of water was severely felt ... these different attacks were still attended with loss on our side, and the redoubt was now become a horrid scene of carnage – many had fallen, and the rest, through heat, exertion, and thirst were almost exhausted most of them, however stood gallantly to their duty, though, in a few, signs of despondency began to appear.

MAJOR SKELLY, 52ND FOOT, ABOUT MYSORE FORCES ATTACKING
THE BRITISH ARMY UNDER CORNWALLIS NEAR THE
MYSORE CAPITAL OF SERINGAPATAM, 1792.[1]

India proved a key sphere of army activity, one that was to be highly significant for the development of the British empire and of the army, for the hybrid (British and non-British) character of the British force structure was especially apparent and successful in India. British regular units there were part of British-led forces that were largely composed of Indians, which had major implications at the tactical, operational, and strategic levels, and in the organisational and command spheres.

There are questions, nevertheless, of relative effectiveness, questions that arose from the number of military players in India. Why was Britain to prove more effective than other outside forces in this period, notably Nader Shah of Persia, the Afghans, and France? Why were the British able to overcome serious failures, especially in 1746 and, far more, 1779–81, and win eventual victory over France, as well as the two leading Indian powers: Mysore and the Marathas, and particularly because the latter two were improving their armies? These triumphs were to be crucial to

Britain's rise to dominate India, and thus to become a European power with a major non-European presence, indeed, an empire that was at once Atlantic and Asian, and that was to last while it combined these characteristics.

In part, this success was due to structural factors, notably the fiscal strength of the East India Company, Mughal and Maratha weaknesses, and different French priorities. Britain proved to be the most successful of the powers that vied for wealth in the period of Mughal decay. Methodical, planned, disciplined, and relatively orderly, British military and administrative structures were important in making value of the crucial ability to buy military service.

Successive wars saw the number of Indian and British troops at the disposal of the East India Company rise from about 54,000 in 1773 to 70,000 in 1794, and 160,000 in 1801, and ensured that the Company's debts trebled between 1793 and 1808.[2] In response, the Company recalled Richard, Marquess Wellesley, the bellicose Governor-General in 1805, and sought peace with the Marathas. But the key point was that, as with the Peninsular War, the British could afford the financial strain,[3] and thus enable the army to fight its position.

As elsewhere, however, the military dimension was crucial: wars had to be fought. In part, this was a matter of tactics, but a willingness to take heavy casualties was also significant, as, in 1807, when the Bengal army of the East India Company attempted to storm the fortress of Kamonah in Uttar Pradesh:

> Out of 300 of the 17th Regiment which headed the storm, 145 are either killed or wounded. No men could behave more nobly than both Europeans and Sepoys, but no courage, no bravery could surmount the obstacles thrown in their way. The ditch was filled with bags of powder covered over with straw. The enemy awaited until our men had advanced within shot point blank. They then opened a most tremendous fire. Our men coolly advanced to the breach. Immediately the enemy set fire to the straw … as fast as our men mounted ladders, they were either shot or scorched with powder bags thrown on them.[4]

Disease also caused large numbers of deaths, and especially so for Europeans, notably cholera, malaria and diarrhoea.[5] Indeed, including replacement recruits who were sent out, the two Hanoverian regiments that served the East India Company from 1781 to 1792 totalled 170 officers and 2,800 men, but, due largely to disease, 69 of the officers failed to return, only four of whom were killed in action, while only about half the men returned fit for further service.

War in India deserves particular attention in this book, especially due to the importance of India to British imperial history, and of being part of the empire to Indian history. Moreover, failure in North America in 1775–83 made India even more significant to British imperial history. It also served as a base for British activity and expansion elsewhere, notably in South-East and East Asia, and East Africa.

Even more attention has to be devoted to the subject due to the extent to which victory was far from inevitable. Indeed, arguably, it was only in 1799–1806 that the situation really changed. Prior to that, there had been particular success in Bengal, but not elsewhere. Hindustan, in the 1780s and early 1790s under the dominance of Mahadji Shinde, his army strong in artillery and infantry,[6] was now more under the threat of the Afghans as an external power than the British. The naval strength of the latter was unmatched, and Mysore's attempt to develop a rival naval force both proved perfunctory and was wrecked by British action; it was only in 1799–1806, however, and then with considerable difficulty, that dominance on land followed.

Success in the Carnatic

Eventual British military success in India was not an inevitable outcome. Indeed, while the British had established a significant commercial presence in the 17th century, in the shape of the East India Company, this presence had proved politically and militarily vulnerable. Moreover, Britain was not the only European power present, and there was no reason to see it as necessarily the most potentially successful. Indeed, the loss of Madras to French attack in September 1746 was a failure that reflected the skill of the French commander, Joseph François, Marquis de Dupleix, and the greater strength of France at this point. Having captured Madras, Dupleix successfully defended it against the Indian allies of the British, and his ally, Chanda Sahib, became Nawab of the Carnatic in 1749 as France sought to establish an effective system of Allied rulers across southern India. The growing British and French presence in India ensured that their rivalry affected and, albeit to a far lesser degree than with North America, was affected by the conflicts there.

The succession struggle in the Carnatic brought the young Robert Clive (1725–74), a captain, to the fore. In 1751 he captured Chanda Sahib's capital, Arcot, without firing a shot, and, with great ability, bravery and presence, held it with 300 men against a 50-day siege by a much larger force, before going on to defeat the retreating besiegers at Arni.

These defeats wrecked the momentum and appearance of success on which Dupleix depended, and his alliance system collapsed. In 1752, both Chanda and a French force surrendered, the latter to Stringer Lawrence, who, having risen to become a major in the regular army and fought at Culloden, had gone to India in 1748 to become commander of the East India Company army, serving there until 1766. An able and energetic commander, Lawrence created a Company field army in the Carnatic, ensuring that the Company was not restricted militarily to a few coastal positions and enabling it to take a more proactive role in regional politics. By 1752, this army amounted to 1,200 European troops and 2,000 *sepoys*. That year, Lawrence defeated a larger force at Bahur outside Pondicherry, the *sepoys* dispersing their French counterparts before British troops, firing as they advanced, drove their French opponents from the battlefield with a bayonet charge.

The battles Lawrence won, such as Golden Rock and Sugarloaf Rock, both in 1753, are now forgotten, but they were crucial to Britain establishing its position in the Carnatic and developing the use of *sepoys*. This position was seen to depend on being able to protect a base area from which to draw supplies. In 1754, the Presidency of Madras issued instructions that, if war broke out with France:

> The principal points in view are, the engaging their main army, the covering the Nawab's districts, by which a revenue will arise to him, and the distressing that of the enemy, which may carry with it a double advantage of diminishing theirs, and adding to his support.

The following year, plans were drawn up on the basis of reducing the area from which the French received contributions.[7] The recipient, John Adlercron, was a member of a Huguenot family who had taken refuge in Dublin from French persecution. He had followed a career in the regular army, been sent to India in 1754 as colonel of a regular infantry regiment, becoming commander in chief, India that year, and being promoted to lieutenant-general in 1760.

Clive to the Fore

In turn, alongside a naval squadron and Maratha allies, Clive, now a lieutenant-colonel in the British Army, captured Gheria in February 1756. Gheria was the west coast stronghold of Tulajee Angria, a Maratha leader whose naval ambitions challenged Britain's naval dominance in Indian waters. That June came a threat from another direction, when Siraj-ud-Daula, the newly acceded Nawab of Bengal, stormed poorly defended Fort William at Calcutta after a brief siege. Clive, then Deputy Governor of Fort St. David at Cuddalore, and Rear-Admiral Charles Watson, the winning combination at Gheria, were instructed to retake Calcutta. Clive was in command of 850 British soldiers and 2,100 *sepoys*, which was at that time a major deployment of British strength; in a sign of subsequent significant change, it would not have been so in Bengal by 1815. This force regained Fort William, largely thanks to the guns of Watson's squadron, the most mobile form of artillery: and Clive pressed on, supported by Watson to gain the French position at Chandernagore.

Suspicious of Siraj-ud-Daula's stance, and mindful of the possibilities to be gained from replacing him as Nawab by one of his generals, Mir Jafar, Clive, with 1,100 British troops, 2,100 *sepoys* and nine cannon, advanced on the capital, Murshidabad, encountering Siraj-ud-Daula's 50,000 strong army at Plassey on 23 June. Major John Corneille noted 'the plan seemed covered with their army.' In a battle that was less dramatic than it was significant, attacks that were not pressed home were repelled by the fire of Clive's force, and an advance by Clive led the Nawab's army, about 68,000 strong, to scatter. Corneille commented that Clive's cannon was more effective than the 'large unwieldy pieces' of his opponent.[8]

Mir Jafar, who joined in at the appropriate moment, was made the new Nawab. Corneille had gone to India in 1754 as Secretary to Adlercorn.

The path from Plassey to British control of Bengal was not smooth, as the British had to face attempts to reimpose a Muslim ascendancy, the problems of establishing a stable regime, and Dutch intervention in 1759, which was defeated by British defensive fire at the battle of Chinsurah on 25 November. The Dutch East India Company had been invited to intervene by Mir Jafar, who wanted the British expelled. In 1760, Mir Jafar was overthrown and replaced by his son-in-law, Mir Kasim.

Backing by the government in London was a key factor, not least in the dispatch of regular forces. A regiment and six warships had been sent to India in 1754, four companies of artillery following in 1755. In face of the arrival of French reinforcements in 1757 and 1758, and of a French revival in southern India that led to an unsuccessful French siege of Madras in early 1759, Clive asked Pitt for assistance in February 1759. Pitt was more aware of the importance of India than George II or Newcastle and, in October 1759, the Duke wrote of the East India Company, 'Mr Pitt is mightily for sending them two battalions', while, of a Scottish regiment that was to be raised, he added 'The king wants it for the army in Germany. Mr Pitt rather designs it, at present, for the East Indies [India].'[9] India was a harsher destination than cooler Germany for native Scots, but that was not an issue. The reinforcements sent in 1759 and 1760 helped Eyre Coote to defeat the French in the Carnatic, with victory over a larger French force at Wandewash (22 January 1760), a victory that owed much to the British artillery.[10]

After the delay of operations against Pondicherry due to heat and disease,[11] the garrison surrendered on 15 January 1761 after a long siege. The resources available were considerable: John Call, a military engineer, noted of his preparations for this task that he would have '30 24-pounders, and 20 18-pounders, besides small guns, 6 large mortars, and 12 Royals or Coehorns [mortars], with ammunition for 40 days firing at 25 cannon per day.'[12] In contrast, the French had held Pondicherry against British attack in 1748, and, earlier, when they had lost it in 1693, it had been to the Dutch. Call (1731–1801) succeeded Benjamin Robins in 1751 as chief engineer and served in India until 1766.

In addition, Clive had established a pattern of attack, as when he told Francis Forde to attack the Dutch force at Chinsurah 'immediately.' John Carnac, a major in the Bengal army, wrote to Clive, his patron, after winning a victory in 1761: 'If I have any merit in our late affair it is entirely owing to the lesson I have learned from you, always to push forward.' A willingness to advance against vastly greater forces was to be crucial to military success in India, and to link Clive to Wellesley. This was not only a matter of the commanders. Carnac noted how his infantry bravely advanced into the face of cannon, as Wellesley's men were to do in his hard-fought victory at Assaye in 1803, adding 'I was so happy as to have under my command a set of people who were as ready to advance as I could be to lead them.'[13]

The 1760s

In 1760, Major John Caillaud, a Culloden veteran who was Commander of the Company's Bengal Army, repelled an invasion of Bihar by Ali Gauhar, the eldest son of the Mughal emperor. Ali Gauhar's army had pressed hard the forces of Britain's ally, the Nawab of Bengal. The battle took place at Sirpur: 'It was then the Major advanced at the head of his sepoys. They drew up quite close to the flank of the enemy while they engaged the Nawab, threw in their fire, then rushed in with their bayonets.' The Nawab's cavalry then attacked and the Mughal forces collapsed.[14] British tactics, based on firing once or twice in close-range volley-fire, and then charging, greatly impressed Indian opponents. Yet, the most significant fighting in India was the Afghan invasion that culminated in victory over the Marathas at the Third Battle of Panipat in 1761.

In contrast, British activity in Bengal was less central or large-scale. There, in 1763, war broke out with Mir Jafar's son-in-law, Mir Kasim, in part due to the heavy financial demands of the British who were helped, after the successful siege of Pondicherry, by the absence of any diversion of their strength.[15] As a result, troops were then moved from the Carnatic to Bengal where Mir Kasim engaged the far less numerous forces of both Crown and Company under Major Thomas Adams at Gheriah and Udhanala. The former, in which part of the British line was breached, was particularly hard fought, but Mir Kasim was heavily defeated. Adams (1730?–64) served in the Low Countries under Cumberland from 1747, and as an officer went with the 84th Regiment of Foot, a new unit raised in 1758 that was sent to Madras in 1759, fighting first in the Carnatic and then in Bengal. Victorious in 1763, he died in Calcutta of ill-health.

In 1764, there were major British victories at Patna (3 May) and Buxar (23 October), the latter a hard-fought struggle of three hours in which 7,000 men defeated Mir Kasim and his allies, Shah Alam II, the Mughal Emperor, and Shuja-ud-Dowla, the Nawab of Oudh, who together fielded a force of 50,000. At Patna, grapeshot halted the advance of hostile infantry, and when a cavalry attack was launched by the Indians, 'a severe fire of artillery soon drove them back.' At Buxar, British firepower proved superior.[16] Buxar was exploited in February 1765 with the capture of Oudh's leading fortresses, which was followed by the Treaty of Allahabad on 12 August 1765. This recognised the British position in Bengal and Bihar, the resources of which enabled the East India Company to act as an effective territorial power, not only on the Ganges plain, but also elsewhere in India.

With an established political and military presence in three parts of India, the British found themselves faced by rivals in each. Campaigning was not easy, with the campaign against Yusuf Khan in the Carnatic in 1763 described thus by John Call:

> We should not be the least uneasy about the certainty of defeating him were it not for the difficulty of penetrating through the woods to get at him ... The narrow roads are at all times difficult to an army, but retrenched and secured as they are at present we are well assured it is impracticable to penetrate by any route but that of marching by the sea side ... Another grand obstacle is the want of water ... as well as rice ... in spite of all we should have marched against him and could have drawn together a body of 600 Europeans ... but such was our weakened state that we could not send half that number into the field.[17]

Indeed, in this case, the British in defeating Yusuf Khan in 1764 benefited from his betrayal by some of his supporters. The episode indicated the degree to which success in the latter stages of the Seven Years' War did not necessarily mean overall superiority, a point that was to be driven home by the wars with Mysore in 1767–9 and 1780–4. Haidar Ali of Mysore respected and feared Brigadier-General Joseph Smith, the commander in chief of the Madras Army, who, having served in the Madras forces since 1749, had considerable relevant experience. However, Smith had insufficient means and it proved difficult to respond successfully to the Mysore cavalry in the war of 1767–9, notably in 1769 when Mysore forces advanced as far as Madras.

The 1770s

There were smaller-scale clashes in the early 1770s, in southern India, the Ganges Valley and western India. For example, in 1773, after the advance of Company troops, Oudh came under Company protection from the Marathas. The following year, the Company helped Oudh occupy neighbouring Rohilkhand, defeating the Rohillas at Lahykiria (Miranpur Katra) on 23 April in one of the many battles of empire that is apt to be ignored. The firepower of the East India Company forces and the Westernised infantry of their Oudh allies saw off the attack of the Rohilla infantry and cavalry, and pursuit by the Oudh cavalry prevented the Rohilla forces from regrouping. In 1775, albeit with heavy casualties, Company troops suppressed a mutiny amongst those of Oudh, reflecting the British role in protecting allies.[18]

The next major struggle for Britain, that with the Marathas, ended in disaster in 1779 when a British force that had advanced from Bombay was surrounded, and, under heavy pressure and with morale and ammunition falling, signed a convention at Wadgam that provided for withdrawal to Bombay. This was a major failure, but, like the failure under similar circumstances of Peter the Great of Russia at Turkish hands at the battle of the River Pruth in 1711, it was not one that was to be fatal.

Moreover, the British position in that particular war was eased by the transfer of troops by means of an epic march of 785 miles across India from Bengal to Surat. The task was formidable. Thus, in June, the expedition was hindered by bad roads, a lack of water and bullocks, and the 'scorching heat.' On 3 June: 'the scorching hot winds with the intense heat of the sun on a dry extensive plain … exposed us to sufferings of the superlative degree. About twenty sepoys dropped down quite exhausted for want of water.' Nevertheless, the march continued, helped by the Maratha failure to block wells. This force, which had used its infantry volleys to drive off Maratha attacks en route, arrived too late to help the Bombay army avoid disaster;[19] once arrived, however, the British, under Lieutenant-Colonel Thomas Goddard, defeated opposing forces in 1780. The fighting was dramatic, as with the capture of Ahmadabad that February: the British arrived on 10 February after the cannon had blown a breach on the 13th, the fortress was stormed at dawn on the 15th, with the defenders taken by surprise, fighting 'nobly, drawing their swords and dealing blows around them even after the bayonets were plunged in their bodies.'[20]

That August, Major William Popham stormed the major hill fort of Gwalior, having ascended the mountain on which it was located and scaled the walls by rope ladder. In the subsequent struggle, the surprised garrison largely fled. Popham (1740–1821), who had served at the capture of Manila in 1762, was to retire as lieutenant-general in 1803, having taken part in the advances on Seringapatam in 1791, 1792 and 1799. The difficulties of such scaling operations as that at Gwalior were highlighted by Lieutenant-Colonel Henry Cosby in 1780, as delays in raising the ladders could prove fatal:

> By this time the enemy's whole force were collected to oppose us ... and rows of pikes presented through every embrasure so that it now became impossible to enter, as a man no sooner got to the top of the ladder, than he was knocked down by a shot or a pike.[21]

Cosby (1743–1822), the son of Captain Alexander Cosby, was born on Minorca, where his father was stationed. Alexander had served in Europe before entering the service of the East India Company as second in command first to Stringer Lawrence and then, in 1759, in the capture of Surat, where he died soon after. Alexander had helped organise the Company forces to fight as regulars on the European pattern. Henry served at the capture of Gheria and in that of Pondicherry in 1761, had extensive experience in the Carnatic in the 1760s and 1770s, and moved between British and Indian service, notably as commander of the Carnatic cavalry, fighting extensively in the Second Anglo-Mysore War. In 1786, Henry Cosby finally left India, having made a large fortune, and he died a lieutenant-general. Cosby was an instance of the frequency of family links in military service, links that were important to personal success, as they provided connections and patronage, and to institutional strength, as they both offered a means for the transmission of experience and helped maintain morale.

The 1780s

In 1781, in campaigning that indicated the difficult context affecting operations as well as variations between particular campaigns, Goddard had less success. Aside from the cost of the Maratha war leading to pressure for its end, there was also concern about the revival of war with Haidar Ali. As in 1778–9, there was an effort to strike at the Maratha centre of Pune (Poona), but, suffering from attacks on his supplies, Goddard was forced to retreat with serious losses. The indecisive nature of the warfare in 1781, one that scarcely looked toward later British success, was due to the greater effectiveness of the Marathas, who increasingly emulated the infantry-artillery combinations of European armies while also maintaining their superiority in cavalry. Other important factors were the problems of terrain and logistics confronting the British, and their need to fight Mysore at the same time. Most British gains were restored to the Marathas by the Treaty of Salbai of May 1782, which committed both parties to resist Mysore, a necessary result for the hard-pressed British.

Meanwhile, the British capture on 19 March 1779 of the French coastal base of Mahé, which Haidar Ali saw as under his protection and through which he acquired French arms, angered Haidar. So also did the British refusal to provide help against the Marathas as they were obliged to do under a treaty of 1769. Anglo-Maratha hostilities in western India gave him an opportunity to attack, and in July 1780, with an army 80,000 strong, largely cavalry, he invaded the Carnatic.

The inadequate and confused British response reflected serious command failings, as well as the availability of only 26,000 troops. On 10 September, the Mysore army attacked a heavily outnumbered force under Colonel William Baillie who drew up his men in a defensive position, only to find that badly disrupted when his numerous camp followers fled. In the end, the square of his troops, under fire from more numerous cannon (about 50 to 10), was fought down by repeated attacks by Mysore cavalry and infantry. Haidar pressed on to make gains, notably Arcot, where the defences were breached in October, while his capture of supplies created serious supply problems for the British.[22]

The British position in the Carnatic was further compromised by French intervention, but Eyre Coote, the talented commander in chief in India, arrived by sea from Calcutta and saved the situation by a series of victories, notably at Porto Novo, Pollilur and Sholinghur on 1 June, 27 August, and 27 September 1781. Coote was in no illusion about the difficulty of his task, explaining later that year his opposition to attacking the Dutch base at Negapatam by referring to:

> every military idea which I have been able to form in the course of forty years service. It is a rule which a soldier ought never to lose sight of – if there is an enemy in the field, anywhere near, and in force, to a fortified town or garrison intended to be attacked, first to beat it, and so effectually as to himself satisfied that it will not be able to rise again in strength sufficient to molest him whilst carrying on the operations of the siege.[23]

Negapatam was captured. However, the French navy (and therefore its British counterpart) became significant factors, Coote writing the following year:

> I wish most anxiously for intelligence of the Admiral and the Fleet being again upon the Coast, as I should hope thereby to have it in my power to move to the southward, as a supply of provisions might then be sent me by sea without which I could not in the present position of Haidar [Ali of Mysore] and the French undertake such an operation to its full extent, at least with that degree of security so necessary to the preservation of our real interest.[24]

Once Coote returned to Bengal, his health wrecked by the 1782 campaign, which was a matter of many moves without significant advantage, the British found it difficult to prevail, not least because of a division between Major-General James Stuart and the Governor of Madras, George, Lord Macartney, a division that captured the distinctive tension affecting British Army operations. Never the easiest of men, Macartney believed it crucial to subordinate military commanders to the civil power and felt that Stuart was less than energetic and competent.

Stuart was indeed slow, but there was also a major difference over strategy, one that captured the extent to which there was rarely a clear optimum solution, a point that tends to be underplayed by subsequent criticism. In this case, whereas Coote and Stuart both felt that French forces should have priority over Haidar and Tipu and that the army should be kept concentrated, Macartney, who felt that harassment by the Mysore cavalry might grind down the army, had Mysore as the main target and wanted to divide the army so that it could fight in different theatres. Stuart countermanded Macartney's orders to make a detachment, only to be suspended from his command, imprisoned and sent back to Britain.

Stuart, who had served at Louisbourg (1758), Belle-Île (1761), Martinique (1762) and Havana (1762), had entered the service of the East India Company in 1775 with the rank of Colonel, becoming commander in chief of the Madras Army in 1776 but being involved in the dispute focused on the arrest of the Governor there earlier that year. Losing a leg to cannon fire at Pollihur in 1781, he severely wounded Macartney in a duel in Hyde Park in 1786.

Tipu Sultan, who had succeeded his father Haidar Ali in December 1782, was affected by the loss of French support with peace in 1783, but he continued to press the British hard, and, in March 1784, the Treaty of Mangalore was based on the *status quo ante bellum*, a return to the situation prior to the war that was scarcely a sign of failure on Tipu's part. Indeed, it had proved far easier for Britain to take French positions, notably Pondicherry again in 1778, than to defeat Mysore.

The local British commander, Colonel William Fullarton, complained in July 1784 that Tipu had failed to fulfil the peace terms and that the British eagerness for peace only led him to be less accommodating, concluding: 'Tippo Sultan or the English must fall, for his conduct is such as cannot be compatible with our safety.'[25] Over the following years, Tipu Sultan weakened the British position across southern India by sapping their allies.[26]

The empire appeared under further threat due to French imperial expansion as well as France's influence with the Dutch. In November 1784, Henry Dundas, a key member of the Board of Control responsible for overseeing the East India Company, in a letter to its President, claimed:

> It must readily occur to everybody, that an exceeding good establishment of artillery, a considerable establishment of cavalry, and a large European force must at all times be kept in India, particularly on the coast … our force now and hereafter must be regulated by the intelligence we have of the force that our European rivals have at Mauritius, Pondicherry, Ceylon and other places. Taking it for granted that India is the quarter to be first attacked, we must never lose sight of having such a force there as to baffle all surprise.[27]

Keen on more direct control, George III complained 'Whilst the army in India remains in such unfit hands as those of a company of merchants I cannot expect any good can be done.'[28] This led to the appointment of Cornwallis as Governor-General and commander in chief in India in 1786, to the plan for a reorganisation of the East India Company army, involving the dispatch of 5,000 troops, and, eventually, to its reinforcement in 1788 by four British regiments, in part in response to reports of French troop movements to an extent linked to the Dutch Crisis of 1787.

The 1790s

War with Tipu resumed in 1790, but the British invasion of Mysore that year and in 1791 failed. Cornwallis, who had already acted to improve the army,[29] took personal charge of operations in 1791, but was hit by poor weather, an epidemic that hit the bullocks that pulled the wagons, and a scorched earth policy by Tipu Sultan, all of which greatly hampered the advance. The battle between British and Mysore forces outside Seringapatam indicated the different nature of the two sides. Major Skelly of the 52nd Regiment recorded:

> While our army was forming, which took up more than an hour for it was necessary to use many precautions against the horse (which was constantly threatening our flanks) the enemy brought a numerous and well served artillery to bear upon us, and we suffered very considerably from their shot.

Another participant wrote that when the Mysore army fell back:

They soon recovered firmness, particularly the cavalry who attacked in their turn, supported by a large body of infantry, with sabre, spear, and pistol. Here was a glorious spectacle! The glittering of the swords in a bright sun shine, and the flashes of the fire arms, on both sides, was grand and awful. Our cavalry found their overmatch and were obliged to give way in a masterly manner wheeling outwards to the right and left into the rear, by a signal from Colonel Floyd, at a moment when the Bengal battalions came up between the two divisions and gave their fire, and perhaps saved the whole corps.

Skelly noted the advance of Cornwallis' army 'in such perfect order, and with such fire resolution as might have commanded victory from better mettled troops than Tipu can bring into the field.'[30]

Cornwallis then advanced on Seringapatam, only to find that it was well-defended and he was short of supplies, which led him to fall back. Major-General Robert Abercromby, the commander in chief of the Bombay Army, who had advanced toward Seringapatam from the west, also had to fall back, his troops suffering greatly from disease and heavy rainfall. Abercromby's career reflected the range of experience that an individual could encompass. Born in 1740, he served in the Seven Years' War and the War of American Independence, before going out to India in 1790, returning home in 1797 with an eye disease he had contracted there.

His older brother, Ralph (1734–1801), who also rose to be a lieutenant-general, again displayed variety in his career, although, like many officers, he did not serve in India. Entering the army in 1756, and serving in Germany during the Seven Years' War, Ralph Abercromby did not serve in the War of American Independence because he sympathised with the American Patriots, and, instead, served in Ireland during the war. The 1790s saw Abercromby a brigade commander under York in the Low Countries, an expedition commander in the West Indies in 1796–7, commander in Ireland in 1798, serving under York in Holland in 1799, and the commander of the expedition to the Mediterranean in 1800, where he was fatally wounded in the battle of Alexandria in 1801. Service under York was a major help to promotion for him and others.

In 1792, Cornwallis advanced anew and more successfully, although the Mysore forces were no pushover, one officer writing: 'the enemy fire heavily at the rate of about 800 shot a day.'[31] Skelly noted of an attack by Tipu's forces near Seringapatam that Cornwallis 'finding that our fire was trifling in comparison to that of the enemy ordered a charge to be made that was immediately executed by the 74th Regiment ... with a spirit which totally disconcerted the enemy they gave way and retreated in some confusion.'[32] Seringapatam was then besieged, with Cornwallis joined by Abercromby. Tipu negotiated peace in order to end the threat, ceding some of his territory.

In a pattern also seen with Indian powers, the British were greatly helped in India by sequential, rather than simultaneous, warmaking, the Third Mysore War being followed in 1794 by the Second Rohilla War. The British under Robert Abercromby, now commander in chief in India, won the battle of Bithura on 26 October against a far larger army under Nawab Ghulam Muhommad of Rampur, although the victory was not easily gained. The initial Indian cavalry charge threw the defence into disorder, but the failure to follow up with another charge, and the preoccupation of the Indian vanguard with looting the British tents, enabled the British to recover and win the battle.

Yet, putting this in perspective, one that greatly helped affect the views of participants, including their willingness to ally with Britain, Zaman Shah of Afghanistan (r. 1793–1800) advanced across the River Indus into northern India on a number of occasions, notably 1796 and 1797. In 1798, it was feared by the British and their allies that the Afghans would advance across north India as far as Oudh, a British protectorate. There was concern about Afghan links in Oudh and, more generally, among the Muslims of northern India.

In response, the British looked at the idea of an Indian alliance against the Afghans involving in particular the Marathas, who had done well in campaigning in Rajputana in the 1780s and 1790s. The British also sought, as part of the widening scope of their power,[33] to persuade Persia to raise its level of military activity in order to dissuade the Afghans from advancing, and also anticipated supplying cannon and munitions to Persia and to principalities that might resist the Afghans, notably Sind. In the event, there was no Afghan advance due to Zaman's rebellious brothers being backed by Persia, and, in 1799, he pulled back to Peshawar. This was the last Afghan invasion of north India.

This episode no more suggested British dominance than the deliberate failure in 1791 to heed Nepalese requests for help against a Chinese invasion about which the British could have done little. Moreover, in India itself, the Marathas were becoming more powerful, as could be seen by their defeat of the Nizam of Hyderabad in 1795. Repeatedly, the British were greatly helped not by victories, but by divisions between the other Indian powers: in 1782, the Marathas had refused Mysore's request to threaten Bengal; in 1784–7, Mysore and the Marathas had fought a war; and, in 1792, the *Peshwā* (the leading Maratha ruler) and the Nizam had joined Britain in getting territory from Mysore. The Marathas suffered greatly from civil war in the 1790s,[34] and the aggression of Daulatrao Shinde (Sindhia) helped lead to support from Baji Rao II, the *Peshwā*, for Britain against Tipu Sultan in 1799. The Nizam also provided the British with backing.[35]

Fearful of links between Tipu and the French, and with Richard Wellesley a more aggressive and politically connected Governor-General than his cautious predecessor, Sir John Shore, the British successfully coordinated forces from Bombay and Madras and maintained the pace of their offensive. As with so many conflicts, the choice made by the opponent was crucial: Tipu failed to display the mobility that he had shown in the previous war, and that his father had displayed. Instead, he concentrated on positional warfare. Having unsuccessfully attacked the British under Major-General George Harris at Malavelly, Tipu retreated into Seringapatam, where a breach made by the effective British artillery was stormed under heavy fire on 4 May. Part of the British force was held in savage fighting until the defenders were outflanked by British troops who had gained the inner rampart and then moved along, throwing the defenders into disorder. Tipu was among those killed.

The victorious British pressed on to capture a series of forts, and the rest of Mysore rapidly surrendered. The British then restored the dynasty displaced by Haidar Ali, although important territories were annexed by the East India Company. Harris (1746–1829), the son of a clergyman, joined the Royal Artillery in 1760, transferring to the infantry in 1762, and first saw active service at Lexington in 1775.

Severely wounded at Bunker Hill, he served in America until 1778, St. Lucia (1778–9), and Ireland, then going to India, where he served in the Third Anglo-Mysore War and became commander in chief of the Madras Army in 1797. After returning home in 1800, he had no more active service. The commander in chief in India at that time, Lieutenant-General Sir Alured Clarke (1644–1832), the son of a judge and former MP, was an old Etonian who was commissioned as an ensign in 1759, served in Germany under Granby and in the American War of Independence, held gubernatorial roles in Jamaica and Canada, and captured Cape Town in 1795 en route to becoming commander in chief of the Madras Army, and going on to be commander in chief in India from 1798 to 1801.

Again, as an instance of sequential warmaking, victory over Mysore provided an opportunity to send troops from India to contribute in 1801 to the attack on the French in Egypt, an area which very much became an aspect of the forward defence for India against both France and Russia.[36]

Victory 1803–18

The Second Maratha War, which began in 1803, was a more complex and longer struggle than the last Anglo-Mysore war, a contrast that reflected the complexity of Maratha politics and the strength of the Maratha forces. The battle of Assaye on 23 September found Arthur Wellesley, later Duke of Wellington, heavily outnumbered and with the Marathas deploying impressive cannon. Keen to fix his opponents' forces, a goal he shared with Nelson, Wellesley used speedy attack to compensate for his numerical inferiority and he relied heavily on bayonet advances and cavalry charges, which scarcely conformed to the standard image of Western armies gunning down masses of non-European troops who relied on cold steel. Casualties accounted for over a quarter of the British force. British losses were fewer at Argaum on 29 November, and, again, it was the British ability to mount attacks that was crucial. This tactical capability reflected Wellesley's creation of a well-supplied army capable of continuous movement and, thus, of putting operational pressure on the Marathas, thus prefiguring his campaign against the French in Spain in 1813.[37]

This campaign was a key element of the process in which, with the British benefiting from the role of their credit in raising troops in the North Indian military labour market, the Marathas were defeated in detail in what was in effect a series of separate campaigns that finally brought peace in January 1806. In winning a series of victories, the British benefited from aggressive, fast-moving leadership, notably by the commander in chief in India from 1801 to 1807 – Gerard Lake, victor of the battles of Laswari on 1 November 1803 and Farrukhabad on 14 November 1804 – and by Wellesley. Lake (1744–1808), who had served in Germany in the Seven Years' War, Yorktown, the Low Countries in 1793–5, and as commander in chief in Ireland in 1798, was a highly talented commander, although his successive attempts to storm Bharatpur in 1805 proved costly mistakes.

There was a determined attempt on the British part to increase mobility, in the shape of light infantry, more cavalry, and the establishment in 1800 of a horse artillery unit, which became permanent in 1809. Mobility was a key element, and against all opponents. Thus, the guerrilla warfare of the rebellion of the Palassi Raja in Wynad entailed mobile British columns which succeeded only in 1806 after several years of conflict. Drawing on his experience of campaigning in the American South, Cornwallis had emphasised the significance of cavalry, writing in 1787 first 'no man in India can be more convinced than I am of the importance of cavalry to our armies' and later:

> I found, in the extensive field in which I acted during my command in the Southern provinces of America, very great advantage from mounting about eighty or an hundred men on ordinary horses, to act with the cavalry. By this means I could venture to detach my cavalry and strike an unexpected blow at a very considerable distance from my army. It occurs to me that in case of an invasion of the Carnatic, you might find a corps of this sort picked from your European infantry ... very useful. It would not only protect the cavalry when detached in their camp or quarters, and assist them when harassed by swarms of irregular horse in the field, but it would enable you frequently either by surprise at night, or ambuscade, to punish considerable parties of plunderers, who are employed in laying waste the country.[38]

This army was to go on to be important across South Asia, defeating the Dutch in Java in 1811 and, having first failed to advance into the interior of Sri Lanka in 1803, succeeding there in 1815, with the task facing its independently advancing columns eased by the unpopularity of the volatile king of Kandy. In Nepal, facing a more difficult opponent, the British initially did badly against the Gurkhas in 1814, in part due to poor generalship, unfamiliarity with mountain warfare, and the Gurkha combination of defensive positions, especially hill forts and stockades, with attacks on British detachments. Attacks on Gurkha positions at Jaithak and Nalapani proved costly for the British and affected the confidence of their commanders. However, victories in 1815 and 1816 brought the war to a successful conclusion in 1816. Such battles as Almora and Maluan (both 1815) are now essentially forgotten, but they reflected the British ability to respond to the challenges of the military and physical environment. The use of heavy cannon and cutting water supplies proved significant in the attack on forts, with that of Almora surrendering on 27 April after gun positions had been brought close. Bold advances were matched with systematic offensive position warfare, and the British also benefited from having larger forces.

In 1817–18, the British went on to defeat the Marathas in campaigns far less difficult than those of 1803–5. As against the Gurkhas, infantry advances played a key role. Thus, at Mahidpur on 21 December 1817, the infantry, under Brigadier-General Sir John Malcolm, advanced under heavy fire from the Maratha artillery. The Maratha infantry mostly retreated, but the gunners continued to fire until bayoneted beside their cannon. A Scotsman, Malcolm (1769–1833), one of many sons of a poor tenant farmer, made his fortune in India, where he became an ensign in the Company's Madras Army in 1783, serving there until 1794 before returning to Britain for his health. Having served under Wellesley and Lake in the 1800s, he also acted in diplomatic roles, notably in Persia.

The Marathas had successfully resisted and eventually overcome the Mughals, but could not do the same to the British. Between 1799 and 1818, Mysore, Nepal, and the Marathas had all been humbled. There were other powerful states that were to fight the British, notably Burma,

Afghanistan, and the Sikhs, but Britain had gained an unassailable position in the imperial stakes.

Reasons for Success

Technological advantages are frequently cited as a reason for Western success. However, given that the role of firepower in that of the Spanish *Conquistadores* in the New World in the early 16th century has been heavily qualified,[39] there is a need to put the British situation in India in context. The weapons they had were more impressive and the firepower they could deploy was far greater than those of the *Conquistadores*. Moreover, Benjamin Robins, a central figure in the developing understanding of ballistics,[40] died in 1751 serving as engineer general and captain of the Madras artillery for the East India Company. Yet, whatever the capability gap, the Indians had plentiful firearms, while those opposed to Britain could acquire expertise and firearms by turning to France. Other factors were relevant to British success, including those of naval support, fiscal capability, and political continuity. Moreover, far from relying on defensive volleys, the emphasis on the attack, including the use of bayonets, corresponded with the Russian operational mode developed by Count Peter Rumyantsev that had been successful against the Turks.

Britain's financial strength helped in the development of the hybrid warmaking that was important to their tactical and operational success, notably of *sepoy* infantry with cavalry and impressive logistics, and also of effective local workers with the Company's finances, thus avoiding the problems of poorly constructed fortresses seen in North America. Cornwallis wrote of the *sepoy* units:

> It is highly expedient and indeed absolutely necessary for the public good that the officers who are destined to serve in those corps should come out at an early period of life, and devote themselves entirely to the Indian service; a perfect knowledge of the language, and a minute attention to the customs and religious prejudices of the *sepoys* being qualifications for that line which cannot be dispensed with … how dangerous a disaffection in our native troops would be to our existence in this country.[41]

Earlier, he had felt less concerned about Tipu 'since I have seen this brigade of *sepoys*. Major Hay's regiment is one of the finest in every respect that I ever saw in any country ... the facility of obtaining good recruits is so great in this country, that we may share almost any numbers of native infantry.'[42]

This indeed served as a basis not only for the expansion of the empire based on expeditions from India but also as a model for activity elsewhere. In 1807, the year after rapidly crushed disturbances among the Madras Army due to the decreasing real value of their pay and the Europeanisation of their dress,[43] Lieutenant-General Urquhart pressed William, Lord Grenville, then the Prime Minister, on the value of hiring native troops, both infantry and cavalry, in all British colonies. He argued that this would save on the dispatch of British soldiers, that the placing of such forces under British officers would accustom them to British discipline, and that these native troops would be able to serve in any part of the world.[44]

Indian rulers tried for the same process of synthesis, but less successfully due to financial, organisational and political factors.[45] The Indian reliance on recruitment via semi-independent figures who, repeatedly, were ready to switch allegiance was a source of weakness. In contrast, the East India Company, while long keen to work within existing Asian frameworks of power,[46] increasingly relied for its army on more direct recruitment and treated officers as a professional body subject to discipline, which, although generally defined by Europeans in their own terms, could be seen as crucial; Dean Mahomet, the son of a *sepoy*, observed in 1772: 'Our men, arranged in military order, fired ... the greater part of them ... giving way to our superior courage and discipline....'[47] George Thomas (c. 1756–1802), an Irish adventurer who served Indian rulers, creating his own principality in 1797–1801, contrasted 'European troops, or Indian troops disciplined and conducted by European officers in which instance they may be considered as a machine actuated and animated by the voice of the commander', with the forces of the Rajah of Jaipur, 'in an irregular army where discipline never obtained.'[48] Such comments risk serious cultural misunderstanding,[49] but any reading of the Maratha

Wars underlines a serious lack of unity among the Marathas that certainly helped the British.

Rather, however, than attributing a lack of unity or order in India simply to some supposed cultural factor, it might be compared with that of the European monarchs opposed to the French Revolutionaries and Napoleon, some of whom proved only too willing to ally with them, or to rest neutral. At any rate, the British forces (understood, throughout, as including the crucial *sepoys*) provided in India a reliance on the attack, whereas, in Europe, the focus was more commonly on the defence. At the same time, there was in truth a mixture of both in most battles, and it was the skill and determination in both that was important to victory.

CHAPTER 7

Fighting in Europe, 1793–1815

When the French cavalry attacked us in our squares (which they did with the most persevering gallantry, never retiring above 100 or 150 paces and charging again) our men behaved as if they were at a field day, firing by ranks and with the best possible aim. Under a most destructive cannonade and having several shells burst in the middle of us, not a man moved from his place ... at the last we became exposed to the united efforts of all their arms and changed from lines to squares and from squares to lines, as the circumstances of the cases required ... There was a moment peculiarly critical and where nothing but the extraordinary steadiness of the troops saved the day.

COLONEL JAMES STANHOPE, 1ST FOOT GUARDS OF WATERLOO.[1]

'By God! I don't think it would have done if I had not been there', Wellington's comment to the diarist Thomas Creevey on 19 June 1815[2] captured an important truth about Waterloo. This indeed was the last major one in Europe to be personally directed by one of the commanders from front-line positions. However, victory at Waterloo was a product not only of his generalship but also of the improvement of the British Army over the previous decade and a half. In contrast, the situation for this army when Napoleon seized power in late 1799 was dire. Defeated on land in the War of American Independence (1775–83), the British Army also had not fared particularly well against Revolutionary France. Indeed, in 1793–5, the army had failed to hold the Low Countries, doing worse than in 1745–8 and also putting in a very different performance to that it was to achieve in 1815.

Years of Peace, 1784–92

The army was weak in part because of the serious blows to morale suffered in the War of American Independence and also due to the poorly handled disbandment of 1783. A low level of peacetime capability had been further manifested in an absence of large-scale manoeuvres and of adequate training. There was nothing equivalent to the annual Prussian manoeuvres. In part, this was in line with the nature of the army as a collection of regiments, but there was also the need to address the unprecedented level of national indebtedness that was a consequence of the American War of Independence.

On 13 June 1783, Colonel Richard Fitzpatrick, the new Secretary at War, presenting the Army Estimates to Parliament, explained the different views on how best to reduce army numbers and advanced his preference for keeping up the number of officers, as they 'required more time' to 'make' than private soldiers:

> Fill up old thin regiments with recruits, and experience had shown, they would much sooner be fit for service, and resist the power of severe climates more effectually, than new regiments composed entirely of raw recruits ... keep up thin regiments with regard to the privates, and as full ones as the circumstances of the times would allow, with regard to the officers.

'Severe climates' was a reference to service in the Caribbean. The Commons was promised by Fitzpatrick the disbanding of 'near 40 regiments' and an annual saving of at least £100,000. The second son of an Earl, Fitzpatrick (1747–1813) had entered the army as an ensign in 1765 and, as captain (and, as an MP), served in North America in 1777–8, including at Brandywine and Germantown, so that he had far more experience for the role than others had done. An ally of Fox, he never fought again, but was Secretary at War in the ministries of 1783 and 1806–7, spoke on military matters in the Commons, for example in the Mutiny Bill in 1786, and rose to be a general in 1803.

The fiscal result of the American War of Revolution was not as serious as in France where it helped cause the politico-governmental crisis leading to revolution. However, in Britain the ministry of William Pitt the Younger that came to power in December 1783, in its determination to tackle the fiscal crisis, spent relatively little on the army. This also owed much to the post-war naval race with France and Spain, and the focus of military expenditure on the Royal Navy owed much to the maritime nature, for Britain, of the crises with France, Spain and Russia in 1787, 1790 and 1791 respectively. In addition, in 1787, during the Dutch Crisis, the emphasis on land was on the hire of nearby foreign troops rather than the use of more distant British Regulars: an agreement to hire Hessian troops was signed and the British government sought also to have Hanoverian troops prepared. The Dutch, Nootka Sound, and Ochakov crises of 1787, 1790 and 1791 respectively, would have had implications for the British Army had they led to war, not least conflict in the West Indies in the first two cases. Nevertheless, the assumptions about conflict in each case focused strongly on the navy.

This situation caused problems when an unprepared Britain went to war in 1793 as, more generally, did the need to increase greatly and rapidly the size of the army and to introduce an effective command and planning structure. The peacetime military system was not up to the challenge of war, and there were no comparisons to the preparations made before entry into the two world wars with Germany, in each of which it also proved necessary to expand the military rapidly. Major-General Charles O'Hara, who had been second-in-command under Cornwallis in 1781, surrendering the latter's sword at Yorktown, complained in 1787 about Gibraltar: 'defenceless works, unserviceable artillery, exhausted stores, weak garrison etc all of which is most true, to a scandalous degree.'[3] It had similarly been in a bad state before the Seven Years' War. When, in 1797, a French expedition approached Fishguard Harbour in Wales, the garrison in the fort there had only three rounds of ammunition each.

Nevertheless, there had been improvements, not least as the immediate pressures of a desperate war ended in 1783, while the Pittite peacetime years were a period of general government reform. As far as the army was concerned, these years saw an increase in the size of the peacetime force and an improvement in the organisation of recruitment. Moreover, the Corps of Engineers was transformed into the Royal Engineers in

1787, and a corps of Royal Military Artificers was created. Tactical conventions were standardised in 1792, army pay appreciably increased in that year, and, in 1793, the Royal Horse Artillery was formed, an important enhancement of the army's mobility and of its battlefield firepower; although Thomas, Lord Pelham, the Home Secretary, criticized the consequences of contracting out services in this case: 'Our ill-judged economy in these matters makes us trust to contracts to supply horses which when called for are never fit for service, kept at grass or in straw yards for the sake of a little saving in their food, and unused to the collar, their shoulders soon gall, they will not draw.' A larger problem was the practice of using civilian drivers to move the guns. The establishment of the Royal Horse Artillery, however, began a practice of the militarisation of both horses and drivers, and it was not long before the Board of Ordnance made similar provision for the foot artillery.[4]

The British were affected by the prestige of the Prussian army which had risen greatly under Frederick II, 'the Great'. William Fawcett, whom we have already encountered in chapter five while serving in the Seven Years' War and will do so again later in this chapter, had translated the regulations for the Prussian infantry into English in 1754 and 1757, and for the cavalry in 1757. From 1764 to 1785, the British kept yearly summaries of the annual Prussian manoeuvres and, in 1782, George III's second son, Frederick, Duke of York, reviewed Prussian garrisons in Westphalia and the troops demonstrated their manoeuvres for him. Cornwallis met Frederick II at the Prussian reviews in 1785, although, in the aftermath of the lessons he had received in America in 1781 about speed and tactical flexibility, he was (correctly) critical of the lack of flexibility in Prussian tactics, a lack that was to hit them hard when fighting the French in the French Revolutionary and Napoleonic wars. Other British officers attended Prussian reviews and visited the sites of Frederick's victories.[5]

The drill manual, and therefore tactics, adopted by Britain in 1792 drew on those by the Prussian Inspector-General and were based on Colonel David Dundas' *Principles of military movements chiefly applied to infantry, illustrated by manoeuvres of the Prussian troops, and by an outline of the British campaigns in Germany* (1788), in short on the experience of Continental European warfare. Nicknamed 'old pivot', Dundas (1735–1820) focused on manoeuvre in formation as the best way to link firepower and mobility, but the system he recommended lacked flexibility and was particularly inappropriate in the face of a rapidly moving and innovative opponent, which was to be the situation in the French Revolutionary Wars.

Dundas understood the need for a unifying doctrine in order to cope with the consequences of variations between the regiments, and such a unification was necessary if regiments were to be able to cooperate. However, this tactical system represented a deliberate rejection of the more flexible tactics of the American War of Independence, and, indeed, Dundas, who was to be commander in chief in 1809–11, belonged to what was termed the 'German' rather than the 'American' school of officership. He had fought at the major Westphalian battles of 1760–1 and had attended Frederick II's 1784 manoeuvres. Dundas placed the organised firepower of the close-order line at the centre of military practice, claiming that such a line could resist cavalry in open country, which was indeed the case, but was much less concerned with light infantry, believing that interest in it had led to a decline in the close-order line. Dundas had issued a call to arms in the *Principles*:

> In order to facilitate the movements of great armies, and to enforce their discipline, it is necessary to organise, divide, subdivide them; to establish such general regulations as may prevent the repetition of a tedious but essential detail at times when action and exertion are required and particularly; to ascertain the duties and attentions of individuals in every situation of march; so that the most concise order may suffice to put the army in motion; and to place it at all times ready to execute with exactness and alacrity such intentions of its commander as may arise from the circumstances of the moment.

Dundas also praised past instructions under which he claimed troops had moved 'as parts of one and the same great machine.'[6] In practice, he knew nothing of Frederick's consideration of new, more flexible tactical ideas in 1768, in particular an advance in open order,[7] a technique British line regiments had acquired during the War of American Independence. Dundas, moreover, did not consider the many failings of the Prussian army in the War of the Bavarian Succession (1778–9), when Frederick failed to defeat Austria.

It is instructive that commanders such as Moore and Wellesley (the future Wellington) were critical of the army in the 1790s, and the campaigns of that decade certainly revealed serious deficiencies in it. Commanding the 33rd Regiment in the Low Countries in 1794–5, Lieutenant-Colonel Arthur Wellesley learned 'what not to do'.[8]

The Low Countries, 1793–9

When the British troops arrived in the Low Countries in 1793, the war had already begun a year earlier, and the French fought alone against a coalition including, from 1793, Austria, Prussia, the Dutch and Spain. With German auxiliaries, 17,000 of whom were hired in 1793, playing a major role in it, the British Army in the Low Countries rose to 37,500 troops by late 1794. This army was commanded by Frederick, Duke of York, who would have been available to command at Waterloo had he not made such a hash of previous commands in the field. In 1815, his first cousin, the Duke of Brunswick, died at Quatre Bras, while William, Prince of Orange, then a general in the British Army, was wounded at Waterloo.

The 1793 campaign is instructive for the light it throws on Waterloo. First and foremost, the value to Wellington of Prussian support in 1815 is readily apparent, because York found himself confronting the problems of cooperating with Allied forces operating to very different agendas. He also suffered in 1793 from the problems of launching an offensive in the face of an undefeated French army, a task that Wellington was spared by Napoleon's decision to attack.

The French army was large thanks to the *levee en masse*, had acquired confidence from success in late 1792 at the expense of Austria and Prussia, conquering Belgium rapidly in November, and successfully combined attacking columns and covering skirmishers. Traditional close-order linear formations were vulnerable to French soldiers in their open order, and also to the French artillery which had become very impressive as a result of reforms from mid-century.[9] In contrast, the relative British neglect of light troops at this stage served them ill. The deadly impact of French artillery was felt by the British from 1793, for example:

> The [Coldstream] Guards marched in excellent order through the wood keeping as good a line as their situation would permit ... the masked [hidden] battery of the French (of which the Guards were completely ignorant) commenced the heaviest firing of grape shot ... within 30 yards.... The second discharge of the French knocked down whole ranks ... as the Prussians observed, what business had the Guards in the wood when it was only the duty of light infantry and riflemen.[10]

Having helped the Austrians capture Valenciennes on 28 July 1793, York, assisted by Hanoverian and Dutch forces, was ordered to besiege the fortified port of Dunkirk, a potent symbol of Anglo-French hostility. This decision was a mistake as, by abandoning the possibility of an Allied concentration of strength and, instead, dividing from the Austrians in order to mount a siege, the British became a more tempting target for French attack. The focus on Dunkirk spoke to British concern in 1815 during the Waterloo campaign about the security of Ostend and the communication, supply (and retreat) routes to Britain. The siege of Dunkirk, however, was delayed by a lack of siege artillery, a problem that had also affected British operations in Belgium in 1744, and, in 1793, after two days of fighting, a large relieving French army pushed back the less numerous British at Hondschoote (6–7 September), obliging York to abandon the siege.

In 1794, the strength of British and Austrian forces in attack was indicated in engagements at Villers-en-Cauchies and Beaumont. In the latter, cavalry attacks on the French flanks defeated advancing columns with heavy casualties. British success culminated at Willems on 10 May: the French cavalry was swept aside and their infantry broken; repeated cavalry attacks supported by infantry and cannon broke a French square. However, on 17–18 May, in the battle of Tourcoing near Tournai, a major clash, the French under Charles Pichegru used their local numerical superiority to defeat British and Austrian forces, driving them from the field. In contrast to Prussian conduct at Waterloo, York's army was given inadequate support by its ally, and the British were forced to stage a fighting retreat.

In an anticipation of a might-have-been arising from a different result at Waterloo in 1815, York, thereafter, retreated, pushed back by stronger French forces, while the Austrians increasingly focused on their ambitions in Poland. Falling back, York, increasingly deprived of Austrian and Prussian support, abandoned Belgium and after failing to hold Nijmegen, the British, now under Lieutenant-General Sir William Harcourt, fell back through the Netherlands during a hard winter. Harcourt was a veteran of the siege of Havana and the American War of Independence. The French were able to benefit from their opponents' retreat by driving them in different directions, the Austrians east and the British north, thus prefiguring what they hoped to do to the British and Prussians in 1815. The British fought well when they engaged in 1794–5, but they were outnumbered and had lost the initiative. Their medical, transport and supply systems proved inadequate, and, in April 1795, after a long retreat through the Netherlands, the remaining British troops were evacuated from Bremen in Germany.

Thereafter, there were a series of unsuccessful British expeditions to the European continent, including one under York to Holland in 1799 which is commemorated in a nursery rhyme about the 'Grand Old Duke of York':

> He had ten thousand men,
> He marched them up the hill,
> And then he marched them down again!

In this expedition, an Anglo-Russian army landed on 27 August, and was initially successful, notably in gaining control of Dutch warships, a key goal. However, the exploitation proved slow and inadequate, which gave the defenders opportunities to prepare, not least with inundations in a landscape that was already difficult. The Allies then used column advances, but found them difficult to coordinate. Moreover, there was not the enthusiastic Dutch popular support that had been envisaged, and Allied numbers were hit by sickness. The last major clash, the battle of Castricum on 6 October, saw the Allies fail to break through and suffer heavier losses, which led to an Allied retreat, including the abandonment of the field hospitals of the British wounded. Concerned about supplies,

York signed the Convention of Alkmaar on 17 October under which the Allies were able to leave.

From 1793 there had been a far broader engagement with conflict in Europe than in the recent wars, which reflected the more limited character of the American War of Independence and even the Seven Years' War, but also the extent of French success and the range of resulting commitments. In 1793–1815, unlike in the War of American Independence, or indeed the War of 1812 (i.e. 1812 to 1815) with the United States, Britain was pledged to an alliance strategy, a strategy that made possible, necessary and sense of, the commitment of key British forces to the Continent. Waterloo was the culmination of this strategy. Moreover, as on the pattern of other forces, there was a substantial learning curve, from major failures in 1794–6 to repeated successes in 1812–15.

British forces were not alone in the 1790s in falling victim to the tactics, numbers and enthusiasm of the Revolutionary French. The armies of Britain's allies were also defeated in what became a general crisis of an entire politico-military system. The formidable challenge posed by the French in part arose from the size of their army, notably due to the conscription introduced in 1793, but also from the novelty of their military methods, particularly attack in column. For the British, there were tactical, command, logistical and institutional issues. In Parliament, in 1797, opposition spokesman (and playwright) Richard Brinsley Sheridan mocked governmental assurances about the ease with which the French would be destroyed: 'I will not remind those gentlemen of their declaration so often made, that the French must fly before troops well disciplined and regularly paid. We have fatal experience of the folly of those declarations; we have seen soldiers frequently without pay, and without sufficient provisions, put to rout the best paid armies in Europe.'[11]

York and Reform

The pace of reform greatly accelerated during the war, as serious deficiencies were highlighted by repeated failure. The rise of the War Office, under the Secretary at War, from 1783, especially from 1809 to 1828 under Henry, 3rd Viscount Palmerston, a Junior Lord of the Admiralty from 1807 to 1809 (and later Prime Minister), and, above him, under the Secretary of State for War from 1794 provided a larger and more effective bureaucracy for the conduct of overseas operations. The Secretary of State for War had a lot of power over operational planning, but the Army commander in chief, situated in the Horse Guards, administered personnel.[12] This process of administrative reform was taken further from 1806 with the appearance of the first of a number of reports by the newly established Commission of Military Enquiry.

Much improvement was due to the efforts of York, who became commander in chief in 1795 and was a more effective administrator than he was a field commander. In the face of defeat, the army needed to be revived, and York took particular care to raise the quality of the officers. He faced a formidable challenge. Britain was up against a strong opponent, and it was necessary both to manage the major expansion in army strength that had begun in 1793 and to cope with the consequences of defeat. York's changes can be seen as part of a period of national reform, one that included the introduction of income tax (1799), parliamentary union with Ireland (1800–1), and the first national census (1801). York was unsuccessful in ending absenteeism among officers, and could not abolish the practice of purchasing commissions (officerships); indeed, Pelham pointed out in 1801 that 'regiments have been raised by persons having real or supposed influence in the counties they resided in; rank has been given as the price of recruits.'[13] Nevertheless, York made this practice less deleterious, both by raising the number of free commissions and by establishing minimum periods of military service as a condition for promotion.

The appointment from 1795 of a Military Secretary to the commander in chief was designed to encourage bureaucratic procedures, especially with regard to appointment and promotions. Also, in 1797, the army first appointed paymasters with an army rank, replacing the former reliance on civilian agents. Colonel Robert Brownrigg (1795–1803) was followed as Military Secretary by Colonel William Clinton (1803–4), Lieutenant-Colonel James Gordon (1804–9), and Major-General Sir Henry Torrens (1809–20). Brownrigg went on to be Quartermaster-General to the Forces (1803–11). Clinton had served under York in the Low Countries and become his aide-de-camp. After being Military Secretary, he was Quartermaster-General in Ireland, and a divisional commander in Spain in 1812–13. Gordon, who had served under Clinton, went on to be Commissary-in-Chief to the Forces from 1809 and Quartermaster-General from 1811 to 1851, a period that reflected the continuity in office that was commonplace in this period. Torrens served in Holland under York in 1799, and had been Wellesley's military secretary in Portugal. Thus, a nexus of administrative experience was developing, one centred on York, and a counterpoint to that of campaign experience to be gained by those who served under Wellington, who commanded the British field army longest in an individual sphere in Europe in this period. Continuity helped provide the basis for a system in which professionalism became more apparent.

York encouraged schemes for military education, especially those of Lieutenant-Colonel John Le Marchant for a military college that would both train cadets and also staff officers. The former was opened in 1802 at Marlow, with Sir William Harcourt as first Governor, and developed into the Royal Military College at Sandhurst; and the second, which opened in 1799 at High Wycombe, developed into the Army Staff College. York was also a supporter of the standardisation of drill, and, in 1796, Sir William Fawcett, who was Adjutant-General to the Forces from 1781 to 1799, published *Instructions and Regulations for the Formations and Movements of the Cavalry*. In its focus on the charge, and its assumption that all cavalry should operate similarly, this, however, underplayed both the need for a range of tasks and the particular value of light cavalry. In the Peninsular War, it proved necessary to adapt doctrine, even ignore it, and to develop through experience the skill of younger officers, using them to replace their seniors.[14]

Consistency was a standard theme in York's policies, and this emphasis on consistency helped to turn a collection of regiments into an army, a development from which Wellington was to benefit greatly in so far as his British units were concerned. Consistency aided the transfer of officers, troops and equipment between units, and improved tactical and operational flexibility; but there was little improvement in some areas of training, such as bayonet training, where a system for the whole army was not introduced until 1857. While presiding over a significant increase in the size of the army, from 40,000 men in 1793 to about 163,000 in 1800, 200,000 in 1809, and over 250,000 in 1813, York also addressed the conditions of the ordinary soldiers, including chaplaincy services,[15] food, accommodation (by means of barracks building), medical care, punishment regimes, and the provision of greatcoats to keep out the cold. In 1793, women had played a key role in prompting and responding to a newspaper appeal for flannel waistcoats and other clothes for British troops in the Low Countries. York also moved in 1800 to get rid of the queue, a form of pigtail used by many British soldiers.

York was a supporter of the cause of light infantry, one associated in particular with Colonel John Moore (1761–1809), a veteran of the War of Independence and of campaigning during the French Revolutionary and Napoleonic Wars in Corsica, St. Lucia, Ireland, and Egypt, who, in 1803, was appointed commander of a new brigade at Shorncliffe Camp in Kent, which was designed to serve as the basis of a permanent light infantry force. Moore had been much impressed by the system of training and manoeuvring light infantry developed by Major Kenneth Mackenzie the previous decade. Particular emphasis was placed upon marksmanship, which was aided by the use from 1800 of the Baker Rifle, a flintlock produced by Ezekiel Baker. Colonel Charles Manningham and Lieutenant-Colonel William Stewart were key figures in developing the Experimental Corps of Riflemen, established in 1800, later the 95th Rifles (1802) and then the Rifle Brigade.

Moore's force was to become the Light Brigade and, subsequently, the Light Division. His career showed the possibility of rapid promotion for the talented son of a Scottish doctor, just as Dundas had been the son of a Scottish merchant. As a lieutenant-general, he was killed at the battle of Corunna on 16 January 1809 while managing, in the face of stronger French forces, the successful evacuation of a force he had led into Spain in a failed attempt to thwart the French conquest of the country. The risk of conflict, both of combat and disease, lessened the availability of talent, and Wellington's career was eased by the death of alternatives, notably Ralph Abercromby (1801, Egypt) and Moore, who were killed in conflict, and Sir Gerald Lake who died in 1809 as a result of sickness.

In turn, Wellington exposed himself to considerable personal danger, notably at Argaum in 1803, but also at Waterloo. Major-General Isaac Brock was killed in action at Queenston Heights in 1812.

Dundas, then General Officer Commanding Northern District, in which role he thwarted a keelmen's strike on Tyneside in 1807, succeeded York, under whom he had served in the Low Countries in 1794–5 and in the 1799 Dutch campaign, his last campaign position, as commander in chief when the latter felt obliged to resign in 1809 after a former mistress, Mary Anne Clarke, testified before the House of Commons that she had sold commissions with York's knowledge, but York returned to his position as commander in chief in 1811, holding the post until he died in 1827. He did not seek operational command, although, born in 1763, he was still relatively young. This decision was important to the Waterloo campaign. Unlike the Dutch at Waterloo, who expected the lacklustre William Prince of Orange, the heir to the throne, to play the key role, both the British and the Prussians relied then on meritocratic choices for command. Although he did not take a battlefield role in Waterloo, York deserves some of the praise for the state and success of the British Army then, and is appropriately celebrated with a commanding statue in Waterloo Place in London completed in 1834. Earlier, in July 1815, he received the thanks of Parliament for his care of the army.

At the same time, York was successful due to governmental support as well as that of an officer corps that was interested in thinking about war as well as learning it on the job. Wellington was not the only up-and-coming officer who read widely on military matters and was part of in effect a British branch of the Military Enlightenment.[16]

The Home Front

Alongside the development of the Regulars, there was a major attempt to supplement strength by raising militia and volunteer units, the Fencibles. These underlined the need for the state to cooperate with local interests in obtaining resources, an aspect of the longstanding balance between the Crown and local interests. Militia colonels regarded their regiments as patronage fiefs, immensely valuable to them as county magnates and public men for both patronage and prestige. As a result, important changes in the militia laws had to be negotiated with the colonels, and even the practice of regular drafts into the army was carefully conducted to protect their interests. Military service by both the militia and the volunteers raised from 1794 under the Volunteer Act was conditional, being dependant on the enabling legislation. The number of militia rose to over 100,000 in the mid-1790s, and volunteer numbers were comparable or greater, rising to over 300,000 at the end of 1803.[17] George III's reviews of the volunteers, including on his seaside trips to Weymouth, helped associate him with the war effort. Before large numbers of spectators, he also reviewed volunteers in Hyde Park on his birthday in 1799 and 1800.

There were calls for a vigorous response to any invasion. In August 1792, prior to Britain entering the war, William, Lord Auckland, a senior diplomat, pressed that war not be conducted:

> ... with the courtesies of the age ... the French troops, however despicable they may be in point of discipline and command, are earnest in the support of the wicked and calamitous cause in which they are engaged ... I sincerely hope that it may be a plan rigorously observed, to disarm every place and district through which the troops may pass, to destroy the arms, to dismantle the fortresses, to demolish the cannon, powder mills etc, and all forges for arms etc, and to issue a notice that any place or district found a second time in arms shall be subject to military execution ... if neglected, there is reason to believe that the impression of the interference will at best be transitory.[18]

In turn, in 1796, Henry Dundas, Secretary of State for War from 1794 to 1801, produced a memorandum outlining the total war envisaged if the French invaded,

> When an enemy lands, all the difficulties of civil government and the restraint of forms cease; every thing must give way to the supplying and strengthening the army, repelling the enemy ... The strongest and most effectual measures are necessary ... The great object must be constantly to harass, alarm and fire on an enemy, and to impede his progress till a sufficient force assembles to attack him ... every inch of ground, every field may to a degree be disputed, even by inferior number ... The country must be driven, and every thing useful within his reach destroyed without mercy.[19]

This anticipated Winston Churchill's language in 1940 when German invasion threatened. Thomas, Lord Pelham, Home Secretary from 1801 to 1803, was also interested in popular mobilisation.[20]

There was, moreover, a process of building, with the construction, from 1792, of barracks to house the expanded forces (in place of the traditional reliance in England on billeting them in inns); as well as of fortifications to resist invasion. These included 103 Martello Towers along the south coast of England, from Seaford, Sussex to Aldeburgh in Suffolk, three in Scotland, and several in Wales built from 1804 under the influence of the impressive defence of the Torra di Mortella on Corsica against British forces in 1794; as well as the mighty Berry Head fortifications constructed to the east of Brixham between 1794 and 1804, the impressive Western Defences above Dover and the Royal Military Canal across Romney marshes.[21] The defensive lines around Plymouth Dock were reconstructed in 1801–16. Although intended as force-multipliers, these defences required significant numbers of troops and cannon, which lessened those available for deployment abroad or for a mobile reserve at home. This also underlined the significance of naval deterrence against invasion for that deployment.

Expeditionary Warfare

The army York was struggling to improve was sent on a series of operations on the Continent, as the British attempted to complement their, generally more successful, attacks on the colonies of France and her allies, by playing their part in coalitions against France by weakening its grip in Europe. Many operations, notably Holland, 1799; Ferrol, 1800; Spain, 1808–9; Walcheren, 1809; and Antwerp, 1814, were failures, with large numbers of troops dying of disease at Walcheren; but there were also valuable successes, particularly in Egypt in 1801, which is covered in the next chapter. A force landing in southern Italy in 1806 defeated an attacking French opponent at Maida thanks to superior firepower,[22] although the British were not able to exploit the victory and returned to Sicily, which they were protecting from French attack The following year, an expedition to

Copenhagen involving a large fleet and 25,000 troops, led to the defeat of a small outnumbered Danish militia force at Koge, the bombardment of Copenhagen, and the enforced handing over of the Danish fleet. This was a major success in the important process by which Britain thwarted the naval consequences of France's ability to extend its alliance system.

The Peninsular War

The key operation was the dispatch of troops to Portugal in 1808, which began Britain's participation in the Peninsular War, in which Portugal resisted French invasion while an uprising challenged Napoleon's attempt to place his brother Joseph on the throne of Spain. This commitment gave Britain an opportunity to contest French power on land.[23] This war made the name of Arthur Wellesley, later Duke of Wellington. Born in 1769, the same year as Napoleon, he was the fourth son of the Anglo-Irish Earl of Mornington. Entering the army in 1787, he purchased a commission as major as well as being promoted to lieutenant-colonel, both in 1793. Wellesley had first seen action in 1794 in the defence of the Netherlands against the French advance, and took part in the subsequent winter retreat. His rapid rise to positions of command made him accustomed to taking responsibility and making decisions. In October 1795, Wellesley's regiment embarked for the West Indies, only to be driven back by storms.

Wellesley's regiment, instead, went to India, arriving in Calcutta in February 1797, and his reputation was to be made there. Wellesley took part in the Mysore campaign of 1799 in southern India, and fought the Marathas in 1803–4 in western India, winning the very hard-fought battles of Assaye and Argaum in 1803, each of which was more difficult in some respects than Waterloo. He returned to Britain 1805. Having taken part in the Danish expedition of 1807, winning at Koge, Wellesley was promoted lieutenant-general in 1808. An MP also from 1806, the well-connected Wellesley was appointed Chief Secretary in Ireland in 1807. The following June, he expressed his confidence about taking on the French, 'first, because I am not afraid of them, as everyone else seems to be; and, secondly, because (if all I hear about their system is true) I think it a false one against steady troops. I suspect all the Continental armies are half-beaten before the battle begins. I at least will not be frightened beforehand'.[24]

In a series of battles in Portugal and Spain (Iberia, the Peninsula), in what proved a long and costly struggle, the British showed that they could repeatedly defeat the French in the open. The disciplined firepower of the British infantry played a major part in Wellington's victories, of which the most important were Vimeiro (1808), Talavera (1809), Busaco (1810), Salamanca (1812), Vitoria (1813) and Toulouse (1814). The French, conversely, suffered from sometimes indifferent command in the Peninsular War, as well as the frequent unwillingness of their generals to cooperate with one another, and Napoleon's inappropriate interference. The French also had generally inadequate battlefield tactics, relying on crude attacks in dense columns which provided easy tactics for the British, as at Vimeiro, Talavera and Busaco, although at Albuera (1811) where the army was under General William Bereford, in part due to command mistakes, the situation proved far less happy for the British.

Wellington was very active in counter-attacks, and the well-timed bayonet charge, launched when the French were disorganised by their approach march and by British fire, was as effective as the volley. Medical records on casualties, and other sources, suggest that the bayonet was essentially a psychological weapon in most Napoleonic engagements. Firepower caused more casualties and was therefore crucial to the decision of the battle. However, the bayonet charge permitted exploitation of the advantage. Such a charge, preceded by a volley, had become a standard British tactic from the late 1750s, used with effect in the War of American Independence, and, with his fine grasp of timing and eye for terrain, Wellington brought the system to a high pitch of effectiveness, notably perfecting keeping the force on the reverse slope of a hill to nullify French artillery fire until the precise moment they deployed into line for the volley and the bayonet attack.[25] The attack was the key to the British victories in the later stages of the war, most notably at Salamanca, Vitoria and Toulouse.

Casualties, however, could be heavy: more than a quarter of the British force at Talavera, and 40 per cent of those at Albuera in 1811 when, in particular, a British brigade was caught unprepared by a cavalry attack on their flank. Only the regiment able to form squares saved itself. The British also lost heavily during the battle to French cannon and infantry fire. Wellington, who was not in command there, commented that another such battle would ruin his army.

At Vimeiro on 21 August 1808, in contrast, the superior firepower of his army and his flexible generalship, not least in manoeuvring attempts to outflank his position, defeated attacking French forces under General Junot, the newly appointed French Governor-General of Portugal. As at Waterloo, Wellesley sheltered his lines of infantry from the French cannon by deploying them behind the crest of the ridge. He placed his riflemen in open order down the slope and used them to prevent the French skirmishers, who advanced before the columns, from disrupting the British lines. Then the advancing French columns were halted by British infantry and cannon fire, before being driven back by downhill charges. The French attacks were poorly coordinated and, having beaten them, Wellesley was on the point of ordering a general attack when he was overruled by a more senior general.

On 27 and 28 July 1809, the French under Marshal Victor attacked the Anglo-Spanish army at Talavera, concentrating their attack on the outnumbered British. Wellesley again employed his infantry firepower to repulse the French columns, but the pursuit of the retreating French threw the British into confusion and fresh French units drove them back. The final French attack on the centre of the Allied line was only just held, with Wellesley committing his reserve, the key element in so many battles of the period, but held it was, although the British suffered 5,400 casualties; more than a quarter of the force.

On 27 September 1810, at Busaco, Wellesley, by now Viscount Wellington, resisted the advancing French under Marshal Masséna in a good defensive position. The French found the British drawn up on a ridge, which denied the French the use of their artillery and cavalry, and their poorly planned attacks were repulsed with nearly 5,000 casualties.[26] Nevertheless, unable to stop Masséna's advance, Wellington fell back to the prepared defensive lines at Torres Vedras, which stretched from the Atlantic to the Tagus and saw off what in effect was a large-scale French siege of Lisbon.

On 22 July 1812, Marshal Marmont was defeated at Salamanca. His strung-out disposition allowed Wellington to defeat the French divisions in detail. Noting that the French were over-extended, Wellington rapidly and effectively switched from defence to attack, and ably combined his infantry and cavalry in the destruction of three French divisions, one of which was ridden down by the cavalry.[27]

The following year, at Vitoria (21 June), Wellington, now also *Generalissimo* of the Spanish armies, again took the offensive, inflicting, in a confused mixture of a number of engagements that proved difficult to bring to the planned-for execution, a serious defeat and 8,000 casualties on the French, for which he was rewarded by being made a field marshal. Beethoven composed 'Wellington's Victory' as a celebration.

The victory enabled Wellington to besiege and capture San Sebastian and Pamplona, both formidable positions. The former fell on 31 August 1813 only after a difficult siege in which the attackers lost heavily in two assaults.[28] Defensive fortifications indeed, posed a challenge to British operations. That year, explaining the weakness of his position on Spain's Mediterranean coast, Lieutenant-General John Murray wrote: 'The French General [Suchet] possessed in every direction fortresses around me to cover his army if defeated, to furnish his supplies, or to retire to if he wished to avoid an action for the purposes of bringing up more troops.'[29] On 8 March 1814, in the Low Countries, the British fought their way into Bergen-op-Zoom, but the fighting then turned against them, the columns that were in the town received insufficient support, and were driven out with 2,100 casualties.

The disciplined firepower of the British infantry played a major part in Wellington's victories. Most British infantry continued to be armed with smooth-bore muskets, because rifled ones (rifles) were expensive and difficult to produce, required special ammunition, and, though more accurate, were much slower to load and fire than smooth bores.

The risk of rust necessitated browning the flintlock muskets with an anti-rusting solvent, which led to them being termed the 'Brown Bess.'

British firepower was more effective than that of the French. Tests carried out by the Prussian general Gerhard von Scharnhorst in 1813 suggested that, whereas French and Prussian flintlocks were more effective at 100 yards, their British counterparts were better at a greater distance and, therefore, more appropriate for engaging French columns at a distance. Furthermore, the large bore of the Brown Bess meant that it could take all calibres of musket ammunition, while the loose fit of the ball helped make ramming it down the barrel easy, and thus contributed to the rate of fire. However, the loose ball would have meant that accuracy was lost with distance.

This firepower was not necessarily immobile, but, rather, often used as a prelude to a bayonet charge. In doing so, Wellington ably executed fire and movement tactics, achieving a success the French were not to display at Waterloo. The British succeeded in the Peninsula in balancing the well-drilled line, that represented the legacy of Frederick the Great of Prussia, and the extensive use of light infantry in battle, and, thereby, the conservatism of an emphasis on linear firepower formations with a greater role for manoeuvrability.[30] The 95th Regiment of Foot armed with 1806 Pattern Baker rifles were important to British success, but the other regiments in the celebrated Light Division were equipped with the Brown Bess.

Wellington was always heavily outnumbered by the French in the Peninsula in both cavalry and artillery, but his troops were among the best in the British Army, a contrast to the situation among his opponents, and a margin of advantage that did not pertain at Waterloo. The British cavalry was to be heavily criticised for its conduct during the Peninsular War, but, aside from the serious problems in maintaining cavalry effectiveness and controlling the tempo of cavalry attacks, there was improvement in this cavalry during the war. This improvement was more generally significant for the army as a whole, and is also instructive in the assessment of British fighting effectiveness in some other wars, notably the two world wars.

Aside from benefiting from good operational intelligence on French moves,[31] Wellington was, as he was again to display at Waterloo, a fine judge of terrain. Moreover, he was adept at controlling a battle as it developed. At Vimeiro, the well-positioned British line succeeded in blunting the attacking French columns, while, at Salamanca, Wellington used his lines in attack with great effect. There was not, however, to be an opportunity for such action at Waterloo until the closing stage of the battle.

Battles have to be set in the context of opposing moves and the operational dimension. In the Peninsula, and again reflecting a deterioration that was to be seen at Waterloo, the French employed inadequate battlefield tactics. In place of *l'ordre mixte*, the interplay of lines, columns and skirmishers that had proved so effective in the 1790s, especially in weakening lines of opposing infantry, the French relied on crude attacks in dense columns. Thus, the firepower of the British lines was not compromised, and the French themselves provided an easy target for the British.

The decline in the quality of the French army, due to near-continual campaigning, affected its tactical sophistication, not to mention its morale. Success in battle had greatly turned on the exploitation of the synergy that had been created between cavalry, close-order infantry, artillery and skirmishers. A combination of attacks by different French arms reduced both the enemy's physical means to resist – by silencing his guns with counter-battery or skirmisher fire, by neutralising his command and control by picking off officers, or by using cavalry, especially to force infantry from lines into defensive squares, thereby cutting their frontage and, thus, firepower – and chipped away at his will to resist. The French, however, experienced great difficulty in Spain in trying to achieve this synergy and to execute these tactics. Problems with the terrain frequently precluded the efficacious use of their often superior cavalry and artillery. Partly as a result, attacks were often executed sequentially by the French, rather than simultaneously, and by one arm, usually the infantry. Much the same happened at Waterloo, although with fewer excuses for Napoleon.

Any French failure to weaken the British lines, by the use of artillery or skirmishers, before the column attack, was especially serious. This failure owed much to Wellington's reverse-slope ploy: his policy of locating his troops behind the crest of hills in order to protect them from artillery and move them unseen to critical parts of the field, which was important, for example, at Busaco and Waterloo. Because of this British deployment and, more generally, the breakdown of their 'system' in engagements with British troops, French infantry columns were too often left exposed to fire from intact, unshaken lines, and with neither the time nor the space to redeploy, a situation that recurred at Waterloo. The French therefore either had to run for it or to try to bludgeon their way through. The latter, however, was often more than flesh and blood could achieve. A bayonet charge against an adversary who stayed ordered and calm, pulling the trigger and throwing up a hail of lead, was generally ineffective, and the French were in a difficult position because this was frequently the situation they faced. Repeatedly, the French advanced and, having taken casualties, retreated, while the British stayed firm.

As a reminder, however, of the operational context of tactical achievement, Wellesley had, after Talavera, to retreat in the face of fresh, larger French forces under the talented Marshal Soult who advanced on his lines of communication. Napoleon's strategy in 1815 did not lead him to seek to do the same: he wanted battle, and not to out-manoeuvre Wellington into retreating. Yet, Wellington's concern about such a move led him to deploy a large force to prevent such an advance past his right flank at Waterloo.

He also expanded his opportunities by his development of logistical capability. Like Marlborough, Wellington employed a magazine system, as opposed to the process of requisition pursued by the French. Nevertheless, Wellington's system relied on support from the host nation, whether Portugal or Spain, as well as a Commissariat that worked for the benefit of the men, and not for the system or themselves. This required Wellington to be able to hold the Commissariat's feet to the fire, which was called 'tracing the biscuit',[32] a reference to the 'hard tack' eaten by the troops.

A persistent problem, more serious than that of personalities, was provided by the convoluted command and administrative system of the army, a system that evolved in the 18th century as a means to prevent the army from overextending itself in politics. The Commissariat came under the Treasury and the Commissary-General, and the latter's large host of deputies and assistants were inevitably under pressure from Whitehall. Wellington did not seek to circumvent this, but he made it clear that what he ordered was what he required. He sacked a few Commissariat generals, and other close personal staff, before getting the men he wanted. By 1812, his shortage of money was a serious problem: the troops had not been paid for five months. When campaigning abroad, it was necessary to pay troops and foreign suppliers in British bullion, the reserves of which fell rapidly. As a result, going off the gold standard was, like the introduction of income tax, a key element in the strengthening of the logistical context and in the strategic dimension to logistics. Due to the length of the commitment, the government faced particular difficulties in meeting Wellington's insistent and strident demands for funds,[33] but his ability to deliver victories helped ensure more resources from London, as did the development of a good working relationship with Robert, 2nd Earl of Liverpool, the Secretary of State for War and the Colonies from November 1809 to June 1812.[34]

Logistical difficulties were eased when distance was lessened. Thus, military success in northern Spain in 1813 enabled the British to use the harbours there, and thereby to shorten the lines of communication that had hitherto been via Lisbon, although there were still problems in developing an effective supply system. For Britain, as for other powers, distance was always easier to overcome when the army was able to operate with naval support. On expeditions, troops carried their supplies with them in store ships, which provided mobility, as with the supplies for 40,000 men for eight months carried by the fleet taking a large expedition to the West Indies in 1795[35] (although the ships did not carry the wagons and draught animals that helped mobility on land). When the British landed in Egypt in 1801 they 'expected no supply from the country ... we have hitherto got water – everything else is landed from the ships.'[36] Wellington repeatedly urged other commanders in Iberia that:

> I recommend to your attention my first campaign in Portugal. I kept the sea always on my flank; the transports attended the movements of the army as a magazine; and I had at all times, and every day, a short and easy communication with them. The army, therefore, could never be distressed for provisions and stores, however limited its means of land transport; and in case of necessity it might have embarked at any point of the coast.[37]

In 1813, Wellington added, 'If anyone wishes to know the history of this war, I will tell them that it is our maritime superiority gives me the power of maintaining my army while the enemy is unable to do so.'[38] This was the thesis and practice of an expeditionary, joint-warfare, operational and strategic culture.

The operational side of logistics attracts most attention, but the strategic dimension was, as in war as a whole, the most significant. The British were unique both because they had money and because their operations required naval support, these factors ensuring very different strategic parameters to those of other powers. If these parameters might seem a long way from commissariat wagoners urging unwilling oxen forward, there was in practice an important linkage, which was important to the need to respond in theatre. The difficulties facing the commissary general were accentuated by the lack of a collective experience. The British Army had encountered major logistical difficulties in Iberia in 1703–13 and 1762, but, by 1808, when new forces were sent, there was no relevant experience. Instead, the experience of operating in the Low Countries in 1793–6 and 1799 had been very different. In part, Iberia posed issues of limited supplies, a harsh environment and a poor road system that were very different to those in the Low Countries, as with the complaints of the garrison commander at Almeida in Portugal in 1808–9: shortages of food, clothing and shoes led British troops to pillage, and the Spanish authorities frequently did not provide the promised supplies.[39] Nevertheless, in part, whatever the area, relations with allies were a similar problem. Some issues faced were also seen in operations in British territories, notably North America in 1754–60, 1775–83, and 1812–15, and Ireland in 1798; in Iberia though, language proved an additional burden, while the poverty of the region put a more acute pressure on food supplies. A key aspect of poverty was the weakness of the communications network.

There was not, however, the problem of operating in hostile territory, until Wellington moved into France, advancing to Toulouse in 1814. Even then, there was concern not to offend local sensitivities, for the British were the allies of the Bourbon cause, committed to a Bourbon restoration, and reliant on local acceptance to move from military output, in the shape of victory, to political outcome in the shape of compliance. This situation was very much linked to the politics of logistics, which took the shape of not angering local opinion.

In contrast, French requisitioning, which so often meant looting, compromised support for client regimes, notably that of Joseph I in Spain, and thus posed a major additional military burden in the shape of the counter-insurgency overlap of obtaining supplies: Spanish guerrilla and regular operations hit French logistics, not least by resisting French requisition parties, notably in the *Montaña* of Navarre. The British were harsh in their treatment of looters, with summary hanging and flogging, both carried out in front of the unit in question in order to drive home the point, and this exemplary punishment was an aspect of the disciplinary system as well as of the 'hearts and minds' dynamic of campaigning. Both aspects were part of the background to successful deployment for battle.

Order and organisation were necessarily a key part not just to effectiveness but also to existence. Operating at a distance in poor foreign countries, and in the face of a powerful opponent, Wellington needed to know that his forces would be able to respond to instructions to move and fight. Wellington used his general orders to that end, and also to ensure predictability and discipline.[40] Once arrived in Lisbon, units were expected to acclimatise and were equipped to march, which involved the issue of camp kettles, medicine chests, entrenching tools, blankets, and tents, and firepower in the shape of 60 rounds of ball cartridge to add to the flintlock and flints. Frequent kit inspections were necessary. The regular marching pace was two and a half miles per hour, but doing so, with the loads carried and in the hot sun, required endurance and fitness.

More generally, the army was held together by the unit cohesion, of generally long-service troops, notably in individual messes as well as regiments. Regimental calls and colours were of significance as part of a masculinity in which, for rankers, bravery was primarily an aspect of group activity. This cohesion was helped by, in comparative terms to other armies, sufficient food, regular pay and an absence of conscription. It is possible to draw attention to deficiencies and to poor discipline, but individual eyewitness accounts to this effect have to be handled with care.[41] A more systemic issue was that of the weakness of care for those suffering from disabilities as a result of injury. Nevertheless, morale was generally good.

Alongside deficiencies, British fighting quality emerged repeatedly. It was evident from the campaigns of 1793–4 and was demonstrated strikingly, before the Peninsular War, in the victories over the French in Egypt in 1801 and at Maida in 1806. Combat required a disciplined willingness to accept hazardous exposure. When troops approached the Egyptian coast in a landing contested by the French in 1801: 'the enemy commenced their attack upon us with round shot and shell which as we approached nearer was changed into the hottest discharges imaginable of grape, canister and musquetry without our being able to make any return. In spite of this destructive opposition the boats still advanced', and, indeed, the landing was successful.[42] Such impressive, disciplined bravery was repeatedly important to success.

CHAPTER 8

The Army around the World, 1793–1815

'Mind your duty, my lads; onwards, onwards, Britain for ever', were the last words I heard our noble Captain Brookman utter.

THOMAS HOWELL OF THE UNSUCCESSFUL
ATTACK ON BUENOS AIRES, 1807.[1]

The fleet arrived in Aboukir Bay on the 1st but contrary winds prevented our disembarkation until the 8th. The French availed themselves of this interval to strengthen their position on the coast, collected about 3,000 men to oppose our landing and lined the whole coast with their artillery. About 2 o'clock in the morning the first division of the army were in the boats and after rowing five hours came within gun shot of the coast when the enemy opened the hottest fire upon us, at first of shell and round shot and, as we approached nearer, of grape shot and musketry. Several boats were sunk, many persons killed, and in one boat alone 22 persons killed or wounded by musketry before the boat took ground, but nothing could withstand the ardent spirit and impetuosity of our troops who forced their landing in spite of every opposition immediately attacked the enemy whom they completely repulsed after an action of about half an hour.

MAJOR HUDSON LOWE, INVASION OF EGYPT 1801.[2]

In response to strategic ambitions, fears and commitments – these three closely entwined – the army, from the outset of the war with France in 1793, needed to operate across the world,[3] a situation that was expanded when the Dutch, Spain, and Denmark joined France. This requirement created organisational and operational problems, as well as those of expectations. There was a combination of local and distant resources, the latter enhanced by the establishment of storage points in the shape of garrisons from which troops could be obtained. Both the ability to move forces long distances and the availability of local support improved the confidence of British military planning. No other state in the world could match this capability: none had such a military system, and therefore none could share these goals.

Operating across the world had implications both for the army as a whole, and for specific individuals and units. The navy could deliver the army, but the latter had only mixed success in then obtaining victory, as the serious failures in 1807 at Buenos Aires and in Egypt indicated. On the other hand, the 1801 expedition to Egypt was a success, the French there being thoroughly defeated, John Moore noting: 'we have beat them without cavalry and inferior in artillery.'[4] Similarly, there was success in Denmark in 1807, Major-General Thomas Grosvenor writing:

> Began the bombardment of Copenhagen at sunset, 3 mortar batteries of twelve each all opened at the same time … The Congreve arrows [rockets] made a very singular appearance in the air. Six or seven comet-like appearances racing together. They seemed to move very slow. The town was set on fire …. The Great Church was on fire to the very pinnacle of the steeple. The appearance was horrifying grand.[5]

Grosvenor (1764–1851), the son of an MP, joined the army in 1779, was in charge of security at the Bank of England during the Gordon Riots in 1780, served in the Low Countries in the mid-1790s and 1799, and was last on campaign in the expedition of 1809. Promoted to full general in 1819, he was advanced to field marshal in 1846.

Variable success, which was only to be expected, was also the case in the War of 1812 (in fact 1812–15) with the United States. The defence of Canada was repeatedly achieved, with the Americans in successive campaigns, unable to advance anywhere near as far as they had done in 1775, but the blows against the Americans in 1814–15 were far more variable in their results, and culminated in a major defeat outside New Orleans in 1815.

Yet, Britain's very capacity to dispatch amphibious operations surpassed that of any other power. Moreover, the very potential in attack brought strategic capability irrespective of what happened. This was important to the significance both of the army and of the navy. The Marines, organised in 1755 and titled Royal Marines from 1802, did not take this role. The number and range of such operations was an indication of the pressure Britain could try to bring on its opponents. Some commitments were very large-scale, notably the West Indies from 1794 and the Peninsular War from 1808. Others could be large-scale, but for a shorter period, especially with the 36,000 troops sent to Holland in 1799, 13,000 to Ferrol in Spain in 1800, 15,000 to Egypt in 1801, 25,000 to Copenhagen in 1807, 10,000 to Sweden in 1808, and 40,000 troops to nearby Walcheren in 1809.

Not all the expeditions succeeded. In 1800, when attempted landings at Belle-Île, Ferrol and Cadiz all failed, Cornwallis described the army as the laughing stock of Europe. More sympathetically, Henry Dundas, the Secretary of State for War, replied to Major-General Thomas Maitland's explanation of why he had decided not to attack Belle-Île: 'It was certainly judicious in you under all circumstances not to expose the troops under your command, by attempting a landing in the face of a superior force, possessing an addition to the natural strength of their position, a strong fortress to support their operations.'[6] Maitland (1760–1824), the second surviving son of a Scottish Earl, became a captain in 1778 and was commander of the force sent to Saint-Domingue in 1797, negotiating an agreement with the rebel leader Toussaint L'Ouverture in 1798. He went on to command in Ceylon, and in 1812 proved a lacklustre commander of a British expedition in eastern Spain, going on in 1813 to be first Lieutenant-Governor of Portsmouth and then Governor of Malta and Lord High Commissioner of the Ionian Islands, products of the gather-all success of British imperialism.

The Walcheren expedition saw 4,000 dying of disease, principally malaria, compared to only 106 killed in the fighting, and many others remained seriously ill thereafter. The campaign was a tribute to naval power, as it was directed (unsuccessfully) against the major naval dockyard at Antwerp. So also with the Holland expedition of 1799, the attack on the port of Ferrol, and the attempt to gain control of the Danish fleet in 1807. There were crucial choices in tasking and deployment. This was seen with the suspicious and critical attitude of Wellington toward commitments other than Iberia. Writing in February 1813 to

Henry, 3rd Earl Bathurst, Secretary for War and the Colonies, about the decision to send a regiment to Canada, Wellington hoped that the British commander there:

> Will not be induced by any hopes of trifling advantages to depart from a strong defensive system. He may depend upon it that he will not be strong enough either in men or means, to establish himself in any conquest he might make. The attempt would only weaken him, and his losses augment the spirits and hopes of the enemy, even if not attended by worse consequences; whereas by the other system, he will throw the difficulties and risk upon them [the Americans], and they will most probably be foiled.[7]

In defence, the army protected colonies, including naval bases such as Gibraltar, Halifax, Antigua and Jamaica. Concerned about the threat to empire, there were efforts to strengthen defences. Québec's fortifications were strengthened after the siege of 1775–6, and a citadel was completed in 1783. At Halifax, the existing citadel was in ruins, and the new one was completed by 1800. To accommodate the fortress, the top of the hill was levelled and lowered, and four bastions surrounded a central barracks and magazine. To provide defence in stages, a note on a British map of 1796 read: 'It is proposed to finish the bastions first because in case of a sudden attack, they can be turned into redoubts by shutting the gorges', a gorge being the rear part of an independent fieldwork or detached outwork.

The major defensive conflict that was prepared for was that of the British Isles from invasion. Indeed, French attacks led to small-scale conflict in Wales (1797) and, at a much larger scale, Ireland (1798). There were longer-term conflicts in defence of the Caribbean colonies against slave rebellion and French attack in the 1790s, and in the protection of Canada during the War of 1812.

Although the troops destined for the Caribbean might have been better used in the Low Countries in 1793–4,[8] attacks on Caribbean positions seemed the most possible, profitable and appropriate way to strike at France, and a key way to strengthen the empire. Such operations would make effective use of the striking power of the navy, and, by taking colonial bases, would lessen the likelihood of successful French attack on nearby British colonies, not least by denying the French bases where they could shelter and resupply any fleet sent to the Caribbean. In 1793, Tobago was rapidly captured by troops from the local British garrisons, an unsuccessful attack was mounted on Martinique, and a position established on Saint-Domingue. In 1794, with 6,000 troops arrived from Britain, and good use of the winter campaigning season, and of assault tactics rather than those of line-and-volley, Martinique, St. Lucia and Guadeloupe were captured, the British being welcomed by the white planters, who were worried about slave rebellion.[9]

However, with disease hitting hard, impetus was lost, and a French force landed on Guadeloupe, and, backed by free blacks and rebel slaves, defeated the British and local royalists, in street fighting on Point-à-Pitre, and drove them from the island. Using revolutionary ideology to build up their military strength, the French had conscripted freed slaves and recaptured St. Lucia in 1795 in what was to be called the First Brigand War, as well as stirring up rebellion on Grenada, St. Vincent and Dominica, in part by means of a black-manned privateer squadron, and driving the British back in Saint-Domingue. The white Royalist slave-owners fled St. Lucia with the British. Slavery was abolished on the island and several planters guillotined.

This was a crisis for the British Caribbean, and therefore for the British imperial system; and was seen in that light. The Caribbean was important to British trade, public finances, and creditworthiness: but now even more so after the loss of the Thirteen Colonies in 1783, and because Britain had been militarily driven from the European Continent, was at war with Spain from 1796, the Dutch, under French control from 1795 till 1814, following France into war with Britain.

In response to the crisis in the Caribbean, 33,000 troops were sent in late 1795 under the talented Major-General Sir Ralph Abercromby, the navy providing crucial 'lift' and mobility, not least matching supplies to troops. Thus, the mighty East Indiamen, the big ships that usually sailed to India, carried 300 tons of provisions each, while the total carried by the fleet was deemed sufficient to sustain 40,000 men for eight months, and amounted to 5,824 tons of pork, beef, butter and flour, and 52,031 bushels of peas. These figures indicated the importance of Britain's Agricultural Revolution and organisational capability to its military action in the Caribbean. So also with the Industrial Revolution as discussed later.

Acting with great energy, Abercromby captured St. Lucia, where British racism made their task more difficult in encouraging opposition,[10] and crushed rebellions in Grenada and St. Vincent in 1796, pressing on in 1797 to capture vulnerable Trinidad from Spain; although failing when he attacked San Juan, the well-prepared key position in Spanish-ruled Puerto Rico. The pace of British conquest continued. The Dutch colony of Curaçao was captured in 1800, and St. Martin, the Danish West Indian islands, and the Swedish island of St. Barthélemy, all in 1801. It was necessary after 1795 to convince actual and potential allies, that Britain, despite her defeats in Europe, was weakening France, and to demonstrate to domestic opinion that the war was not without point and profit.

Yet, aside from the death of sailors, 45,000 British troops were lost in the West Indies in 1793–1801, over 96 per cent to disease, principally malaria and yellow fever, about 14,000 of them on Saint-Domingue, and these casualty rates affected morale, leading to desertion. If the British had not deployed troops for conquest, they would have had to send them there to protect the colonies against both the French and slave risings. Nevertheless, the losses were savage given the high death rate they represented, one about seven times that of the British garrison in Canada, and given the overall size of the entire army, the absence of conscription, and the need to men for the navy. The 'opportunity cost' was also high in terms of what else could have been done with these men. There was an equivalent in the very heavy losses of troops in the capture of Havana in 1762 and the argument that this loss of skilled men compromised the military response to the American rebellion in 1775. To remind us of the rippling effects of these losses in British society, Jane Austen's sister Cassandra became engaged to the Reverend Thomas Fowle in 1795, but he accompanied his patron, the libidinous William, 7th Lord Craven, to the West Indies as a regimental chaplain and died there in 1797 from yellow fever. She never married.

The Peace of Amiens, which Cornwallis helped negotiate in 1802, meant the restoration of all these British gains, bar Trinidad from a

Spain that was not in a position to complain; so that the islands had to be captured anew after war with France resumed in 1803. That year, St. Lucia and Tobago were easily taken and the French plan for an attack on Antigua thwarted, but, after a failed British attempt in 1803, Curaçao was not captured until 1807, a year after the last French squadron in the Caribbean to risk combat was destroyed in the battle of San Domingo. When war was declared against Denmark in 1807, St. Croix was quickly taken. In turn, French squadrons arrived in the Caribbean, most prominently in 1805 when ransoms to be spared devastation were obtained from Dominica, St. Kitts, Nevis and Montserrat, but to no lasting effect.

There were also successes in other regions, notably West and South Africa. In the latter, British forces were successful in 1795 and 1806, with the battles in each case won by the British, that of Blaauwberg in 1806 seeing a British bayonet charge playing a major role.

There were also major failures in trans-oceanic operations. In 1806, Lieutenant-General John Hely-Hutchinson, who had served with great success in Egypt in 1801, capturing Alexandria, claimed that the country could easily be conquered, 'a corps of 4 or 5000 infantry, 7 or 800 cavalry with a proportion of artillery will be sufficient to accomplish this object… This operation would certainly be only a march.'[11] In fact, an expedition to Egypt in 1807, designed to thwart the possibility of French intervention, that reflected growing British sensitivity about possible opponents on routes to India, ended in failure. Having captured the port of Alexandria with ease, the British marched overland to attack Rosetta, only for the troops to take heavy casualties from snipers in the narrow streets of the town and to retreat. A subsequent advance on Rosetta ended in failure in the face of larger Egyptian forces. Hely-Hutchinson himself did not serve on campaign after 1801, although he was a colonel until his death in 1832 and a member of the House of Lords from 1801.

Also in 1807, a poorly commanded and coordinated attack on Spanish-ruled Buenos Aires met strong resistance in the barricaded streets and failed with heavy casualties, leading to a humiliating surrender. Looking ahead to more recent difficulties, the problems of staging attacks in towns was amply demonstrated at both Buenos Aires and Rosetta. Street-fighting rewarded detailed knowledge of the terrain, rather than general firepower, and also placed a premium on small-unit effectiveness for which the training of the parade ground and the linear tactics of the battleground were little preparation.

The greatest loss in British expeditions was that to disease and notably so in the Caribbean, and as a result of Walcheren in 1809. Yellow fever and malaria were the key killers. Such losses on distant operations far outweighed those from combat, but also made the latter more serious. These losses also underlined the harshness of military service.[12]

Thereafter victory was the norm outside Europe, with 1809 seeing the major success of the fall of Martinique when a shell from the besiegers detonated the principal magazine in Fort Desaix, the major French position, Thomas Browne recording next day: 'The inside of the work presented a shocking spectacle of ruins, and blood, and half buried bodies, and was literally ploughed up, by the shells we had thrown into it.' With concern about disease leading to instructions to avoid a lengthy campaign, the British then turned against Guadeloupe, first instituting a close blockade in order to encourage the garrison to surrender, while the use of smallpox vaccine also helped the British forces cope with the challenge of disease. Guadeloupe, St. Eustatius, St. Martin and Saba, the last three without a fight, were rapidly taken in February 1810; a marked contrast with the total disaster that awaited the British near New Orleans in January 1815. The French had now been driven from the West Indies.

Subsequently, in 1811, the British achieved a new success for them when they captured Batavia (Djakarta) and, with it, Java, a campaign involving larger forces (11,000 troops), and tougher opposition than that with 1,700 troops launched against Manila in 1762. This was a range of action no other state could match, one dependent on cooperation between army and navy.

Handed back to France in 1814, the French Caribbean islands were swiftly captured anew in 1815 after Napoleon seized power again. The rapid British success indicated the strength and dominance in the Caribbean of a military system that prefigured that later there of America. Lieutenant-General Sir James Leith, a veteran of the Peninsular War, the Governor and captain general (commander in chief) of the Leeward Islands, moved rapidly, sending troops to Martinique from nearby St. Lucia. They landed on 5 June and occupied all the strong positions, helping to stop a revolution in favour of Napoleon. There was similar success on Marie-Galante, but on Guadeloupe the situation was more difficult, and an insurrection, mounted by coincidence on 18 June, the day of Waterloo, succeeded with the support of the local authorities. Napoleon was proclaimed Emperor there the next day, replacing Louis XVIII.

In reply, Leith, covered by Rear-Admiral Sir Philip Charles Dunham, the commander in chief of the Leeward Islands station, landed his men on 8 August. Advancing rapidly in columns the next day, the British prevented the French from concentrating, and, on the tenth, the French surrendered, Leith being helped by bringing the news of Waterloo to Guadeloupe. Some French soldiers deserted, refused to surrender, and took refuge in the woods on the island where low-level guerrilla opposition continued, but it had no future.

In 1790, George III had responded to the prospect of war with Spain and attacks on the Spanish Caribbean (a war that did not break out) by suggesting that 'the measure of raising Blacks is much improved by attaching ten men to each company', and, in 1794, the British used specially raised units of slaves under white commanders, units capable of moving rapidly and acting as light infantry, which was an aspect of the flexibility of the imperial slave system. These became eight West India regiments in 1795, a number raised to twelve by 1798; but a practice opposed by the local settlers and legislatures, notably on Jamaica. About 13,400 slaves were purchased to fight in the regiments between 1795 and 1808. The Eighth West India Regiment fought bravely in the capture of St. Martin from the French in 1801, but mutinied in Dominica in 1802 fearing they would be sent to work in the cane fields, a mutiny, in which white officers were killed, that led to a bloody response by other military units. As a reward for service, all of the slaves serving in the army were freed in the Mutiny Act of 1807, thus increasing the number of free blacks in the British colonies.[13]

The very varied nature of local contribution to the military system was shown not only by the slave units of the period but also by the settlers who fought Aboriginal groups in Australia in an often brutal struggle. The first frontier war there broke out in 1795.[14]

The War of 1812

This conflict displayed an impressive degree of capability and effectiveness for the British military system because it was already fully stretched until the spring of 1814 in war with Napoleonic France. Moreover, with different institutional support, the attacking Americans were a far more formidable force than the Patriots who had invaded Canada in 1775 only to be defeated in 1776. The War of 1812 also reflected the range of the British war-effort on land, with Regulars, Canadian volunteer units who were to prove impressive,[15] and Allied First Nations/Native Americans all fighting the invaders, while more Regulars were launched in amphibious attacks on America in 1814–15. In June 1812, there were only 9,777 Regulars in Canada, and no significant reinforcements arrived that year. There was also scant artillery, although many volunteers came forward,[16] the Canadian militia was untried, and the centres of population in the St. Lawrence valley were vulnerable to attack from the United States.

Although the continued war in Europe, and more particularly Iberia, affected the numbers of Regulars available, by the summer of 1813 their number had been increased to over 20,000. This buildup in part reflected the end of French resistance in the West Indies. Had the Americans attacked earlier then the British would have been under more significant pressure in the New World.

The fighting in the War of 1812 was mostly a matter of what were small-scale battles by the standards of the Napoleonic battlefield. Rapid advances on the battlefield, sometimes successful, sometimes not, were a key element, with commanders showing their mettle in knowing how to shape such engagements. Thus, Shadrach Byfield of the 41st Foot wrote of the River Raisin battle in January 1813:

> Under cover of a wood we approached near to them unperceived. We formed the line and had a view of them as they surrounded their fires ... Before daylight we had charged them several times, thinking that we were close up their lines;

but our men were so cut up that after every attempt we were obliged to retreat to the cover of a rising piece of ground with considerable loss.

This battle, in which Byfield was wounded, was a British victory, and with most of their opponents killed or captured,[17] which underlines the extent to which battles were in part a matter of almost separate engagements grouped together, a process encouraged if the terrain or cover ensured discontinuities in the deployment of units. That May, Byfield recorded an unsuccessful clash with an American relief column near Fort Meigs, Ohio: 'We charged them close under the fort, but were obliged to retreat because of their great guns.'[18]

At the same time, rapid-attack tactics were not the sole story for the British. Thus, at Crysler's Farm in the St. Lawrence Valley on 11 November 1813, the Americans deployed a larger force, but their attack, launched in miserable rain, was not coordinated, the troops became disordered, and the superior fire discipline of the British Regulars powerfully contributed to the failure of the American assault. The close-range rolling volleys from the British infantry were supplemented by cannon firing shrapnel shells which had been adopted by the army from 1803 and used from 1804. After suffering more than 400 casualties, compared to 180 British, the Americans drew back. To the late David Chandler, for long the doyen of British military historians of the period, the battle established 'the superiority of British linear tactics in the open against less well-trained opponents used to forest warfare.'[19]

This is a questionable assessment, for it is always dangerous to read general conclusions about military quality from individual engagements, just as it is unhelpful to explain the result of such engagements by virtue of a supposed understanding of aggregate military quality. The last is not a terribly helpful concept, however much it matches the tendency to adopt an approach based on national strategic culture, institutional sociology, or ethno-assumptions as in discussion of a supposed British way of war. While that approach has its value, it is necessary, in discussing particular battles, to give due weight to the circumstances of the day, to individual units, commanders, and terrain, and to their interaction; and the same is the case, albeit with different elements, of campaigns. At Crysler's Farm, there was a well-balanced defence, with the standard

British linear position also part of a defence in depth that included a skirmish line.

As a reminder of the contemporaneous range and effectiveness of their military, 1812 had seen not only the start of the War of 1812, but also both victory at Salamanca and the intrepid Brigadier-General Robert Gillespie depose the Sultan of Palembang in Sumatra and capture the Sultan of Yogyakarta's royal residence in Java; while the day before Crysler's Farm, on 10 November 1813, Wellington had outflanked and stormed the French defences on the River Nivelle. Gillespie, who had served in the West Indies, and suppressed the Vellore Mutiny of *sepoys* in India in 1806, was shot dead by a Nepalese defender when trying to storm the hill fort at Khalanga on 31 October 1814, his reputed last words 'One more for the honour of Down', his native part of Ireland. He was posthumously knighted. Like Wellington, Gillespie is a reminder of the leadership, experience and continuity of service of many British officers, which was important to their combat effectiveness.[20] So also with ordinary soldiers, many of whom served on more than one continent.[21]

As a result in part of the battle at Crysler's Farm, the most powerful American attempt to conquer Canada failed. In addition, there was an operational defence in depth, with a large British force ready to defend Montréal, including five regular battalions. The fighting on that frontier in Canada closed in 1813 with an extensive use of bayonets in a successful surprise night attack on Fort Niagara on 19 December.

In 1814, troops were also provided for the naval forces off North America, but the range of British commitments was such that only 2,400 men were sent. Their commander, Sir Thomas Sidney Beckwith (1770–1831), was a skilled leader of light troops with the sort of experience that most non-American generals could not mount. The son of a major-general, he had entered the army in 1791 and served in India, was a protégé of Moore, served at Copenhagen in 1807, fought extensively in the Peninsula, including at Vimeiro in 1808, and rose to be a lieutenant-general and commander in chief of the Bombay Army, only to die in India of disease. Beckwith's instructions from Bathurst drew attention to what he could achieve:

The number and description of the force placed under your command, as well as the object of the expedition itself, will point out to you that you are not to look to the permanent possession of any place, but to the reembarking the force as soon as the immediate object of each particular attack shall have been accomplished.... As the object of the expedition is to harass the enemy by different attacks, you will avoid the risk of a general action, unless it should become necessary to secure your retreat.[22]

In 1814, 16,300 additional troops were sent to North America, a result of the fall of Napoleon. In the meanwhile, an outnumbered British force was driven off by American defensive firepower in the battle of Chippawa on the Niagara Front on 5 July. The extent to which in battle there could be repeated attacks and counterattacks was subsequently shown in the night battle of Lundy's Lane (25 July), a contact-battle in which both sides claimed victory, an outcome already seen at Monmouth Court House in 1778. With the many wounded, Major-General Phineas Riall on the British side having an arm amputated, the aftermath of the battle was grim, but the need for life to go on was reflected in the journal of Lieutenant John Le Couteur of the 104th Foot: 'A great camp kettle of thick chocolate revived us surprisingly, though we devoured it among dead bodies in all directions.'[23] The son of a lieutenant-general, he survived and rose in the regular army but only to be a captain in the army and a colonel in the militia, because he left the army when his regiment was disbanded in 1818.

The battles in the 1814 Niagara Front campaign revealed the difficulties of controlling engagements, both from a distance and on the ground, as well as the role of risk. Commanders took the chance of battle, but, as at sea, with which there were many tactical and operational similarities, found it hard to control its flow and tempo, not least because of the difficulty of coordinating forces; and of creating and then using reserves. Poor visibility was one reason why it was difficult to manoeuvre units on the battlefield, especially once they were engaged. Even in clear weather, there was a limit to what could be seen with the naked eye or with the telescope. With limited mapping and no facilities for aerial reconnaissance, generals had very limited knowledge of the terrain and of the position or movements of opposing forces, and many battles revolved around the surprise deployment of units. As a result, the ability to understand the lie of the land, and to assess the possible military consequences, was a very important aspect of generalship. Aside from a lack of information, tactical flexibility was also lessened by poor battlefield communication, a problem accentuated at night. It was particularly difficult to keep units in touch, which was necessary in order to prevent gaps that could be exploited by opponents, not least by mounting flank attacks.

In August 1814, a force under the talented Major-General Robert Ross landed on the Patuxent River, fifty miles from Washington. At Bladensburg on 24 April, Ross found 6,500 Americans, mostly militia, drawn up under Brigadier-General William Winder behind a branch of the Potomac River. Despite being outnumbered, without cavalry, and heavily outgunned in artillery, the British attacked, boldly led by Ross, who bravely commanded from the front. The British troops advanced across the river and attacked the Americans in the front and flanks, defeating them after three hours of combat. Ross reported: 'the enemy was discovered strongly posted on very commanding heights … a position which was carefully defended by artillery and riflemen.' Thanks to a good attack, however, 'this first line giving way was driven on the second which yielding to the irresistible attack of the bayonet and the well-directed discharge of rockets got into confusion and fled leaving the British masters of the field', and having captured ten canon.'[24]

The young Peter Bowlby (1791–1877), who had become an ensign in the 4th Regiment of Foot in 1808, and was already a veteran of the disastrous Walcheren expedition of 1809 and of the Peninsular War, recorded:

> The weather was dreadfully hot and the road deep in sand.... Arrived at Bleydensburg [sic] we saw the American army marching from Washington to a position a mile in front. We had to pass the stream by a wooden bridge in single file. Fortunately it was covered from the American position by a turn in the road under the wood. As soon as the leading regiment, the 85th, cleared this, they extended to the right and advanced in light infantry order over a tolerably open country, the 4th regiment doing the same to the left. In front we had a wood occupied by the Americans and some high ground to the right to the wood occupied also by columns of the Americans and some field artillery, Commodore

Barney and his guns playing down the high road. The 85th first reached him and all his men were cut down at their guns. The American army then retreated in great haste on Washington. On approaching the wood I received a shot in the shin which splintered the bone but did not break it. I tied a handkerchief round it and marched with the regiment to Washington.[25]

Bowlby returned in time to serve at Waterloo and rose to become a captain. It is worth citing another participant, an American, Joshua Barney, who was in command of naval cannon, which underlines a point more generally true for all battle accounts, that they are those of individual participants and substantially reflect their position, experience, and commitments. Having described deploying his cannon and awaiting the British arrival:

During this period the engagement continued the enemy advancing, our own army retreating before them apparently in much disorder, at length the enemy made his appearance in the main road, in force, and in front of my battery, and on seeing us made a halt. I reserved our fire. In a few minutes the enemy again advanced, when I ordered an 18 lb to be fired, which completely cleared the road, shortly after a second and a third attempt was made by the enemy to come forward but all were destroyed. The enemy then crossed over into an open field and attempted to flank our right. He was there met by three twelve pounders, the marines under Captain Miller and my men acting as infantry, and again was totally cut up. By this time not a vestige of the American army remained except a 5 or 600 posted on a height on my right from whom I expected much support, from their fine situation. The enemy from this period never appeared in force in front of us. They pushed forward their sharp shooters, one of which shot my horse under me, who fell dead between two of my guns. The enemy who had been kept in check by our fire for nearly half an hour now began to outflank us on the right, our guns were turned that way. He pushed up the hill, about 2 or 300 towards the corps of Americans ... who, to my great mortification, made no resistance, giving a fire or two and retired .... Finding the enemy now completely in our rear the wounded Barney gave the order to retire, only to be captured and well-treated.[26]

The battle descriptions yet again showed that, whatever the environment, the well-timed bayonet charge, launched when opponents were already disorganised by heavy British fire, remained a standard tactic, as it had been from the late 1750s. This method expanded the range of tactical problems opponents could anticipate as the British did not have to charge, but could yet readily switch from a firefight to the charge.

The British followed up the battle of Bladensburg by briefly occupying Washington, burning down public buildings as the Americans had done in Canada, and also, allegedly, because some Americans fought on while no ransom was provided. The subsequent advance on well-fortified Baltimore, a very different proposition to Washington, was a failure. Nevertheless, it was one that the British, without being defeated, sensibly pulled back from at the end of a campaign in which with a modest use of forces they had underlined American vulnerability.[27]

British tactics, however, failed dismally on 8 January 1815 in a poorly managed attack on the American lines outside New Orleans.[28] The British did not use their attack on the other side of the river to bring pressure to bear on the defenders while on the main front, where they were organised in four columns, key units had not taken their positions before the advance was launched, and the sugarcane bundles and ladders designed to allow the troops to cross the canals were not brought to the fore, all of which led to the subsequent court-martial and cashiering (dismissal from the army) of Lieutenant-Colonel Thomas Mullins of the 44th Foot. Moreover, the main column was directed against the strongest part of the American defences, in the mistaken belief that it was the weakest. In practice, American defensive firepower was formidable and the British attack, in tightly packed formations, moving forward over the cane stubble on a narrow front, provided a good target. Whereas the British cannon focused on the American artillery, the latter fired on the British infantry causing heavy casualties with grape and canister shot. Instead of pressing home the attack, the British infantry slackened, losing impetus and the initiative, and increasing their vulnerability to American fire. The 44th broke and fled, although doggedness led other troops to stand under fire. Bowlby's account brought together the initial confusion and the decimating American firepower:

> The 44th Regiment being ordered to carry fascines and ladders across the ditch and breastwork, but missed finding them in the dark. They were sent to bring them, and when they came up the men were quite exhausted. Passing to the front it now became daylight, the enemy opened a tremendous fire, they threw down

the fascines and ladders and rushed through the regiment in the rear throwing them into confusion … I received a shot wound in the head striking over the right eye which left me insensible on the ground. There were a few riflemen to protect the wounded, and the enemy not having come out from their works, in half an hour I was able to rise and walk off the field.[29]

Joseph Hutchinson of the 7th Royal Fusiliers was in a force under Lieutenant-Colonel Benny that attacked the redoubt on the Mississippi on the right of the American front line:

After marching a short distance on a pretty good road by the river side we quitted it and remained in column covered by the 43rd company in extended order until a rocket which had been the arranged signal was let off upon which we gained the road and marched rapidly forward, still covered by the skirmishers.

But we had scarcely advanced one hundred yards when it became suddenly broad daylight and we were saluted by two field pieces filled with grape shot. The troops on the road who had escaped the fire inclined to the left and got on the banks of the Mississippi. And dashed on in double time and got into the Redoubt without further opposition. After remaining in the Redoubt a short time during which Colonel Benny was killed, finding no support was coming and our men being killed I who was the senior officer in the Redoubt gave orders to retire – which was done, but before we could get out of range of the guns of the enemy they fired another round of grape and committed great destruction. On assembling the troops when out of fire, only fifteen men was found serviceable out of 85 of which the company was composed one hour before. I received seven shots through my clothes and cape.

The battalion which had acted in line as the reserve in the attack of the morning, had approached near the works and been so long detained in covering the retreat of the attacking column that it was deemed more advisable to remain lying down where they were then retiring for half a mile across perfect flat exposed to the fire of the whole American lines, and continued in that disagreeable situation until dark at night, a period of twelve or fourteen hours very much exposed and cost many men.[30]

The more pithy *Annual Register* wrote of 'an enterprise which appears to have been undertaken with more courage than judgment.'

The nature of military service, notably the unpredictability of survival, emerges from the accounts of contemporaries. So also their resilience, a key element in the continued ability to engage in sequential campaigning and to put up with the hardships and risks of campaigning. As a result, it is appropriate to end this chapter with Hutchinson, a young but experienced veteran, when returning from failure in New Orleans to a warship:

> It is quite impossible to describe my feelings in finding myself in comparative comfort, for on disembarking 20 days before we were desired only to take what we had on our backs and in consequence for those days we have had our clothes off. I now found my baggage on board. ... and after a good dinner and a glass of comfortable grog [rum and water] turned in to bed and got a comfortable sleep without the dread of having a shell tumble on us every instance.[31]

CHAPTER 9

The Army as a Political Force

> This is essentially a military government. The regular army is too strong
> for the unarmed millions, who would otherwise not allow the government
> to stand for six months; and while the government has the direction of
> the army, the latter will continue to be paid, and the former supported
> by the bayonets in its authority.
>
> RICHARD RUSH, AMERICAN ENVOY IN BRITAIN, 1820.[1]

The situation in Britain was far more complex than the markedly hostile
Rush argued. Not least, he did not capture the range of social, political
and ideological factors making for stability and cohesion. Nevertheless,
Rush appreciated the role of force in ensuring control. A very different
view was offered in 1780, when, concerned about the pressure of conflict
on many fronts, the talented Secretary at War Charles Jenkinson was
nevertheless clear when he wrote to Lord Amherst, the commander in
chief, that he was opposed to conscription:

> I am convinced that any plan of compulsion … is not only contrary to the nature
> of the government of this country, but would create riots and disturbances which
> might require more men for the purpose of preserving the peace, than would
> be obtained by the plan itself … besides that men who are procured in this way
> almost constantly desert, or at best make very indifferent soldiers.[2]

More generally, the army, itself enjoying considerable continuity due
to regimental pride, was a force for national stability, but what that
should and could mean was unclear. There was certainly an opportunity
through military service for elite benefit, expansion and cohesion. Indeed,

alongside the ability to reach out to those not in the senior ranks of the élite, indeed including those who did not come from the land, the army was closely linked to the governing group. 182 army officers were MPs in 1715–54, and those who turned against the government were dismissed, as William Pitt was in 1736.[3] In 1754–90, 208 army officers sat in the Commons.[4] War markedly increased the number of regiments and led to an increase in military enthusiasm among the existing élite. In 1759, Thomas Dampier, Lower Master at Eton, noted: 'There is such a military spirit in the young gentry of the nation at present.' Two years earlier, Charles, 3rd Duke of Richmond, a lieutenant-colonel although only 22, wrote to his younger brother, Lord George Lennox, who was eventually to become a general, complaining of his own inexperience and claiming that he was unsuitable for any post of responsibility:

> Persons of rank should be prefer'd young and out of their turns. Everybody says so, but why, because they are the persons to whom the nation should choose to entrust their safety in giving them command as having so much property.

Richmond, who rose to be Master-General of the Ordnance in 1782–3 and 1784–95 and a field marshal in 1796, was far more radical than most. In 1758, both brothers took part in the successful attack on the French port of Cherbourg, while Richmond served at Minden. An MP from 1761 to 1790, Lennox was with the opposition during the American War of Independence.

The views of the élite were heeded in military matters. John, 4th Earl of Sandwich wrote to an unnamed senior minister in about 1760, seeking the removal of troops from Huntingdon, a borough where he had great influence, and put him in mind:

> of what he said in the beginning of the sessions of the House, that no Member of Parliament had ever applied to him to remove the troops from any place where they were complained of, but that he had complied with his request.

The context was the Seven Years' War and the revival of French invasion plans. The forces the French planned to land were by no means small: the plan outlined at the French council on 14 July 1759 called for 48,000 troops.[5] This posed a challenge for British defences and assumptions about the military. In 1757, Cumberland had mocked Pitt's support for the militia: 'I have wrote my humble opinion for the raising more troops, but I don't know whether the dauntless Man Mountain [Pitt] will think it proper, or perhaps intend to meet the enemy at their landing in person at the head of his new valiant militia. If so, what has Old England to fear.'[6] Two years later, prior to the total defeat of the French Brest fleet in Quiberon Bay on 20 November 1759, Charles, 2nd Marquess of Rockingham, recorded:

> I had some conversation a few days ago with Mr Pitt, who I find still continues desirous that no strength (that can be had) should be now neglected for the security of this country. All the militias which are in readiness are called out.[7]

Nevertheless, despite all Pitt's praise for the militia, especially at politically opportune moments when Tory support was being wooed, he was aware that it was not as effective as the army, not least because national military training was not possible.[8] In reality, as in 1588, 1692, 1744, 1779 and 1805, Britain was fortunate in 1759 that no invasion was mounted, although any French force that landed would have faced significant logistical problems, as well as the probability that its maritime lines of communication would have been cut. Moreover, after the '45, military value was gained from large-scale recruitment in Scotland, notably in the Highlands, and the opposition at Tranent in Scotland to the 1797 Militia Act was suppressed in 1797 with several protestors killed.

The tension over troop numbers within the ministry in 1759 and on other occasions reflected a sense of menace but also the pressure of rival demands, including the finances and competing tasks. In 1759, Pitt was determined to maintain substantial forces in North America and to send sufficient troops to prevent the defeat in Germany of the British and British-Allied army under Prince Ferdinand of Brunswick. After the Prince's victory at Minden that year, Pitt suggested that Ferdinand be provided with 10,000 new men, including two men out of every company in Britain and 600 Highlanders. Newcastle, more concerned by the prospect of invasion, was unenthusiastic.[9] To secure his ends, Pitt was against withdrawing any troops from America or Europe, refusing to be distracted by the threat of invasion, and pressed for the raising of fresh troops in Britain.[10] Ultimately, the politics of the ministry was crucial to the tasking of the military.

The absence of insurrection in the British Isles in the decades after the battle of Culloden in 1746 ensured that the role of the army as a force for stability was less prominent than its role against invasion. War with France in 1778 revived concern about national defence, so that, that year, the militia was embodied while Parliament approved an increase in its size and George III played a conspicuous role in reviewing militia units. The situation became more urgent, first with the Gordon Riots in 1780, and subsequently, and more consistently, during the crisis and sense of crisis created by rivalry with Revolutionary France, with a war and insurrection panic in 1792 which led to the movement of troops nearer to London, followed by the declaration of war in 1793. These crises brought to the fore a reliance on the prospect of force seen for example with an election riot in Leicester in 1790 where 'it was not till after the military were called in, and the Riot Act read, that the mob was dispersed.'[11] The army remained the main buttress to law and order until the establishment of the police, and this role ensured a mixed reputation.

The army continued to play a major role in control of Ireland, notably in response to the 1798 rising. There was no comparable need to face rebellion in mainland Britain, but the government's strategy for the war involved action against domestic radicalism, as well as a major attempt to encourage loyalism. Neither might appear to have a role in any account of military history, but this is mistaken, as the ratio between domestic opposition and loyalism was crucial to military capability. This was particularly true of raising volunteer support, which was seen as a key resource in the face of the threat of French invasion, and one that permitted the dispatch of more regular troops abroad.

Indeed, local volunteers acted successfully against the small French force that invaded Wales in 1797. The 1,400 strong *Légion Noire* (named after their dark-brown coats, captured from the British and dyed), commanded by the American Colonel William Tate, landed in Pembrokeshire. Once landed, the French seized food and alcohol, while the defending Pembroke Yeomanry, only 190 strong, retreated. However, the defence was rallied by John, 1st Lord Cawdor, the local landowner, who, lacking military experience, assembled a 600-strong force and advanced with determination. Intimidated by this advance and affected by a collapse of confidence, Tate surrendered on 24 February. Seeking to exploit social strains, the French had planned to win the support of the local poor and disaffected, and to press on to attack and burn Bristol. However, although the invasion force included two troops of grenadiers, much of it was composed of jail-sweepings and Tate was not up to the task.

More generally, large-scale volunteering ensured that the situation prefigured that of the Home Guard in World War Two, although, in the French Revolutionary War, there was felt to be a far more potent threat from domestic opposition – as indeed there was, particularly in Ireland. As a result, loyalist volunteers were seen as crucial in the defence against radicalism, as were the Cinque Port Light Dragoons in suppressing the protest at Tranent in 1797. This defence was regarded as a central war goal. Moreover, the issues of political radicalism made agrarian and industrial disorder more disturbing,[12] as with the response to the Luddites in the early 1810s. However, the use of military force against food riots had already increased, while the capability for action rose with the revival of the militia, which was embodied (assembled under military discipline) in 1792, the improvement in capability due to barracks and roads, and a greater willingness, in the midst of an international crisis, to use force, so that, by 1795–6, the military were used in about half of riots and, by 1800–1, about two-thirds.[13]

The role of local communities in volunteering and, indeed, in the recruitment of regular troops, meant that their cooperation, and notably that of the social élite, was necessary.[14] Far, however, from this being a source of weakness, it was an aspect of the broadly based nature of British military power, one that was particularly seen with the army due to this very local reliance which was found across the country. To a degree, this reliance was an aspect of the emphasis on law and order that provided a role and need for the socially prominent. They were significant as Lord-Lieutenants, Justices of the Peace (JPs), and militia officers. Much work was devoted to the walls, gates and lodges that provided bounds to the estates of the stately homes of the period. These were not designed to provide protection against attacking troops, but rather to protect the estate against criminals, notably poachers and, from the late 1770s, game preserves were increasingly protected by spring guns and mantraps. Moreover, the approach from the landscaped grounds to the house was easy for people, with the major obstacle being the ha-ha, a ditch to keep the cattle away from the house itself. The new neo-Gothic architectural style was not designed to provide strength and was almost a parody of medieval fortification.

As JPs, the élite were at the forefront of the relationship between local communities and the army, and local records demonstrate the scale and intensity of the relationship, not least in terms of recruitment, provisions for quartering troops, the provision of wagons, assistance for individual soldiers and their families when they moved about the country independently of the army, relief for former soldiers and their family, and dealing with deserters. Indeed, a sad aspect of the army experience was the need many later had for poor relief.[15]

A key episode in British military history was short-lived and therefore underrated, but in 1798 it revealed the different directions that could have taken and the necessity to fight in order to maintain empire. An Irish rebellion and the supporting French invasion force were totally defeated. Ireland was governed with scant concern for the views and interests of the bulk of the population, but, although there was much popular protest in the shape of mobs defending livelihoods and customary practices,[16] the level of revolutionary resistance that this encouraged was low. In part, this was because of economic growth. As Ireland was drawn more fully into the market economy, its agricultural sector experienced growing diversification and commercialization. Textile production also developed markedly. Moreover, far from the Catholic majority being an amorphous mass of downtrodden victims, they were a flexible group that came to play a more central role in politics and a more active role in society.

A combination of social stresses and agrarian discontents led to outbreaks of organized violence in parts of Ireland, especially by the Houghers of 1711–12, the Whiteboys of 1761–5 and 1769–76, the Oakboys of 1763, the Steelboys of 1769–72, and the Rightboys of 1785–8. However, these outbreaks were sporadic, although troops were used against them. In addition, arson, cattle-maiming and attacks on agents, while very unsettling to local landowners, was not a serious military threat to the state. They were not part of a guerrilla resistance determined to seize control of the countryside. It was therefore possible for the government in London to regard such violence as a minor military priority.[17]

In contrast, the French Revolution radicalized Irish discontent, weakened patterns of social control, and provided the possibility of foreign support for a large-scale rebellion. Government concessions on Catholic rights failed to prevent the rise of radicalism, as did the loyalty of the Irish Catholic Church, which was concerned about the anti-Christian posture of the French Revolutionaries. The United Irishmen, founded in 1791, largely as a Presbyterian movement pressing for political reform, was banned in 1794, but it reformed as a secret society that was openly republican and increasingly Catholic, and began to plot revolution. In 1796, a supporting French invasion attempt was thwarted by a violent storm.

That year, growing British concern led to the adoption of a proactive policy towards possible internal discontent, including an Insurrection Act that decreed harsh penalties for administering and taking illegal oaths, and also authorized curfews and searches for concealed weapons. *Habeas Corpus* (defence against imprisonment without trial) was suspended, and a largely Protestant Irish Yeomanry, an armed constabulary nearly 20,000 strong by the end of 1796, was established. This essentially sectarian policy alienated Catholic support. Calling on the army to disarm potential opponents helped to militarize the situation. The army violently disarmed the United Irishmen's Ulster network in 1797, while, as the United Irishmen movement sought to win Catholic backing, they alienated Protestant support.

Rising sectarian violence and harsh repression by the British Army culminated in rebellion in 1798. However, the arrest of the Leinster provincial committee of the United Irishmen in March and of the organizers of a projected uprising in Dublin, gravely handicapped the rebels. Lord Edward Fitzgerald had planned an insurrection in Dublin, to be followed by coordinated risings elsewhere, but the scheme was nipped in the bud. Fitzgerald was seized on 19 May, four days before the projected rising, and the Yeomanry occupied key positions in Dublin, where there was no rising. Controlling the major towns, the government dominated the communication foci, and this helped them retain the initiative. The rebels were only able to mount a serious military challenge in County Wexford where the local garrison was weak. The rising began on the evening of 26 May, the blazing heather highlighting the meeting points. Having successfully ambushed a detachment of overconfident militia next day at Oulart Hill, the United Irishmen overran most of the county, establishing the Wexford Republic. However, attempts to exploit the situation by advancing further afield, notably on Dublin, were checked in early June. At the same time, a badly prepared and led rising in Ulster failed. In Wexford, in turn, the poorly led United Irishmen concentrated at Vinegar Hill, losing the operational and strategic initiatives. The British Army under Lieutenant-General Gerard Lake, who went on to be commander in chief in India, attacked the rebels, many of whom had to use pikes, on 21 June, although estimates of the size of the two sides varied. The rebels fought for two hours, suffering heavy casualties, not least under the bombardment by the British cannon which used both shrapnel and grape shot. Under heavy pressure, the United Irishmen finally retreated when their ammunition ran out. Their cohesion lost and, many returning home, they suffered heavy losses in government punitive operations over the following weeks. The insurgents had suffered from military factors, notably a shortage of muskets, ammunition, provisions, discipline, training and, particularly, cannon. The degree to which Irish political opinion was divided, and many Catholics unwilling to support the insurgents, was also highly significant. This element tends to be underplayed in the national historical account.

A French supporting force did not land until 22 August, but was only 1,100 strong and, although defeating a largely militia force at Castlebar on 20 August, it and supporting Irish rebels were eventually forced to surrender at Ballinamuck on 8 September by a far larger British force under Cornwallis (26,000 troops to 2,350). Defeat at Castlebar had led to the dispatch of numerous reinforcements. After Ballinamuck about 200 Irish prisoners were hanged.

Organized and effective resistance to British authority was now at an end, but, in County Wicklow, a band under Michael Dwyer continued to defy the government, successfully employing guerrilla tactics, until Dwyer surrendered in 1803 in the aftermath of the failure of Robert Emmet's rising in Dublin. A United Irishman, Emmet launched his small-scale rising by marching on Dublin Castle, but his poorly organized men were dispersed by the garrison and the rising collapsed. In Ireland certainly, Rush's assessment was not without weight, although it was far less pertinent as far as Britain was concerned. Moreover, about a third of Wellington's army in the later stages of the Peninsular War were Irish.

CHAPTER 10

Culmination, 1815

With his fine grasp of timing and eye for terrain, Wellington brought the British Army system to a pitch of effectiveness at Waterloo. Yet, he complained that because, in part due to their dispatch in 1814 to fight the United States (the regiments had sailed direct from the Gironde), he lacked his Peninsular War army at Waterloo, the battle proved much more difficult than his successes in the Peninsula. Not only had many of the British units at Waterloo not served under him, but, more particularly, many of the British units (and their German, Dutch and Belgian counterparts) there had had no experience of battle. Indeed, to a certain extent, the situation repeated that in the American War of Independence. Then, the British suffered from the heavy losses that their army that had conquered Canada from France in 1758–60 had taken from tropical diseases, especially yellow fever, when capturing Havana from Spain in 1762. As a result, there was a greater reliance in 1775–6 on troops that had not hitherto experienced battle.

In practice, neither the British nor the French were on peak form at Waterloo, as the French army had suffered greatly from the unsuccessful invasion of Russia in 1812, in troop losses and, even more, in those of cavalry horses, many of which had been eaten. Nevertheless, Napoleon had more of his veterans present at Waterloo than Wellington. Such deficiencies put a premium on command skills and, in particular, on making the best use of what was available. Wellington, however, failed operationally on 15–16 June 1815 because he did not understand sufficiently clearly what the French, who had the initiative, were trying to do in driving the British and Prussian forces apart, so as to hit them separately. First blood for the British was an encounter-battle at Quatre Bras on the afternoon of the 16th. Major-General Lord Edward Somerset, the commander of the First (Household) Cavalry Brigade, recorded in his diary:

> The action was extremely sharp. The French brought a very superior force into the field; notwithstanding which the British troops maintained their position with the greatest bravery and resisted the attacks of the enemy's cavalry; although unsupported by the British cavalry which had not yet come up. The action continued till night, but the enemy could gain no advantage. The loss was considerable on both sides.[1]

A son of the Duke of Beaufort, Somerset (1776–1842) had joined the army in 1793, and crucially served as an aide de camp to York during the 1799 campaign. He served in the Peninsular War, winning glory at Salamanca.

The French, under Marshal Ney, had enjoyed a good numerical advantage at the outset, but, with understandably poor intelligence about developments, misjudged the battle, launching piecemeal attacks and failing to outmanoeuvre the defenders. Wise after the event, Jérôme Bonaparte, a divisional commander in the battle, was to claim 'the campaign was lost at Quatre Bras by Ney's unaccountable conduct.'[2] As the Prussians, hit hard by Napoleon on the 16th at Ligny in a larger-scale clash than Quatre Bras, then retreated, Wellington, now seriously exposed to the risk of flank attack, also fell back on the 17th. The skills he and the army showed that day were important to survival and therefore to eventual victory at Waterloo. A skilful disengagement followed by an effective rearguard action, neither the easiest of tasks, prevented the French from exploiting the withdrawal, although, as a reminder of the need to use more than one source, views varied. An officer of the 10th Hussars commented:

> The retreat in rain … was against us – besides that our cavalry had suffered in the retreat as the Seventh Hussars had had the worst of it with the [French] Lancers on the chaussée [road], which is favourable to the lancers as they can only be attacked in front.[3]

Somerset provided a more sanguine account:

> As soon as the main body had moved off, a considerable force of the enemy's
> cavalry made a sudden attack on the rear [light cavalry] … and after some time
> drove them back on the Heavy Brigade which had retired up the hill beyond
> it. At this movement, Lord Uxbridge directed the 1st Regiment of Life Guards
> which had been placed on the road, to advance and charge, which order they
> executed with the greatest gallantry. Twice they attacked the French cuirassiers
> in the most brilliant manner, and with complete success, and thus checked the
> rapid advance of the enemy.[4]

The Duke proved especially good at making the best use of what he had
on the day of Waterloo, 18 June, both in making his dispositions and in
responding to French attacks. Wellington had 68,000 troops on or near
the battlefield, 31,000 of them British, holding the route to Brussels
against attacks by Napoleon's 72,000. Wellington was encouraged by
a Prussian promise that four corps would be sent to his aid, while the
unevenness of his army helped encourage him to rely on a defensive
deployment anchored on British units.

Conversely, as, throughout the campaign, French intelligence and
staff work were inadequate, Napoleon, who was ill, underestimated
Wellington's generalship, and on the battlefield there was no effective
coordination of French infantry, cavalry and artillery. The British line
was not weakened by prior engagement, and British firepower decisively
defeated a number of separate and poorly coordinated French assaults.

Yet, for all Napoleon's failings, the French were still a formidable army,
willing to take heavy casualties, and Wellington regarded Waterloo, in
which he suffered over 15,000 casualties in what was a long struggle,
as his hardest battle, describing it as a 'pounding match.' Napoleon
was frustrated by the overnight rain, which had left the clay soil soggy,
and delayed (perhaps fatally) the start of the battle as the cannon were
hauled into position. Having defeated with steady volleys the French
infantry attempt to smash through its centre, an achievement brought to
culmination in a British cavalry assault on those French units, Wellington's
army was attacked in mid-afternoon by the French cavalry. The defence
against the latter, however, was multi-layered, with the British cannon
in advance, the infantry squares providing mutually supportive fire, and

the British cavalry in reserve ready to counterattack should the French penetrate past the frontline squares. This was both a coordinated defence and a defence in depth, and none of the squares broke.

A French infantry attack in the centre then captured the farmyard of La Haye Sainte, when the remains of the garrison, their ammunition exhausted, withdrew at 6 pm, putting the British under pressure. However, by then, the French right was under heavy pressure from the advancing Prussians.

Other than a long day, the experience of battle hit the emotions and senses of the soldiers, the blows being countered by training, the pressure of the moment, orders, and the example of comrades. The physical and psychological strains of repelling and awaiting attack were considerable, while casualties remained lying alongside those who fought on. The smoke lay thick in the heavy, hot afternoon air, and was accentuated by the sweat of men and horses who thronged the small battlefield, the sweat contributing to a potent mix of smells including copious quantities of human and animal urine and faeces, as well as the sulphur in the gunpowder. The noise also pressed hard, Edward Neville Macready of the 13th Foot finding the roaring of the cannon and the shouting together producing the impression 'of a labouring volcano.'[5]

The attack by the Imperial Guard was the final throw of Napoleon's dice against Wellington, but this too was stopped by British fire, both cannon and infantry, a British artillery lieutenant recording that:

> Upon reaching the crest of our position they [the French] attempted to deploy into line; but the destructive fire of our guns loaded with canister shot, and the well directed volleys from the infantry prevented their regular formation. They remained under this fire about ten minutes advancing a little, but finding it impossible to force our position they gave way and went to the right about: upon which the Duke ordered a general charge to be made and in a moment our infantry and the French were so mixed together that an end was put to our firing for the day.[6]

Wellington then ordered a general advance. Earlier, either flank attacks, which Napoleon neglected, or yet more frontal assaults might have succeeded; but the arrival of Prussian support in the battle helped close Napoleon's options and assisted Wellington greatly in its later stages.[7]

After the battle, Wellington and the Prussians advanced into France, capturing Paris. Napoleon surrendered to a British warship and was taken to the South Atlantic island of St. Helena, where he died in 1821, his imprisonment a consequence and demonstration of British power. The career of his gaoler, the Irish-born Major-General Sir Hudson Lowe (1769–1844), Governor of the island from 1815 to 1821, was a testimony to the range of British power. Lowe's father was an army surgeon, and the young Hudson accompanied his father's regiment to the West Indies and America, while he served in Gibraltar (1787–93), Toulon (1793), Corsica (1793–6), Elba (1796–7), Portugal, Minorca, Egypt (1800–1), Malta, Italy (1803–9), the Ionian Islands (1809–12), France (1815), and, after St. Helena, in Antigua and Ceylon (1825–30). From 1815 until it ended in 1818, Wellington, as another sign of British significance in Europe, was in charge of the Allied forces that occupied much of France.

As a wartime commander, Wellington was energetic in confronting logistical issues, and good at the problems of managing alliance forces, tasks he had had to learn in India, where the British relied on *sepoys*, native troops in their employ, as well as on native allies, and, even more so, on the Peninsula, where he had to deal with both the Portuguese and the various Spanish elements.[8] Alliance dynamics were a key element of the British military effort in 1815, and, had he failed in these, then Wellington's skill as a commander of British units would have been of far more limited value, not least as the British alone would have been heavily outnumbered by the French. In this skill at alliance management, Wellington matched the ability of Marlborough as British commander in the Low Countries. That both men campaigned on the Continent underlined the need for consistent qualities if Britain was to be successful. As with Marlborough, Wellington had to be able to manage both the Dutch and those German forces that were either part of his army or fighting alongside it. The Prussians fought alongside the British in both wars.

When, conversely, during the Seven Years' War, the British were not allied with the Dutch or the Austrians (then the rulers of Belgium), they had not been able to operate in the Low Countries. Instead, allied with Prussia and Hesse-Cassel, and able to rely on the king's Hanoverian dominions, the British forces had operated further east, between the Rivers Rhine and Elbe in Germany, and as part of a multi-state army under Ferdinand of Brunswick. The supply routes ran through the German port of Emden. During the American War of Independence, the British had lacked even this possibility. In 1815, in contrast, Wellington was able to rely on a stronger alliance system, and this permitted him to operate in Belgium. Without an alliance system, such operations would not have been possible other than as coastal raids. At the same time, the alliance system had strategic consequences, not least the need to protect Britain's allies. Wellington had repeatedly shown perforce in the Peninsula that he was willing to withdraw in the face of advances of larger French armies and to abandon Spanish and Portuguese cities, but this flexibility was not really present in 1815, as such losses might lead to local weaknesses for the coalition, especially in encouraging Belgian dissatisfaction with Dutch rule.

Britain had fought France for longer than any combatant, keeping the resistance to Napoleon alive in 1810–12, but, in 1812–14, it was Russian, Prussian and Austrian forces that had defeated him. In the subsequent peace settlement, the Congress of Vienna, Britain had to accept their expansionism as the price of alliance, although it also served to contain France and limit its future potential. Yet, the British made an important contribution in the Peninsular War, and this distraction of French forces, which was understandably trumpeted by the British government, made an impact elsewhere in Europe. The British had found a way to use their limited military power to maximum effect, something that was far harder in the Low Countries which was far closer to the centre of French military power. The alternative policy in World War One of fighting Germany on its major front proved far more punishing.

In addition, helped by an effective recruitment system that drew on a growing population, the strength of state finances, good working systems, notably the role of Horse Guards, and a degree of cohesion and purpose, the army expanded considerably. By 1813, the army had expanded to a quarter of a million strong. This was without the need for conscription, although militiamen were in practice drafted into enlisting.[9]

A relatively more positive account of the British Army accords with assessments of pre-1789 Continental armies emphasising commitment, unit cohesion, and enthusiasm for aspects of the job, rather than coercion.[10] Far from the troops being the 'scum of the earth', they were, as Wellington pointed out in 1814, 'fine fellows', many from an artisanal background affected by the harsh economy of debt and credit that was accentuated by severe wartime disruption of the economy, as well as the impact of technological change.[11] Many troops were the younger sons of yeomen farmers or tradesmen who would not inherit the land or the family business as would older sons, and were therefore typically listed in muster rolls as 'labourers.'

As with other aspects of British society in period, for example religious observance and rural social relations, it is possible to emphasise very contrasting aspects for what in practice was a range of behaviour. Moreover, unsurprisingly, these were influenced by circumstances, such as the drama and shock of the storming, after heavy casualties, of positions, notably Badajoz in 1812. At the same time, institutional pressure, in the shape of encouragement, training and discipline, and the example and discipline exerted by fellow-soldiers, all helped lessen the range of behaviour and shape the effective code.

Victories in the Peninsular War and at Waterloo greatly improved the reputation of the British Army and helped strengthen it in public approval. The dominant image of this war on land is of Waterloo, of lines and squares of infantry bravely fighting off larger numbers of attacking French. Images of resolute masculinity were to be much celebrated in subsequent paintings, notably *The 28th Regiment at Quatre Bras* (1875) and *Scotland Forever!*, the charge of the Royal Scots Greys by Elizabeth Thompson, Lady Butler (1881), but also in the memory of participants. Claiming of Waterloo 'there has not been such a hard contested battle since the Great Roman War', Private John Abbott wrote: 'we fixed our bayonets and gave the proud messieurs such a dressing as they will ever think of.'[12]

Conclusion

It was there [on 17 June 1815] that Hodges was taken and left for dead by them (beasts!) after he surrendered ... They [the French] are brutes. Bravely certainly ... but insulting when successful – and treacherous – and, as far as I saw, abject in defat – The Lancers piked off Hodges in cold blood and the prisoners of the Life Guards – because they said we used rockets in the pursuit. Men [the French at Waterloo, 18 June] threw down their arms, appeared to surrender – then took them up again and fired at those who spared them. I saw one of them sabred for this act and rejoiced at it. You will think I am getting savage – but you know how often I have said I thought mercy absurd at the beginning of a rout ... I could not help saving some – had I known what was happening at the time to [Major] Howard [of the Tenth Hussars] my feelings might have been different – in charging the infantry he was shot in the mouth and perhaps in the head even brain – for he fell senseless to the ground – a brute stepped out and beat his head with the butt end of a musket. I declare it casts a cloud over our success whenever I think of his loss and of his sweet young wife and child.

OFFICER OF THE 10TH HUSSARS,
AFTER WATERLOO.[1]

The army as much as the navy made the empire, and thus both laid the basis for what became the modern Anglophone world. The army, and military force as a whole, however, was frequently contentious, both throughout the period and beyond. The deadly charge of the Yeomanry (not regular troops) on a political meeting in St. Peter's Field, Manchester on 16 August 1819, with 18 killed, gave rise to the use of the term Peterloo as a conscious echo of and comparison with Waterloo. The army, in truth, had been crucial to the stability of the political system, to the rise of imperial power, to security and to expansion. Moreover, the significance of the army emerges clearly in the comparative context, with both Western and non-Western powers defeated, and repeatedly so, from France to the Marathas.

There has been a tendency to underplay the achievements of the army, one seen in other periods of military history, a tendency that raises instructive questions about the nature of British strategic culture. For long, the focus in Britain was on the Royal Navy, not only in political support and cultural attention, but also in ideology as expressed in both history and political discussion. It was as if a freedom-loving island nation should not have to rely on an army. This was also an attitude seen in the other political culture derived from Britain in this period, that of the United States, and notably so with the attitude of Thomas Jefferson, who was very much a supporter of militia rather than regular troops.

British Army campaigns were reliant on naval support. John Chetwynd, the English envoy in Turin, commented in 1704 about the plan to send a fleet to the Mediterranean: 'Unless there are 10,000 soldiers aboard the fleet it will not have that respect paid to it which it deserves.'[2] Yet, the soldiers could not operate at all without the fleet. In 1760, Frederick II pressed on the value of the British 'alarming their [French] coasts … with apprehension of descent … raise great murmurings among the people … and might strengthen the hands of those ministers who were disposed to peace.'[3] Coote wrote from southern India in 1782:

> I wish most anxiously for intelligence of the Admiral and the Fleet being again upon the coast, as I should hope thereby to have it in my power to move to the southward, as a supply of provisions might then be sent me by sea without which I could not in the present position of Haidar [Ali of Mysore] and the French undertake such an operation to its full extent, at least with that degree of security so necessary to the preservation of our real interests.[4]

Service in the army, however, was not an add-on to the history of the period, but a central feature of public culture, and one linked to a willingness to sustain a long-term struggle. The large number who came forward to serve in volunteer and militia units exemplified this point and underlined the multifaceted character of Britain as a military power. Moreover, the role and image of the army changed. Associated in the late seventeenth and early eighteenth centuries with authoritarianism and foreign models of governance, the image had been largely negative. Instead, the image became largely positive, and especially toward the close of the period. This was seen in literature, for example in the novels of Jane Austen: General Tilney was a manipulative snob, but Colonel Brandon a hero. George Wickham, not an officer in the Regulars, was a rogue, but Colonel Fitzwilliam a figure of attractive sagacity. Indeed, the army had become an important part of Britain's self-image and identity, and was sustained by, and itself sustained, a military culture in British society, with a situation very different to that of the reservations about a standing army a century earlier.

This portrayal reflected the successes of Wellington, culminating with Waterloo, a victory in both defence and then offence, which drove out images of failure, as at Buenos Aires in 1807 and New Orleans earlier in 1815. The pressure on commanders such as Wellington reflected the circumstances of battle, but also a type of warfare in which much independence arose from the effects of a decentralised system of command.[5] Throughout, there was no process of inevitable achievement or immutable success and it can be difficult to determine where to place the emphasis. The Ordnance department complained in 1702 that 'too often the bombs and shells have been filled with sand instead of proper ingredients', but between 1701 and mid-1704 it was able to issue 56,000 muskets. So also with the supply of shot and shells during the Seven Years' War: not all demands were met, but a large amount of munitions was distributed. Between 1795 and 1815, the British produced at least 3,212,000 small arms and in 1814 there were 743,000 serviceable muskets in store.[6]

There were repeated failures, in North America, the West Indies, Western Europe, and India, notably, for the last, in 1779, 1780, 1782, 1790 and 1804. So also with the Peninsula. In 1812, the focus is on Wellington's victory at Salamanca in July followed by the occupation of Madrid on 12 August. However, Wellington was forced to retreat that autumn in the face of larger French forces after his attempts to storm the fortress of Burgos had failed, not least because he had insufficient artillery. This failure, which arose from Wellington's risky tactics and strategy, prefigured the defeat of Wellington's brother-in-law at New Orleans in

January 1815. The British suffered many casualties in the retreat from Burgos in 1812, in part because of a breakdown of the supply system.

At this stage, the situation did not seem too different from that in Spain in the War of the Spanish Succession (1701–13), and that commitment had ultimately ended in failure and a sense of concern about British capabilities. In 1711, prefiguring Montgomery's anxieties about losses in 1944, John, 2nd Duke of Argyll, the commander in chief of British forces in Spain, observed 'I am sure if any misfortune should happen that it would be impossible to get our troops recruited again next year', adding:

> If we are not successful in a general attempt, this late great advantage is thrown away and we are undone, and should we succeed unless the affair chances to be a battle of Ramillies or Blenheim in short that they are entirely routed, I do not know if it will prove greatly to our advantage … my humble thoughts are to shun unnecessary risks.[7]

His recipient, Major-General Thomas Whetham (c. 1665–1741), the son of a London lawyer and grandson of a Civil War colonel, became an ensign in the infantry in 1685, thereafter serving in Scotland, the West Indies, and Spain, and Scotland, including against the '15, and holding military positions until his death.

Wellington, in contrast, was to be more successful in 1813 than 1812, in part because he was able to sustain the results of victory at Vitoria. At the same time, in part this was a matter of benefiting from advantage elsewhere in the shape of the collapse of Napoleon's position in Germany in the face of Britain's allies. This was crucial to his overthrow in 1814, an overthrow that was to lead to a peace treaty that awarded Britain extensive colonial gains. The European operations of the British Army was important to this process as it kept Britain more central in European power politics than it might otherwise have been and thereby lessened the risk of a peace settlement that minimised British interests.

The Napoleonic Wars, more particularly Wellington's campaigns, dominated postwar British perceptions of the army. The Duke's long period of influence and the careers of those who had served under him helped ensure that this history remained the present, and to an unprecedented degree. Command continuity was shown with Fitzroy,

Lord Raglan (1788–1855), ninth son of the Duke of Beaufort, who became a cornet of dragoons in 1804 and aide-de-camp to Wellington from 1808, becoming his Military Secretary in 1810. He lost an arm at Waterloo. Military Secretary at the Horse Guards from 1827 to 1852, he became Master-General of the Ordnance in 1852 and a rather unimaginative commander of the British troops in the Crimean War from 1854 until his death from dysentery.[8] Raglan was compared to Wellington by Sir James Graham, 1st Lord of the Admiralty:

> If the poor old Duke had lived to see your triumph, how justly proud he would have been of victories won by his pupil and by his dearest and most trusted friend. Indeed, he still lives in the army which he trained and in the general whom he taught to conquer.... This is indeed treading in the steps of your great master.[9]

Of other major commanders, Henry Hardinge (1785–1856), who succeeded Wellington as commander in chief in 1852, had entered the army in 1799, playing an active role in the Peninsular War, lost a hand at Ligny, was Secretary at War in 1828–30 and 1841–4, and second in command in the Sikh War in 1845–6. The son of an officer, Hugh Gough (1779–1869), entered the army in 1794, served in the French Revolutionary and Napoleonic Wars, notably in the Peninsular War, and went on to command British forces in China (1839–42) and India (1843–9), defeating the Sikhs. Charles Napier (1782–1853), the eldest son of a colonel, took up active service in the army in 1799, served in the Corunna campaign, being badly wounded, and then again in the Peninsula in 1810–12, and in 1842 was appointed commander of Indian Army within the Bombay Presidency, in which role he conquered Sindh.

Alongside the personal and career memories of the Napoleonic Wars, there were also plentiful first-hand accounts, including from the junior ranks, and a mass market fed by an entrepreneurial world of print, as with *Recollections of Rifleman Harris* (1848), George Gleig's *The Subaltern* (1825), Captain James MacCarthy's *Recollections of the Storming of the Castle of Badajos* (1836). Gleig (1796–1888), who had served in the Peninsular campaigns of 1813–14 and became Chaplain-General, also published *Sketch of the Military History of Great Britain* (1845), *Waterloo* (1847) and biographies of Clive (1848) and Wellington (1862). A veteran of the war, William Napier, a brother of Charles Napier, produced a *History of the*

War in the Peninsula (1828–40), of which several editions, abridgements and translations appeared. He was involved in controversy, publishing *Observations Illustrating Sir John Moore's Campaign* (1832) in response to criticism expressed by another veteran, Moyle Sherer, in his *Popular Recollections of the Peninsula* (1823). Sherer also published a commercially successful *Life of Wellington* (1830–2).

After the Crimean War, there was to be a growing sense that reform was necessary, and that features such as the selling of commissions and the use of patronage rather than merit had damaged the army. This was more a guide to the assumptions of the second half of the 19th century than the realities of earlier effectiveness. Indeed, as the past then slipped into heroic recollection, the role of Britain's army in the long struggle from 1689 to 1815 became a more patchy series of collective memories. However, this role should be understood not as a series of separate conflicts, but as an interrelated whole that reflected the interaction of Britain's military commitments: in the British Isles, in Europe, and further afield. And so also with the careers of soldiers, from privates to generals. This was a global army that made a world empire.

Abbreviations

Add	Additional Manuscripts to the British Library
AE	Paris, Ministère des Rélations Extérieures
AST	Turin, Archivio di Stato
Beinecke	New Haven, Connecticut, Beinecke Library
BL	London, British Library
Catton	Catton Papers, Derbyshire Record Office, formerly Derby Library
Chewton	Chewton House, Chewton Mendip, Waldegrave Papers
Cobbett	W. Cobbett (ed.), *Parliamentary History of England from ... 1066 to ... 1803* (36 vols, 1806–20)
Cornwallis	C. Ross (ed.), *Correspondence of Charles 1st Marquess Cornwallis* (1859)
CP	Correspondance Politique
CRO	County Record Office
Cumb. P	Papers of William, Duke of Cumberland
Durham, Grey	Durham, University Department of Palaeography, papers of 1st Earl Grey
Eg.	Egerton Manuscripts
Farmington	Lewis Walpole Library, Farmington, Connecticut
HL	Huntington Library, San Marino, California
HMC	Historical Manuscripts Commission
Hotham	Hull, University Library, Hotham Papers
IO	India Office Papers
JMH	*Journal of Military History*
LM	Lettere Ministri
Lo	Loudoun Papers

MD	Mémoires et Documents
Me	Nottingham, University Library, Mellish Papers
NA	London, National Archives, formerly Public Record Office
NAS	Edinburgh, National Archives of Scotland
NeC	Nottingham, University Library, Newcastle-Clumber papers
NRO	Northumberland Record Office
PRONI	Belfast, Public Record Office of Northern Ireland
RA	Windsor Castle, Royal Archives
SP	State Papers
WO	War Office Papers

Selected Further Reading

The extent of relevant manuscript and printed primary sources, as well as the volume of valuable secondary works, is such that the entire book could be devoted to them. Instead, I focus on some important works published since 1990, in the knowledge that primary sources and earliest studies can be pursued through their footnotes and bibliographies. In addition, those interested in the subject are advised to follow the relevant periodical literature, notably the *Journal of the Society for Army Historical Research* and the *Journal of Military History*.

Unless otherwise stated, all books are published in London.

Alavi, S., *The Sepoys and the Company. Tradition and transition in northern India 1770–1830* (Delhi, 1995).

Anderson, F., *Crucible of War: The Seven Years' War and the Fate of Empire in British North America, 1754–1766* (New York, 2000).

Bartlett, T. and K. Jeffery (eds), *A Military History of Ireland* (Cambridge, 1996).

Berkeley, A. D. (ed.), *New Lights on the Peninsular War* (Almada, 1991).

Brumwell, S., *Redcoats: The British Soldier and War in the Americas, 1755–1763* (Cambridge, 2002).

Bryant, G. J., *The Emergence of British Power in India, 1600–1780: A Grand Strategic Interpretation* (Woodbridge, 2013).

Buckley, R. N., *The British Army in the West Indies: Society and the Military in the Revolutionary Age* (Gainesville, Fl., 1998).

Campbell, M., *The Maroons of Jamaica, 1655–1796: A History of Resistance, Collaboration and Betrayal* (Trenton, Nj., 1990).

Carpenter, S. D. M., *Southern Gambit: Cornwallis and the British March to Yorktown* (Norman, Ok., 2019).

Chandler, D. and I. Beckett (eds), *The Oxford Illustrated History of the British Army* (Oxford, 1994).

Chet, G., *Conquering the American Wilderness. The Triumph of European Warfare in the Colonial Northeast* (Amherst, Mass., 2003).

Childs, J., *The Nine Years' War and the British Army. The Operations in the Low Countries* (Manchester, 1991).

Colley, L. J., *Britons. Forging the Nation 1707–1837* (New Haven, Conn., 1992).

Collins, B., *War and Empire: The Expansion of Britain 1790–1830* (2010).

Conway, S., *The War of American Independence 1775–1783* (1995).

Conway, S., *War, State, and Society in Mid-Eighteenth-Century Britain and Ireland* (Oxford, 2006).

Cooper, R. G. S., *The Anglo-Maratha Campaigns and the Contest for India* (Cambridge, 2003).

Coss, E., *All for the King's Shilling: The British Soldier under Wellington, 1808–1814* (Norman, Ok., 2010).

Davies, H., *Wellington's Wars: The Making of a Military Genius* (New Haven, Conn., 2012).

Dyde, B. S., *The Empty Sleeve: The Story of the West India Regiments of the British Army* (1997).

Fletcher, I., *The Wars of Oblivion. The British Invasion of the Rio de la Plata, 1806–1807* (Tunbridge Wells, 1991).

French, D., *The British Way in Warfare 1688–2000* (1990).

Gregory, D., *Minorca, the Illusory Prize. A history of the British occupations of Minorca between 1708 and 1802* (1990).

Guy, A. J., *Oeconomy and Discipline. Officership and Administration in the British Army, 1714–63* (Manchester, 1985).

Guy, A. J. (ed.), *The Road to Waterloo. The British Army and the Struggle against Revolutionary and Napoleonic France, 1793–1815* (Stroud, 1990).

Hall, C., *British Strategy in the Napoleonic War, 1803–1815* (Manchester, 1992).

Harding, R. H., *Amphibious Warfare in the Eighteenth Century. The British Expedition to the West Indies 1740–1742* (Woodbridge, 1991).

Hayter, A. J., *The Army and the Crowd in Mid-Georgian England* (1978).

Henshaw, V., *Scotland and the British Army, 1700-1750: Defending the Union* (2014).

Houlding, J. A., *Fit for Service: The Training of the British Army, 1715–1795* (Oxford, 1981).

Kennedy, C. and M. McCormack, (eds), *Soldiering in Britain and Ireland, 1750–1850: Men at Arms* (Basingstoke, 2013).

Linch, K. and M. McCormack (eds), *Britain's Soldiers: Rethinking War and Society, 1715–1815* (Liverpool, 2014).

Linch, K., *Britain and Wellington's Army. Recruitment, Society and Tradition, 1807–15* (Basingstoke, 2011).

McCormack, M., *Embodying the Militia in Georgian England* (Oxford, 2015).

Muir, R., *Britain and the Defeat of Napoleon 1807–1815* (New Haven, Conn., 1996).

Muir, R., *Tactics and the Experience of Battle in the Age of Napoleon* (New Haven, Conn., 1998).

Muir, R., *Salamanca, 1812* (New Haven, Conn., 2001).

Muir, R., *Wellington: The Path to Victory 1769–1814* (New Haven, Conn., 2013).

Oates, J., *The Last Battle on English Soil: Preston 1715* (Farnham, 2015).

Pittock, M., *Culloden* (Oxford, 2016).

Robertson, I., *A Commanding Presence: Wellington in the Peninsula, 1808–1814, Logistics, Strategy, Survival* (Stroud, 2008).

Steele, I. K., *Betrayals. Fort William Henry and the 'Massacre'* (Oxford, 1990).

Steele, I. K., *Warpaths. Invasions of North America* (Oxford, 1994).

Stone, L. (ed.), *An Imperial State at War. Britain from 1689 to 1815* (1994).

Tracy, N., *Manila Ransomed. The British Assault on Manila in the Seven Years' War* (Exeter, 1995).

Zerbe, B. *The Birth of the Royal Marines, 1664–1802* (Woodbridge, 2013).

Endnotes

Preface

1   Richard Browne to father Jeremy, 14 Aug. 1759, BL. RP. 3284.

Introduction

1   Cobbett, XI, 467.
2   Northampton, Northamptonshire CRO. L (C) 1734.
3   S. Kinkel, *Disciplining the Empire: Politics, Governance, and the Rise of the British Navy* (Cambridge, Mass., 2018).
4   *Morning Post*, 17 Mar. 1786.
5   NA. SP. 82/64 fol. 220.
6   Bod. MS. Eng, Hist. c.314 fols 46, 51. Current value about £8.5 million.
7   Étienne François, Duke of Choiseul, key French minister, to Ossun, envoy in Madrid, 5 Apr. 1762, AE. CP. Espagne, 536 fol. 25.
8   BL. Add. 32820 fol. 44; NA. SP. 78/323 fols 272–3.

Chapter 1

1   The last Irish and Royalist forces in Ireland formally surrendered at Cloughoughter on 27 April 1653. In Scotland, Dunnottar Castle was the last Royalist stronghold to fall, which it did on 24 May 1652.
2   I. Gentles, *The New Model Army in England, Ireland, and Scotland, 1645–1653* (Oxford, 1992); H. Reece, *The Army in Cromwellian England, 1649–1660* (Oxford, 2013); M. Bennett, *Cromwell at War: The Lord General and his Military Revolution* (2017).
3   J. Childs, *The Army of Charles II* (1976).
4   J. Childs, *The Army, James II, and the Glorious Revolution* (Manchester, 1980); J. Childs, *General Percy Kirke and the Later Stuart Army* (2014).
5   Anon., *Seasonable and Affecting Observations on the Mutiny Bill* (1750), 66.

6 Jenkinson, *Discourse* (1757), 66.

7 N. Rogers, *Mayhem: Post-War Crime and Violence in Britain, 1748–53* (New Haven, Conn., 2012).

8 S. Banks, *A Polite Exchange of Bullets: The Duel and the English Gentleman 1750–1850* (Woodbridge, 2010).

9 M. Mattfeld, *Becoming Centaur: Eighteenth-Century Masculinity and English Horsemanship* (University Park, Penn., 2017).

10 Fox to Devonshire, 31 Jan. 1756, Chatsworth, papers of 3rd Duke, History of Parliament transcripts.

11 J. Brewer and E. Hellmuth (eds), *Rethinking Leviathan: The Eighteenth Century State in Britain and Germany* (Oxford, 1999), 53–70.

12 Stair to Stanhope, 5 Feb. 1715, NAS. GD. 135/137 no. 41.

13 Horatio Walpole to Townshend, 18 May 1722, NA. SP. 84/278 fol. 122.

14 Notes on the debate, BL. Add. 47000 fols 64–6.

15 Newcastle to Robert Keith, envoy in Vienna, 6 Jul. 1753, NA. SP. 80/192.

16 J. N. P. Watson, *Marlborough's Shadow: The Life of the First Earl Cadogan* (2003).

17 Townshend to Newcastle, 24 Jul., 7 Aug. 1725, NA. SP. 43/6 fols 244, 282.

18 Sir John Graeme, Jacobite envoy in Vienna, to John Hay, Earl of Inverness, Jacobite Secretary of State, 5 Oct., 2 Nov., 7, 14, 21 Dec. 1726, Hay to Graeme, 16 Nov. 1726, RA., Stuart Papers, 97/139, 98/132, 99/130, 151, 166, 99/39.

19 Brigadier-General James Cholmondely to George, 3rd Earl of Cholmondely, 19 Nov. 1745, Chester, CRO., DCH/X/9a/11.

20 Wade to Henry, 3rd Viscount Lonsdale, 13 Dec. 1745, Carlisle, Cumbria CRO., D/Pen Acc 2689.

21 R. A. Cumb. P., 7/279, 288, 291, 306; Durham, CRO., D/Lo/F/745/57; C. J. Terry (ed.), *The Albemarle Papers* (2 vols, Aberdeen, 1902), I, 114.

22 Chatsworth, papers of 3rd Duke.

23 C. Duffy, *The Best of Enemies: Germans against Jacobites, 1746* (2013).

24 I. G. Brown and H. Cheape (eds), *Witness to Rebellion: John Maclean's Journal of the 'Forty-Five and the Penicuik Drawings* (Edinburgh, 1996), 35–7; Duffy, *The '45: Bonnie Prince Charlie and the Untold Story of the Jacobite Rising* (2003).

25 J. Black, *Culloden and the '45* (Edinburgh, 1990); M. Pittock, *Culloden* (Oxford, 2016).

26 I. M. McCulloch, *Sons of the Mountains: The Highland Regiments in the French and Indian War, 1755–1767* (Fleischmanns, Ny., 2006); S. Reid, *Wellington's Highland Warriors: From the Black-Watch Mutiny to the Battle of Waterloo* (2010); V. Henshaw, *Scotland and the British Army, 1700–1750: Defending the Union* (2014); T. Royle, *Culloden: Scotland's Last Battle and the Forging of the British Empire* (2016); M. P. Cziennick, *The Fatal Land: War, Empire and the Highland Soldier in British America* (New Haven, Conn., 2015); P. O'Keeffe, *Culloden: Battle and Aftermath* (2021).

27 W. J. Shelton, 'The Role of Local Authorities in the Provincial Hunger Riots of 1766', *Albion*, 5 (1973), 50–66.

28 William, 3rd Duke of Devonshire, Lord Lieutenant of Ireland, to Henry Legge, 14 Feb. 1740, Catton, WH 3429, 123.

29 Bedford, Bedfordshire CRO., Lucas papers 30/9/17/3.

30 HL. Montagu papers no. 4557.

31 Friedrich Wilhelm von der Schulenburg, a key Hanoverian courtier, to Baron Görtz, 7 Dec. 1717, Darmstadt, Staatsarchiv, Gräflich Görtzisches Archiv, F23 fol. 124; H. E. Smith, 'The Hanoverian Succession and the Politicisation of the British Army,' in A. Gestrich and M. Schaich (eds), *The Hanoverian Succession: Dynastic Politics and Monarchical Culture* (Farnham, 2015), 207–26.

32 D'Aix, Sardinian envoy, a military figure, to Victor Amadeus II, 12 Jul. 1728, AST. LM. Ing. 35.

33 J. Niemeyer, *Die Revue bei Bemerode, 1735. Eine kulturgeschichtliche und heereskundliche Betrachtung zu einem Gemälde von J.F. Lüders* (Beckum, 1985).

34 Zamboni to Landgrave of Hesse-Darmstadt, 19 Jan. 1748, Darmstadt, Staatsarchiv, E1 M10/6.

35 A. J. Guy, *Oeconomy and Discipline: Officership and Administration in the British Army 1714–63* (Manchester, 1985).

36 BL. Add. 35406 fol. 136, 35407 fol. 17.

37 HMC, *Polwarth V*, 30.

38 Horatio Walpole to Trevor, 29 Apr. (os) 1740, Aylesbury, Buckinghamshire CRO., Trevor papers vol. 21.

39 *Gentleman's Magazine*, XXVI, 408.

40 BL. Add. 9176 fols 32, 34; Horatio Walpole to Trevor, 10 Aug. (os) 1740, Aylesbury, CRO., Trevor papers, vol. 22.

41 Lowther to Spedding, 18 Nov. 1740, Carlisle, Cumbria CRO., D/Lons./W.

42 Marlborough to Stair, 27 May 1740, Beinecke, Osborn Shelves, Stair Letters, no. 51.

43 J. Severn, *Architects of Empire: The Duke of Wellington and His Brothers* (Norman, Ok., 2007).

44 R. Middleton, 'The Duke of Newcastle and the conduct of patronage during the Seven Years' War 1757–1762', *British Journal for Eighteenth-Century Studies*, 12 (1989), 178–9.

45 J. Potter to Henry Legge, Secretary to the Lord Lieutenant of Ireland, 31 Jan. 1740, Catton, WH 3429, 95.

46 James, 2nd Lord Tyrawley to Henry Pelham, Chancellor of the Exchequer, 11 June 1740, NeC., 109.

47 Richmond to Grey, 27 Apr. 1782, Durham, Grey, no. 61.

48 Memoranda on state of Hanoverian army, 1715, Paris, AE. CP. Brunswick-Hanovre, 45 fols 4–5.

49 *Sense,* Part II, Chapter 9.

Chapter 2

1   Reading, Berkshire CRO. Trumbull papers 133/11/1.

2   John Royland Hughes to Burland, Taunton, Somerset CRO., Trollop-Bellow papers, DD/TB 16 FT18.

3   Townshend to Horatio Walpole, 27 Aug., reply 10 Sept. 1725, BL. Add. 48981 fols 106–13, 117–22.

4   Newcastle to Cumberland, 18 Mar. 1748, John, 4th Earl of Sandwich to Cumberland, 7, 19, 17 Apr. 1748, RA. Cumb. P., 32/337, 33/272, 114,112, 134, 295.

5   B. P. Hughes, *Firepower: Weapons Effectiveness on the Battlefield, 1630–1850* (1974).

6   R. Holmes, *Redcoat: The British Soldier in the Age of Horse and Musket* (2002).

7   *The Journal of Major John Norton* (1816), 308.

8   Beinecke, Osborn Shelves, pc 224, 22 Sept. 1708.

9   M. Crumplin, *Men of Steel: Surgery in the Napoleonic Wars* (Shrewsbury, 2007) and *Guthrie's War: A Surgeon of the Peninsular War and Waterloo* (Barnsley, 2010).

10 P. Levrau, 'Crippled by a Musket Shot and a Sabre Slash', in D. Money (ed.), *1708: Oudenarde and Lille* (Cambridge, 2008), 70.

11 D. Chandler, *The Art of Warfare in the Age of Marlborough* (1976); C. Jorgensen et al, *Fighting Techniques of the Early Modern World* (Steeplehurst, 2005); G. Dempsey, *Albuera 1811: The Bloodiest Battle of the Peninsular War* (2008).

12 W. C. Horsley (trans), *The Chronicles of an Old Campaigner* (1904), 184–5.

13 J. B. Hattendorf et al (eds), *Marlborough: Soldier and Diplomat* (Rotterdam, 2012).

14 Richards diary, BL. Stowe MSS. 467 fols 21–3.

15 J. A. Houlding, *Fit for Service: The Training of the British Army, 1715–1795* (Oxford, 1981).

16 Townshend to Robert Walpole, 18 Oct. 1723, NA. SP. 43/5 fol. 135.

17 Private and Separate Instructions for Richard Sutton, 25 Mar., Townshend to Sutton, 2 May 1727, NA. SP. 81/122.

18 Delafaye to Waldegrave, 15 Feb. 1733, Chewton, papers of 1st Earl Waldegrave; Sir Thomas Robinson to Earl of Carlisle, 3 Feb. 1733, HMC., *Carlisle*, 100.

19 AE. MD. Ang. 55.

20 General Diemar, envoy of Hesse-Cassel, to Prince Eugene, Austrian Minister of War, 18 Feb. 1735, Vienna, Haus-, Hof-, und Staatsarchiv, General Korrespondenz, 85a fol. 566.

21 Edward Weston to Robert Trevor, 23 Feb. 1742, Farmington, Weston papers vol. 13.

22 Carteret to Robinson, 2 Mar. 1742, BL. Add. 23810 fol. 226.

23 Onslow Burrish, British agent in Belgium, to Carteret, 30 Apr., 16, 19 May 1732, NA. SP. 77/92 fols 21–2, 31–2, 34–5.

24 Burrish to Carteret, 5, 19, 22 May 1742, NA. SP. 77/92 fols 24, 35–6.

25 Belle-Île memoire, 19 Mar. 1742, AE. CP. Bavière, 97 fols 245–6.

26 John Cope to Colonel John, 4th Earl of Loudoun, 29 Jul., 19 Aug. 1742, HL. Lo. 10975–6.

27 Philip Brown in Barbara Andrews to Elizabeth Baker, Aylesbury, Buckinghamshire CRO. D/X 1069/2/115. This complements the letter from Brown to his brother published in the *Journal of the Society for Army Historical Research*, 5 (1926); Leonard to Molly Robinson, 18 June 1743, Warwick, The Queen's Own Hussars Regimental Museum.

28 Goodwood Mss, correspondence of second Duke.

29 Wade to John, Lord Carteret, Secretary of State for Northern Department, 10, 20 June 1744, Bod. Ms. Eng. Hist. C.314 fols 15–16.

30 Aylesbury, Buckinghamshire CRO. D/X 1069/2/116.

31 Stone to Edward Weston, 13 Aug. 1745, Farmington, Weston papers, vol. 16; Newcastle to Henry, 3rd Viscount Lonsdale, 5 Sept. 1745, Carlisle, Cumbria CRO, D/Pen Acc. 2689; Trevor to Thomas Robinson, 30 Sept. 1745, BL. Add. 23821 fol. 107.

32 L. Vergez, *Roucoux 1746 : Bataille et combats pendant la guerre en dentelles* (Le Coudray-Macouard, 2017).

33 Newcastle to Harrington, 14 June 1745, NA. SP. 43/37.

34 Thomas Orby Hunter, Deputy Paymaster of the Forces in Flanders, to Henry Pelham, First Lord of the Treasury, 22 Nov. 1746, 28 Feb. 1747, Beinecke, Osborn Shelves, Pelham Box.

35 Newcastle to Harrington, 21 May 1745, NA. SP. 43/37.

36 Newcastle to Cumberland, 5 Apr. 1748, RA, Cumb. P. 33/273.

37 Edmund Martin to 2nd Duke of Richmond, 19 Aug. 1748, Goodwood Mss. 107 no. 685.

38 R. Whitworth (ed.), *Gunner at large. The diary of James Wood RA. 1746–1765* (1988), ix–x.

39 'M Pitt's points', 21 Sept. 1753, BL. Add. 32995 fols 29–30.

40 Anon., *Reflections upon the Present State of Affairs* (1755), 8.

Chapter 3

1 A. Lyons, *The 1711 Expedition to Quebec* (2013).

2 Rivers to Marlborough, 19 June 1703, BL. Add. 61306 fol. 106.

3 A. Charbonneau, Y. Desloges and M. Lafrance, *Québec: Ville fortifiée du XVIIe Siècle* (Québec, 1982).

4 K. McLay, 'Sir Francis Wheeler's Caribbean and North American Expedition, 1693: A Case Study in Combined Operational Command during the Reign of William III', *War in History*, 14 (2007), 383–407.

5 D. W. Boyce, '"As the Wind Scatters the Smoke": The Tuscaroras in the Eighteenth Century', in D. D. Richter and J. H. Merrell (eds), *Beyond the Covenant Chain: the*

Iroquois and their neighbors in Indian North America, 1600–1800 (Syracuse, 1987), 151–63.

6   Colonial Office reports by Trelawny, G. Metcalf, *Royal Government and Political Conflict in Jamaica, 1729–1783* (1965); M. Campbell, *The Maroons of Jamaica, 1655–1796: A history of resistance, collaboration and betrayal* (Trenton, Nj., 1990).

7   R. Law, '"Here is no resisting the country". The realities of power in Afro-European relations on the West African "Slave Coast"', *Itinerario*, 18 (1994), 55–6.

8   A. Deshpande, 'Limitations of military technology. Naval warfare on the West Coast, 1650–1800', *Economic and Political Weekly*, 25 (1992), 902–3.

9   R. H. Harding, *Amphibious Warfare in the Eighteenth Century. The British Expedition to the West Indies 1740–1742* (Woodbridge, 1991), 83–122.

10 Oglethorpe to Walpole, I Oct. 1739, Cambridge, University Library, Correspondence, no. 2926.

11 P. Spalding, *Oglethorpe in America* (Chicago, Ill., 1977).

12 Stewart to John, 2nd Earl of Stair, 10 Sept. 1741, Beinecke, Osborn Shelves, Stair Letters, no. 70.

13 A. J. Smithers, *The Tangier Campaign. The Birth of the British Army* (Stroud, 2003).

Chapter 4

1   'A scheme for the improvement and employment of His Majesty's Forces in America', sent by Townshend to Newcastle, 13 Sept. 1754, BL. Add. 32736 fol. 515.

2   BL. Add. 45662 fols 33–4.

3   *London Chronicle*, 1 Jan. 1758; Henry Meredyth to Sir Robert Wilmot, 19 Apr. 1755, Catton, WH 3448.

4   J. Grenier, *The Far Reaches of Empire: War in Nova Scotia, 1710–1760* (Norman, Ok., 2008).

5   Council memorandum, 21 Aug. 1753, BL. Add. 32995 fol. 27.

6   Council meeting, 26 June 1754, BL. Add. 33029 fol. 124.

7   'A scheme', 13 Sept. 1754, BL. Add. 32736 fol. 515.

8   T. R. Clayton, 'The Duke of Newcastle, the Earl of Halifax, and the American origins of the Seven Years' War', *Historical Journal*, 24 (1981), 571–603.

9   D. Graham, 'The planning of the Beauséjour operation and the approaches to war in 1755', *New England Quarterly*, 61 (1968), 551–66.

10 M. C. Ward, '"The European Method of Warring is not practiced here": The failure of British military policy in the Ohio Valley, 1755–1759', *War in History*, 4 (1997), 247–63.

11 Sackville to Wilmot, 6 Aug. 1755, Catton, WH. 3448.

12 M. McCormack, 'Citizenship, Nationhood and Masculinity in the Affair of the Hanoverian Soldier, 1756', *Historical Journal*, 49 (2006), 971–93.

13 S. M. Pargellis, *Lord Loudoun in North America* (New Haven, Conn., 1933).

14 G. Plank, *Rebellion and Savagery. The Jacobite Rising of 1745 and the British Empire* (Philadelphia, Penn., 2006).

15 HL. Lo. 2765A.

16 I. K. Steele, *Betrayals: Fort William Henry and the 'Massacre'* (Oxford, 1990); B. Hughes, *The Siege of Fort William Henry: A Year on the Northeastern Frontier* (Yardley, Penn., 2011).

17 C. A. Crouch, *Nobility Lost: French and Canadian Martial Cultures, Indians and the End of New France* (Ithaca, Ny., 2014).

18 Earl of Ilchester (ed.), *Letters to Henry Fox* (1915), 116–17.

19 Robert, 4th Earl of Holdernesse, Secretary of State, to Cumberland, 7 Sept. 1757, BL. Eg. 3442 fol. 236.

20 George Ross to Brigadier Forbes, 7 Oct. 1757, NAS. GD. 45/2/20/3; *Centinel*, 11, 12 Oct. 1757; *Herald*, 20 Oct. 1757.

21 Viry, Sardinian ambassador, to Charles Emmanuel III, 7 Oct. 1757, AST. LM. Ing. 62.

22 For support for militia, see also *Monitor*, 1 Oct. 1757.

23 Holdernesse to Cumberland, 6 Oct., and to Andrew Mitchell, envoy in Berlin, 10 Oct. 1757, BL. Eg. 3442 fols 279-80, NA. SP. 90/70.

24 Holdernesse to Mitchell, 25 Feb. 1758, NA. SP. 90/71.

25 John Calcraft to Lieutenant-Colonel Hale, 27 Aug. 1758, BL. Add. 17494 fol. 17.

26 R. Chartrand, *Ticonderoga, 1758* (Oxford, 2000); I.M. McCulloch, 'The Battle of Ticonderoga, 2008', *JMH*, 72(3) (2008), 889-900.

27 BL. Add. 45662 fols 6–7.

28 A. J. B. Johnston, *Endgame 1758: The Promise, the Glory and the Despair of Louisbourg's Last Decade* (Lincoln, Nb., 2008); H. Boscawen, *The Capture of Louisbourg, 1758* (Norman, Ok., 2011).

29 S. Brumwell, *Redcoats: The British Soldier and War in the Americas, 1755–1763* (Cambridge, 2002); D.R. Cubbison, *All Canada in the Hands of the British: General Jeffery Amherst and the 1760 Campaign to Conquer New France* (Norman, Ok., 2014).

30 Pitt to Loudoun, 4 Feb. 1757, HL. Lo. 2765A.

31 Wolfe to Colonel Charles Hotham, 9 Aug. 1758, Hotham, DDHo/4/7.

32 Joseph Yorke to Holdernesse, 11 Apr. 1758, NA. SP. 90/71.

33 Holdernesse to Mitchell, 27 June 1758, NA. SP. 90/71.

34 Anon. Journal, possibly by Henry Fletcher, Providence, Rhode Island, John Carter Brown Library, Codex Eng. 41; M. C. Ward, *The Battle for Quebec 1759: Britain's Conquest of Canada* (Stroud, 2005).

35 D. J. Blackmore, '"Destructive and Formidable": British Infantry Firepower, 1642–1765', (DPhil., Nottingham Trent, 2012).

36 G. E. Aylmer and R. Cant (eds), *A History of York Minister* (Oxford, 1977), 247.

37 BL. Add. 45662 fol. 43.

38 Yorke to Hotham, 26 May 1759, Hotham, DDHo 4/9.

39 Holdernesse to Yorke, 17 Aug., 21 Sept. 1759, NA. SP. 84/485.

40 Bedford to William Pitt the Elder, 29 Aug. 1759, Woburn, Bedford Estate Office.

41 Devonshire to Legge, 24 Mar. 1740, Catton, WH 3429, 154.

42 Sackville to Holdernesse, 2 Aug. 1759, BL. Eg. 3443 fol. 235.

43 Sackville to Holdernesse, 2 Aug. 1759, BL. Eg. 3443 fol. 234.

44 P. Mackesy, *The Coward of Minden* (1979). Sackville changed his name after inheriting the property of Lady Elizabeth Germain.

45 *Monitor* 25 Aug. 1759.

46 Joseph to Philip Yorke, 23 Mar. 1753, BL. Add. 35363 fol. 324.

47 Hatton to Holdernesse, 18 Jul., 13 Aug. 1758, BL. Eg. 3443 fols 34, 42, 48. See also Hatton to Samuel Martin, 3 Sept. 1758, NA. T1/384/54.

48 A. D. Francis, 'The Campaign in Portugal, 1762', *Journal of the Society for Army Historical Research*, 59 (1981), 25–43.

49 Lord Tyrawly to Pombal, Portuguese First Minister, 24 Jul. 1762, PRONI, T 2812/8/48.

50 Lieutenant-General Henry Conway to Charles Townshend, Secretary at War, 5 May 1761, NA. WO. 1/165, 39.

51 Ibid. 20 Sept. 1762, 182.

52 Folliott to Colonel Douglas, 26 Sept. 1762, HL. Lo. 8607.

53 Marlborough to his wife, 30 June 1758, BL. Add. 61667.

54 Hodgson to Lord Barrington, Secretary at War, 29 Apr. 1761, NA. WO. 1/165, 340.

55 T. Keppel, *The Life of Augustus, Viscount Keppel* (2 vols, 1842), I, 320.

56 Francis to Jeremy Browne, 26 Oct. 1762, BL. RP. 3284.

57 Townshend to 3rd Earl of Bute, 17 Sept. 1761, Mount Stuart, Bute papers, 7/23.

58 Fawcett to James Lister, 24 Oct. 1760, Halifax, Calderdale Archives Department, SH:7/FAW/60.

59 Lieutenant-General Conway to Barrington, 25 Apr., Conway to Townshend, 5 May 1761, NA. WO. 1/165, 33, 39.

60 Fawcett to Lister, 5 Dec. 1759, Halifax SH:7/FAW, 58.

61 Sackville to Holdernesse, 10 Sept. 1758, BL. Eg. 3444 fol. 66.

62 A. Starkey, *War in the Age of Enlightenment, 1700–1789* (Westport, Conn., 2003); D. Grebs, 'The Making of Prisoners of War: Rituals of Surrender in the American War of Independence, 1776–83', *Militärgeschichtliche Zeitschrift*, 64 (2005), 1–29.

63 Lieutenant-Colonel Charles Russell to wife, 5 Jul. 1743, BL. Add. 69382.

64 Fawcett to Lister, 24 Oct. 1760, Halifax SH:7/FAW/60.

65 Conway to Townshend, 15 Jul. 1761, 15 Aug., 20 Sept. 1762, NA. WO. 1/165, 95–6, 141–2, 183.

66 Granby to Townshend, 24 Sept. 1762, NA. WO. 1/165, 190–1.

67 *Royal Magazine* 1 (1760), 190.

68 Houlding, *Fit for Service*, 138–9.

69 G. Chet, *Conquering the American Wilderness. The Triumph of European Warfare in the Colonial Northeast* (Amherst, Mass., 2003), 141.

70 Charles Areskin, Lord Tinwall, to John, 4th Marquess of Tweedale, 18 Sept. 1745, NA. SP. 54/26 fol. 92. See also, Lord Glenorchy to Tweedale, 1 Sept. 1745, Edinburgh, National Library of Scotland, Yester papers, vol. 7071 fol. 3.

71 Anon., *A Letter to the People of England, Upon the Militia* (1757), 10; M. McCormack, *Embodying the Militia in Georgian England* (Oxford, 2015).

72 Memorandum by Newcastle, 18 Feb. 1760, BL. Stowe 263 fol. 16.

73 Bampfylde to John, 4th Duke of Bedford, Lord Lieutenant of Devon, 10 Aug. 1759, Exeter, Devon CRO, L1258, M/Militia/3.

74 Fortescue to Bedford, Aug. 1759, Ibid.

75 AE. CP. Ang. 440, fols 26–7, 231–7.

76 Marlborough to his wife, 30 June 1758, BL. Add. 61667, fol. 22.

77 G. Yagi, *The Struggle for North America, 1754–1758: Britain's Tarnished Laurels* (2016).

Chapter 5

1 Bull to Amherst, 15 Apr. 1761, NA. CO. 5/61 fol. 277.

2 J. Oliphant, *Peace and War on the Anglo-Cherokee Frontier, 1756–63* (Baton Rouge, La, 2001); D.J. Tortora, *Carolina in Crisis: Cherokees, Colonists, and Slaves in the American Southeast, 1756–1763* (Chapel Hill, Nc., 2015).

3 M. Grant, *General James Grant of Ballindalloch, 1720–1806* (1930); P. D. Nelson, *General James Grant* (Gainesville, Fl., 1993).

4 M. C. Ward, *Breaking the Backcountry: The Seven Years' War in Virginia and Pennsylvania, 1754–1765* (Pittsburgh, Penn., 2003), 253.

5 M. N. McConnell, *Army and Empire: British Soldiers on the American Frontier, 1758–1775* (Lincoln, NB, 2004), 147.

6 P. Spero, 'Lord Dunmore's Victory: Turning Pennsylvania into Virginia', *Consortium on the Revolutionary Era: Selected Papers, 2007*, 109–19.

7 D. Preston, *Braddock's Defeat: The Battle of the Monongahela and the Road to Revolution* (Oxford, 2015).

8 F. Anderson, *A People's Army: Massachusetts Soldiers and Society in the Seven Years' War* (Chapel Hill, Nc., 1984).

9 J. Bullion, 'The ten thousand in America. More light on the decision on the American army, 1762–1763', *William and Mary Quarterly*, 3rd ser. 43 (1986), 646–57, esp. 651–2, and 'Security and economy: the Bute administration's plan for the American army and revenue, 1762–1763', Ibid., 45 (1988), 499–509, esp. 507.

10 Fawcett to George, 22 Feb. 1786, A. Aspinall (ed.), *The Later Correspondence of George III, 1783–1810* (5 vols, Cambridge, 1962–70), I, 211.

11 S. Brumwell, *Redcoats: The British Soldier and War in the Americas, 1755–1763* (Cambridge, Mass., 2002).

12 J. G. McCurdy, *Quarters: The Accommodation of the British Army and the Coming of the American Revolution* (Ithaca, NY, 2019).

13 M. M. Mintz, *the Generals of Saratoga: John Burgoyne and Horatio Gates* (New Haven, Conn., 1990).

14 P. Papas, *Renegade Revolutionary: The Life of General Charles Lee* (New York, 2014).

15 Evelyn to Sir Frederick Evelyn, himself a veteran of Minden, 23 Apr., 19 Aug. 1775, BL. Evelyn papers LE1.

16 Gage to Viscount Barrington, 26 June 1775, BL. Add. 73550.

17 J. Gwyn, *Frigates and Foremasts: The North American Squadron in Nova Scotia Waters, 1745–1815* (Vancouver, 2003).

18 A. O'Shaughnessy, *The Men Who Lost America: British Command during the Revolutionary War and the Preservation of the Empire* (2013).

19 Humphrey Minchin MP to Amherst, 9 Sept. 1779, and draft answer, NA. WO. 34/118 fols 95–6.

20 NAS. GD. 26/9/513/15.

21 Congreve to Reverend Richard Congreve, 4 Sept. 1776, Stafford, Staffordshire CRO., D1057/M/F/30.

22 J. Piecuch (ed.), *Cavalry of the American Revolution* (Yardley, Penn., 2012).

23 NRO. 1314/6.

24 BL. Add. 32413 fols 14, 16–17.

25 NAS. GD. 26/9/513/7.

26 NRO. 1314/7.

27 Halifax, SH 7/JL/1, 15.

28 NAS. GD. 26/9/513/16.

29 Napier to Lord Dalhousie, Governor-General of India, 27 June 1849, BL. Add. 49106 fols 1–4.

30 T. W. Braisted, *Grand Forage 1778: The Battleground around New York City* (Yardley, Penn., 2016).

31 Rainsford to Amherst, 4 Aug. 1779, NA. WO. 34/117 fols 27–8; Anon, undated memorandum, NA. PRO. 30/11/258 fols 7–8.

32 NA. WO. 34/125 fol. 10.

33 BL. Add. 32413 fol. 12.

34 J. Burgoyne, *A State of the Expedition from Canada .... By ... Burgoyne* (London, 1790), 120; D. R. Cubbison, *Burgoyne and the Saratoga Campaign: His Papers* (Norman, Ok., 2012).

35 T. Corbett, *No Turning Point: The Saratoga Campaign in Perspective* (Norman, Ok., 2012).

36 K. J. Weddle, '"A Change of Both Men and Measures": British Reassessment of Military Strategy after Saratoga, 1777–1778', *JMH*, 77 (2013), 837–65.

37 BL. Add. 34416 fols 156, 271.

38 J. D. Grainger, *The Battle of Yorktown, 1781. A Reassessment* (Woodbridge, 2005).

39 R. Smith, 'The Failure of Great Britain's "Southern Expedition" of 1776: Revisiting Southern Campaigns in the Early Years of the American Revolution, 1775–1779', *Florida Historical Quarterly*, 93 (2015), 387–414.

40 D. Twohig, *The Papers of George Washington: Revolutionary War Series, VIII* (Charlottesville, Va., 1998), 454.

41 NA. PRO. 30/8/5.

42 D. Smith, *William Howe and the American War of Independence* (2015); S. R. Taaffe, *The Philadelphia Campaign, 1777–1778* (Lawrence, Ks., 2003).

43 H. C. Syrett and J. E. Cooke (eds), *The Papers of Alexander Hamilton* (New York, 1961–87), I, 220.

44 NA. WO. 34/115 fol. 71.

45 S. D. M. Carpenter, *Southern Gambit: Cornwallis and the British March to Yorktown* (Norman, Ok., 2019).

46 J. Buchanan, *The Road to Charleston: Nathanael Greene and the American Revolution* (Charlottesville, Va., 2019).

47 D. Stoker and M. W. Jones, 'Colonial military strategy', in D. Stoker, K. J. Hagan and M. T. McMaster (eds), *Strategy in the American War of Independence* (2010), 5–34.

48 Robertson to Amherst, 27 Dec. 1781, NA. WO. 34/142 fol. 48.

49 NA. WO. 34/126 fols 86–7.

Chapter 6

1 Skelly narrative, 7 Feb. 1792, BL. Add. 9872 fols 136–7.

2 K. Roy, *War, Culture and Society in Early Modern South Asia, 1740–1849* (Abingdon, 2011), 57–8; A. Webster, *The Twilight of the East India Company – The Evolution of Anglo-Asian Politics, 1790–1860* (Woodbridge, 2009), 52.

3 J. Cuenca-Esteban, 'The British Balance of Payments, 1772–1820: India Transfers and War Finance', *Economic History Review*, 54 (2001), 67.

4 I. Gordon, *Soldier of the Raj* (Barnsley, 2001), 92–3.

5 M. Harrison, 'Disease and medicine in the armies of British India, 1750–1830: the treatment of fevers and the emergence of tropical therapeutics', *Clio Med*, 81 (2007), 87–119.

6 J. N. Sarkar, *Sindhia as Regent of Delhi* (Bombay, 1953).

7 Presidency to Adlercron, 20 Dec. 1754, Holdernesse to Adlercron, 4 Apr. 1755, BL. Eg. 3488 fols 28, 65.

8 BL. IO. Mss. Eur. B215, printed as M. Edwardes (ed.), *Major John Corneille, Journal of My Service in India* (1966), 121, 124.

9 Newcastle to Hardwicke, 15 Oct. 1759, BL. Add. 32897 fol. 87.

10 Coote's report, 13 Feb. 1760, BL. IO. H/Misc./95, 552–5.

11 President and Council at Madras to Court of Directors of East India Company, 31 Jul. 1760, BL. IO. H/Misc./96, 56.

12 John Call to [Colonel Draper?], 15 Jul. 1760, BL. IO. H/Misc./96, 29.

13 Carnac to Clive, 24 Jan. 1761, BL. IO. Mss. Eur. G37, Box 29.

14 Ironside to John Holwell, 23 Feb. 1760, BL. IO. Mss. Eur. G37, Box 28 fol. 58.

15 Carnac to Clive, 26 Apr. 1763, BL. IO. Mss. Eur. G37, Box 30 fol. 56.

16 Journals of Colonel Alexander Champion and Captain Harper, BL. IO. H/Misc/198 99–107, BL. IO. Mss. Eur. Orme OV219, 39–44.

17 Call to Clive, 25 May 1763, BL. IO. Mss. Eur. G37 Box 30 fols 70–1; S.C. Hill, *Yusuf Khan: the Rebel Commandant* (1914).

18 R. B. Barnett, *North India Between Empires. Awadh [Oudh], The Mughals, and the British, 1720–1801* (Berkeley, Calif., 1980).

19 Narrative of the proceedings of Colonel Leslie, letters from Lieutenant-Colonel Goddard, General Orders by Goddard, BL. Add. 28215, 29119, 38402.

20 Extract from a letter from an officer in Goddard's force, 25 Feb. 1780, BL. IO. Mss. Eur. Orme 197 95–100.

21 Cosby to --, 15 Oct. 1780, BL. IO. Mss. Eur. Orme 197, 148.

22 J. Sarkar, 'Haidar Ali's Invasion of the Eastern Carnatic, 1780', in I. Habib (ed.), *Resistance and Modernisation under Haidar Ali and Tipu Sultan* (New Delhi, 1999), 21–34; G. Kaliamurthy, *Second Anglo-Mysore War: 1780–84* (Delhi, 1987).

23 Coote to George Macartney, Governor of Madras, 31 Oct. 1781, BL. Add. 22439 fols 62–3.

24 Coote to Macartney, 1 May 1782, BL. Add. 22440 fol. 16.

25 Fullarton to Duke of Dorset, ambassador in Paris, 28 Jul., Fullarton to Marquess of Carmarthen, Foreign Secretary, 29 Jul. 1784, Maidstone, Kent Archive Office C188./23, BL. Eg. 3504 fol. 15.

26 P. Nightingale, *Trade and Empire in Western India, 1784–1806* (Cambridge, 1970), 13, 37–9, 44; T.G. Fraser, 'India 1780–86', in P. Roebuck (ed.), *Macartney of Lisanoure, 1737–1806* (Belfast, 1983), 201–2.

27 Dundas to Viscount Sydney, Nov. 1784, NA. PRO. 30/11/112 fol. 60.

28 George to Pitt, 23 Sept. 1784, A. Aspinall (ed.), *The Later Correspondence of George III* vol. I (Cambridge, 1962), no. 128.

29 R. Callahan, *The East India Company and Army Reform, 1783–1798* (Cambridge, Mass., 1972); F. and M. Wickwire, *Cornwallis. The Imperial Years* (Chapel Hill, NC, 1980), 98–173.

30 BL. Add. 9872 fols 97–8, 36747C fols 28–30.

31 BL. Add. 57313 fol. 13.

32 Skelly, BL. Add. 9872 fol. 134.

33 M. E. Yapp, *Strategies of British India: Britain, Iran and Afghanistan 1798–1850* (Oxford, 1980).

34 S. Gordon, *Marathas, Marauders and State Formation in Eighteenth-Century India* (Delhi, 1994).

35 I. Habib, *State and Diplomacy under Tipu Sultan: Documents and Essays* (Delhi, 2001).
36 E. Ingram, *In Defence of British India. Great Britain in the Middle East, 1775–1842* (1984).
37 T. Cornell, 'The Military Revolution, Effectiveness, Innovation, and the Duke of Wellington', *Consortium on Revolutionary Europe 1750–1850. Selected Papers* (1996), 252–9.
38 Cornwallis to Sir Archibald Campbell, 7 Jan., 11 Oct. 1787, NA. PRO. 30/11/159 fols 23, 83–4.
39 M. Restall, *Seven Myths of the Spanish Conquest* (Oxford, 2003), 143.
40 B.D. Steele, 'Muskets and Pendulums: Benjamin Robins, Leonhard Euler, and the Ballistics Revolution', *Technology and Culture*, 35 (1994), 354.
41 Cornwallis to Henry Dundas, President of the Board of Control, 4 Apr. 1790, NA. PRO. 30/11/151 fol. 40.
42 Cornwallis to John Shore, 15 Oct. 1787, NA. PRO. 30/11/165 fol. 56.
43 J. W. Hoover, *Men Without Hats: Dialogue, Discipline and Discontent in the Madras Army, 1806–1807* (New Delhi, 2007).
44 Urquhart to Grenville, 27 Jan. 1807, BL. Add. 59282 fol. 156.
45 K. Roy, 'Military Synthesis in South Asia: Armies, Warfare, and Indian Society, c. 1740–1849', *Journal of Military History*, 69 (2005), 689–90.
46 D. Veevers, *The Origins of the British Empire in Asia, 1600–1750* (Cambridge, 2020).
47 M. H. Fisher (ed.), *The Travels of Dean Mahomet: An Eighteenth-Century Journey Through India* (Berkeley, Calif. 1997), 55.
48 BL. Add. 13579 fols 7–8.
49 See the criticism by Cooper, *Anglo-Maratha Campaigns*, 310–11.

Chapter 7

1 Stanhope to Duke of York, 19 June 1815, BL. Add. 34703 fol. 22.
2 J. Gore (ed.), *The Creevey Papers* (1948), 141–2.
3 O'Hara to Sir Evan Nepean, Oct. 1787, PRONI, T.2812/8/50.
4 Memorandum, BL. Add. 33120 fol. 162; N. Lipscombe, *Wellington's Guns: the Untold Story of Wellington and His Artillery in the Peninsula and at Waterloo* (Oxford, 2013), 18–21.
5 Colonel Richard Grenville to George III, 13 Sept. 1782, BL. Add. 70956; C. Ross (ed.), *Correspondence of Charles, First Marquis Cornwallis* (3 vols, 1859), I, 212; Captain John Barker to Sir Robert Murray Keith, envoy in Vienna, 9 June, Colonel Gordon to Keith, 8 Sept. 1787, BL. Add. 35539.
6 Dundas, *Principles*, BL. Add. 27600 fol. 44.
7 Gates, *Light Infantry*, 30–1; C. Duffy, *Army of Frederick the Great*, 155–6.

8   Philip, 5th Earl of Stanhope, *Notes of conversations with the Duke of Wellington* (1889), 182; Moore diary, BL. Add. 57326 fol. 11.

9   R. Muir, *Tactics and the Experience of Battle in the Age of Napoleon* (New Haven, Conn., 1998).

10 R. Williams to Marquess of Buckingham, 11 May 1793, BL. Add. 59279 fols 23–4.

11 Sheridan, 4 Apr. 1797, W. Cobbett (ed.), *Parliamentary History of England*, 33 (1818), cols. 226–7.

12 R. J. W. Knight, *Britain against Napoleon: The Organisation of Victory, 1793–1815* (2013), 104.

13 Pelham to Henry Addington, First Lord of the Treasury, 23 Sept. 1801, BL. Add. 33120 fol. 59.

14 M.T. Gerges, 'Those Complicated Maneuvers of Dundas: British Cavalry Doctrine, 1793–1814', *Consortium on the Revolutionary Era: Selected Papers* (2006), 240–51.

15 For initial strength and weaknesses, M. Snape, *The Royal Army Chaplain's Department, 1796–1953: Clergy under Fire* (Woodbridge, 2008), 29–32.

16 I. D. Gruber, *Books and the British Army in the Age of the American Revolution* (Chapel Hill, NC., 2010); C. Pichichero, *The Military Enlightenment: War and Culture in the French Empire from Louis XIV to Napoleon* (Ithaca, NY, 2017).

17 J. Cookson, *The British Armed Nation, 1793–1815* (Cambridge, 1997).

18 Auckland to Morton Eden, 10, 31 Aug. 1792, BL. Add. 24444 fols 55, 169, 179.

19 Dundas, memorandum, Oct. 1796, BL. Add. 59280 fols 189–90.

20 Pelham, 'Further Considerations on the Plan for a General Enrolment of the People', 2 Jul. 1803, BL. Add. 33120 fol. 135.

21 M. Duffy, 'Coastal Defences and Garrisons, 1480–1914', in R. Kain and W. Ravenhill (eds), *Historical Atlas of South-West England* (Exeter, 1999), 161–2; R.G. Glover, *Britain at Bay: Defence Against Bonaparte, 1803–14* (1973).

22 R. Hopton, *The Battle of Maida 1806: Fifteen Minutes of Glory* (Barnsley, 2002).

23 The best study is C. Esdaile, *The Peninsular War: A New History* (2002). See also his *Peninsular Eyewitnesses: The Experience of War in Spain and Portugal, 1808–1815* (Barnsley, 2008); C. Hall, *British Strategy in the Napoleonic War, 1803–1815* (Manchester, 1992); D. Gates, *The Spanish Ulcer: A History of the Peninsular War* (1986); R. Muir, *Britain and the Defeat of Napoleon, 1807–1815* (New Haven, Conn., 1996).

24 C. Oman, *Wellington's Army* (1912), 79.

25 P. Griffith (ed.), *Wellington Commander* (Chichester, 1985); R. Muir, *'So Brilliant a Victory': Wellington at Salamanca* (New Haven, 2001).

26 D. Horward, *The Battle of Bussaco* (Tallahassee, Fl., 1965).

27 R. Muir, *Salamanca, 1812* (New Haven, Conn., 2001).

28 B. Collins, *Wellington and the Siege of San Sebastian, 1813* (Barnsley, 2017).

29 Murray to Wellington, 23 June 1813, NA. WO. 1/259, 88.

30 J. R. Arnold, 'A Reappraisal of Column Versus Line in the Peninsular War', *JMH*, 68 (2004), 535–52.

31 H.J. Davies, *Spying for Wellington: British Military Intelligence in the Peninsular War* (Norman, Ok., 2018).

32 W. Reid, 'Tracing the Biscuit: The Commissariat in the Peninsular War', *Militaria. Revista de Cultura Militar*, 7 (1995), 101–8.

33 NA. WO. 6/35, 118–19, 5, 17, 331, 54–9, 75–9; C.D. Hall, *British Strategy in the Napoleonic War 1803–1815* (Manchester, 1992), 20–1; F.O. Cetre, 'Beresford and the Portuguese army, 1809–1814', in A.D. Berkeley (ed.), *New Lights on the Peninsular War* (Almada, 1991), 149–56.

34 J. Moon, *Wellington's Two-Front War: The Peninsular Campaigns at Home and Abroad, 1808–1814* (Norman, Ok., 2011).

35 M. Duffy, *Soldiers, Sugar and Seapower: The British Expeditions to the West Indies and the War Against Revolutionary France* (Oxford, 1987), 190–1.

36 Colonel John Moore to his father, John, 16 Mar. 1801, BL. Add. 59281 fol. 69.

37 J. Gurwood (ed.), *The Dispatches of Field Marshal, the Duke of Wellington* (12 vols, 1837–8), IX, 363, X, 162, 479–80.

38 R. W. Hamilton (eds), *Letters and Papers of Sir Thomas Byam Martin* (1898), II, 409.

39 Memorandum of 17 Dec. 1808, Exeter, CRO., Guard's letterbook, 49/33 fol. 10; M. Glover, 'Sir John Cradock and the Garrison of Almeida', *Journal of the Society for Army Historical Research*, 54, no. 220 (winter 1976), 225–30; I. Robertson, *A Commanding Presence: Wellington in the Peninsula, 1808–1814 – Logistics, Strategy, Survival* (Stroud, 2008).

40 S. Petty, 'Wellington's General Orders, 1808–1814', in C.M. Woolgar (ed.), *Wellington Studies* I (Southampton, 1996), 139–63.

41 E. J. Coss, *All for the King's Shilling: The British Soldier under Wellington, 1808–1814* (Norman, Ok., 2010), but see review by S.H. Myerly in *Journal of British Studies*, 50 (2011), 761–3; G. Daly, *The British Soldier in the Peninsular War: Encounters with Spain and Portugal, 1808–1814* (Basingstoke, 2013) and '"The sacking of a town is an abomination": siege, sack and violence to civilians in British officers' writings on the Peninsular War – the case of Badajoz', *Historical Research*, 92 (2018), 160–82.

42 BL. 56088 fol. 5.

Chapter 8

1 C. Hibbert (ed.), *A Soldier of the Seventy-first* (Moreton-in-Marsh, 1996), 9.

2 Hudson Lowe to his father, also Hudson, 29 Mar. 1801, BL. Add. 36297C fols 12–13.

3 B. Collins, *War and Empire: the Expansion of Britain 1790–1830* (2010).

4 Moore to his father, 25 Mar. 1801, BL. Add. 59281 fols 74–5.

5 BL. Add. 49059 fols 27, 30.

6 Dundas to Maitland, 16 June 1800, NA. WO. 6/21, 21.

7   Wellington to Bathurst, 10 Feb. 1813, J. Gurwood (ed.), *The Dispatches of Field Marshal, the Duke of Wellington* (1838), 108; N. Thompson, *Earl Bathurst and the British Empire* (Barnsley, 1999), 63.

8   M. Duffy, *Soldiers, Sugar and Seapower: The British Expeditions to the West Indies and the War Against Revolutionary France* (Oxford, 1987).

9   S. Brown, *By Fire and Bayonet: Grey's West Indies Campaign of 1794* (Solihull, 2018).

10 C. Robertson, 'Racism, the Military, and Abolitionism in the Late Eighteenth- and Early Nineteenth-Century Caribbean', *JMH*, 77 (2013), 439–47.

11 Hely-Hutchinson memorandum, 22 Nov. 1806, BL. Add. 59282 fols 76–81.

12 T. H. McGuffie, 'The Short Life and Sudden Death of an English Regiment of Foot', *Journal of the Society for Army Historical Research*, 33 (1955), 16–25; R.N. Buckley, 'The Destruction of the British Army in the West Indies 1793–1815: A Medical History', Ibid., 56 (1978), 79–92 and *The British Army in the West Indies: Society and the Military in the Revolutionary Age* (Gainesville, Fl., 1998).

13 B. S. Dyde, *The Empty Sleeve: The Story of the West India Regiments of the British Army* (1997).

14 J. Connor, *The Australian Frontier Wars, 1788–1838* (2nd edn, Sydney, 2005).

15 R. Feltoe, *Redcoated Ploughboys: The Volunteer Battalion of Incorporated Militia of Upper Canada, 1813–1815* (Toronto, 2012); W. Johnston, *The Glengarry Light Infantry, 1812–1816* (Charlottestown, 2012).

16 Major-General Isaac Brock to Robert, 2nd Earl of Liverpool, Prime Minister, 25 May 1812, BL. Bathurst papers 57/21 fol. 82.

17 NAM. 1968–07–339–1, 13.

18 NAM. 1968–07–339–1, 8–11.

19 D. Chandler, *Atlas of Military Strategy: The Art, Theory and Practice of War, 1618–1878* (1980), 116–17.

20 B. Collins, 'Effectiveness and the British Officer Corps, 1793–1815', in K. Linch and M. McCormack (eds), *Britain's Soldiers. Rethinking War and Society, 1715–1815* (Liverpool, 2014), 57–76.

21 D. E. Graves, *Fix Bayonets! A Royal Welch Fusilier at War, 1796–1815* (Toronto, 2006).

22 W. S. Dudley (ed.), *The Naval War of 1812: A Documentary History* (Washington, 1985), II, 325.

23 D. E. Graves (ed.), *Merry Hearts Make Light Days: The War of 1812 Journal of Lieutenant John le Couteur* (Ottawa, 1993), 176.

24 NA. WO. 1/141.

25 NAM. 2002–02–729–1.

26 *Naval War of 1812* III, 207–8.

27 J. McCavitt and C. T. George, *The Man Who Captured Washington: Major-General Robert Ross and the War of 1812* (Norman, Ok., 2016).

28 D. R. Hickey, *Glorious Victory: Andrew Jackson and the Battle of New Orleans* (Baltimore, MD., 2015).

29 NAM. 2002–02–729–1.
30 NAM. 2001–09–36–1.
31 NAM. 2001–90–36–1.

Chapter 9

1   Rush to James Madison, former American president, 30 Aug. 1820, Philadelphia, Pennsylvania Historical Society, Am 13520.
2   Jenkinson to Amherst, 24 Oct. 1780, NA. WO. 34/127 fol. 155.
3   R. R. Sedgwick (ed.), *The House of Commons 1715–1754* (2 vols, 1970), I, 141–4.
4   L. Namier and J. Brooke (eds), *The House of Commons 1754–1790* (3 vols, 1985), I, 138–43.
5   C. Nordmann, 'Choiseul and the Last Jacobite Attempt of 1759', in E. Cruickshanks (ed.), *Ideology and Conspiracy. Aspects of Jacobitism, 1689–1759* (Edinburgh, 1982), 201–17.
6   Cumberland to Fox, 29 Aug. 1757, Ilchester (ed.), *Letters to Henry Fox*, 118.
7   Rockingham to Sir George Savile, 15 Nov. 1759, Bod. MS. Eng. Lett. C144 fol. 280.
8   J. R. Western, *The English Militia in the Eighteenth Century* (1965), 127–61, 302.
9   Memoranda for George II, 14, 16, 21 Aug., Newcastle to Hardwicke, 31 Aug. 1759, BL. Add. 32894 fols 182, 237, 333, 32895 fol. 91.
10 Newcastle to Andrew Stone, 1 Aug. 1759, BL. Add. 32893 fol. 404.
11 *Jackson's Oxford Journal*, 3 Jul. 1790.
12 R. Wells, *Insurrection: The British Experience 1795–1803* (Gloucester, 1983).
13 J. Bohstedt, 'The Waning of the Moral Economy: Military Force and the Politics of Provisions, 1740–1820', *Consortium on Revolutionary Europe, 1750–1850: Selected Papers, 1999*, 140–50.
14 J. E. Cookson, *The British Armed Nation 1793–1815* (Oxford, 1997).
15 J. E. O. Screen, 'The Eighteenth-Century Army at Home as reflected in Local Records', *Journal of the Society for Army Historical Research*, 88 (2010), 217–32.
16 Timothy D. Watt, 'Taxation riots and the culture of popular protest in Ireland, 1714–1740', *English Historical Review*, 130 (2015): 1447.
17 J. S. Donnelly, 'The Whiteboy Movement, 1761–5', *Irish Historical Studies*, 21 (1978): 20–54.

Chapter 10

1   NAM, 1968–07–344–1, 6–7.
2   Anon. account of conversation with Jérôme, 10 May 1823, BL. Add. 34703 fol. 66.
3   Anon. memorandum, 21 June 1815, BL. Add. 34703 fol. 33.

4   NAM, 1968–07–344–1, 8–9.
5   C. Divall, *Redcoats Against Napoleon: The 30th Regiment During the Revolutionary and Napoleonic Wars* (Barnsley, 2009).
6   William Sharpire to Siborne, 6 Dec. 1834, BL. Add. 34704 fol. 16.
7   J. Black, *The Battle of Waterloo* (New York, 2010).
8   I. Robertson, *A Commanding Presence: Wellington in the Peninsula, 1808–1814, Logistics, Strategy, Survival* (Stroud, 2008).
9   K. Kinch, *Britain and Wellington's Army: Recruitment, Society and Tradition, 1807–15* (Basingstoke, 2011).
10 I. Berkovich, *Motivation in War: The Experience of Common Soldiers in Old-Regime Europe* (Cambridge, 2017).
11 J. Uglow, *In These Times: Living in Britain through Napoleon's Wars, 1793–1815* (2014).
12 NAM. 1976–07–34–1.

Conclusion

1   Anon. memorandum, 21 June 1815, BL. Add. 34703 fol. 33.
2   Chetwynd, out-letter book, 25 June 1704, Stafford, Staffordshire CrO. D649/8/2, 56.
3   Andrew Mitchell, envoy in Berlin, to Robert, 4th Earl of Holdernesse, Secretary of State in the Northern Department, 20 Apr. 1760, NA. SP. 90/75.
4   Coote to Macartney, 1 May 1782, BL. Add. 22440 fol. 16.
5   J. B. Hattendorf, *England in the War of the Spanish Succession. A Study of the English View and Conduct of Grand Strategy 1701–1713* (1987).
6   E. Scouller, *The Armies of Queen Anne* (Oxford, 166), 201, 197; Charles Frederick MP, Surveyor-General of the Ordnance, to Holdernesse, 7 Feb. 1758, BL. Eg. 3443; fol. 3; D. W. Bailey and D. Harding, 'From India to Waterloo: the "Indian pattern" musket', in Guy (ed.), *The Road to Waterloo*, 56.
7   Argyll to Whetham, 26 Nov. 24 Dec. 1711, Cambridge, University Library, Add. Mss. 6570 fols 59, 67.
8   J. S. Sweetman, *Raglan: From the Peninsula to the Crimea* (1993).
9   Graham to Raglan, 8 Oct., 22 Nov. 1854, BL. Add. 79696 fols 131, 135.

Index